DARK SPIRITS

Monsters, Demons, and Devils

Richard Estep

DETROIT

ABOUT THE AUTHOR

Photograph by Ali Cotton, Bleu Cotton Photography.

Richard Estep is the author of numerous books, ranging from paranormal non-fiction and UFOlogy to history and current affairs. These books include *Serial Killers: The Minds, Methods, and Mayhem of History's Most Notorious Murderers; The Serial Killer Next Door: The Double Lives of Notorious Murderers; Grifters, Frauds, and Crooks: True Stories of American Corruption;* and *The Handy Armed Forces Answer Book*. He is a regular columnist for *Haunted Magazine* and has written for the *Journal of Emergency Medical Services*. Richard appears regularly on the TV shows *Haunted Files, Haunted Hospitals, Paranormal 911,* and *Paranormal Night Shift,* and has guested on *Destination Fear* and *A Haunting*. He makes his home in Colorado, with his wife and a menagerie of adopted animals.

Richard Estep

DARK
SPIRITS

Monsters, Demons,
and Devils

DETROIT

Cover-Ups and Secrets: The Complete Guide to Government Conspiracies, Manipulations & Deceptions
by Nick Redfern
ISBN: 978-1-57859-679-9

Demons, the Devil, and Fallen Angels
by Marie D. Jones and Larry Flaxman
ISBN: 978-1-57859-613-3

The Dream Encyclopedia, 2nd edition
by James R. Lewis, Ph.D.; and Evelyn Dorothy Oliver, Ph.D.
ISBN: 978-1-57859-216-6

The Dream Interpretation Dictionary: Symbols, Signs, and Meanings
by J. M. DeBord
ISBN: 978-1-57859-637-9

Earth Magic: Your Complete Guide to Natural Spells, Potions, Plants, Herbs, Witchcraft, and More
by Marie D. Jones
ISBN: 978-1-57859-697-3

The Encyclopedia of Religious Phenomena
by J. Gordon Melton
ISBN: 978-1-57859-209-8

The Fortune-Telling Book: The Encyclopedia of Divination and Soothsaying
by Raymond Buckland
ISBN: 978-1-57859-147-3

The Government UFO Files: The Conspiracy of Cover-Up
by Kevin D. Randle
ISBN: 978-1-57859-477-1

Haunted: Malevolent Ghosts, Night Terrors, and Threatening Phantoms
by Brad Steiger
ISBN: 978-1-57859-620-1

Hidden History: Ancient Aliens and the Suppressed Origins of Civilization
by Jim Willis
ISBN: 978-1-57859-710-9

Hidden Realms, Lost Civilizations, and Beings from Other Worlds
by Jerome Clark
ISBN: 978-1-57859-175-6

The Horror Show Guide: The Ultimate Frightfest of Movies
by Mike Mayo
ISBN: 978-1-57859-420-7

The Illuminati: The Secret Society That Hijacked the World
by Jim Marrs
ISBN: 978-1-57859-619-5

Lost Civilizations: The Secret Histories and Suppressed Technologies of the Ancients
by Jim Willis
ISBN: 978-1-57859-706-2

The Monster Book: Creatures, Beasts, and Fiends of Nature
by Nick Redfern
ISBN: 978-1-57859-575-4

Monsters of the Deep
by Nick Redfern
ISBN: 978-1-57859-705-5

Near Death Experiences: Afterlife Journeys and Revelations
by Jim Willis
ISBN: 978-1-57859-846-5

The New Witch Your Guide to Modern Witchcraft, Wicca, Spells, Potions, Magic, and More
by Marie D. Jones
ISBN: 978-1-57859-716-1

The New World Order Book
by Nick Redfern
ISBN: 978-1-57859-615-7

Nightmares: Your Guide to Interpreting Your Darkest Dreams
by J. M. DeBord
ISBN: 978-1-57859-758-1

Real Aliens, Space Beings, and Creatures from Other Worlds,
by Brad and Sherry Hansen Steiger
ISBN: 978-1-57859-333-0

Real Encounters, Different Dimensions, and Otherworldly Beings
by Brad and Sherry Hansen Steiger
ISBN: 978-1-57859-455-9

Real Ghosts, Restless Spirits, and Haunted Places, 2nd edition
by Brad Steiger
ISBN: 978-1-57859-401-6

Real Miracles, Divine Intervention, and Feats of Incredible Survival
by Brad and Sherry Hansen Steiger
ISBN: 978-1-57859-214-2

Real Monsters, Gruesome Critters, and Beasts from the Darkside
by Brad and Sherry Hansen Steiger
ISBN: 978-1-57859-220-3

Real Vampires, Night Stalkers, and Creatures from the Darkside
by Brad Steiger
ISBN: 978-1-57859-255-5

Real Visitors, Voices from Beyond, and Parallel Dimensions
by Brad and Sherry Hansen Steiger
ISBN: 978-1-57859-541-9

Real Zombies, the Living Dead, and Creatures of the Apocalypse,
by Brad Steiger
ISBN: 978-1-57859-296-8

The Religion Book Places, Prophets, Saints, and Seers
by Jim Willis
ISBN: 978-1-57859-151-0

Runaway Science: True Stories of Raging Robots and High-Tech Horrors
by Nick Redfern
ISBN: 978-1-57859-801-4

The Sci-Fi Movie Guide: The Universe of Film from Alien to Zardoz
by Chris Barsanti
ISBN: 978-1-57859-503-7

Secret History: Conspiracies from Ancient Aliens to the New World Order
by Nick Redfern
ISBN: 978-1-57859-479-5

Secret Societies: The Complete Guide to Histories, Rites, and Rituals
by Nick Redfern
ISBN: 978-1-57859-483-2

The Spirit Book: The Encyclopedia of Clairvoyance, Channeling, and Spirit Communication
by Raymond Buckland
ISBN 978-1-57859-790-1

Supernatural Gods: Spiritual Mysteries, Psychic Experiences, and Scientific Truths
by Jim Willis
ISBN: 978-1-57859-660-7

Time Travel: The Science and Science Fiction
by Nick Redfern
ISBN: 978-1-57859-723-9

Toxin Nation: The Poisoning of Our Air, Water, Food, and Bodies
by Marie D. Jones
ISBN: 978-1-57859-709-3

The UFO Dossier: 100 Years of Government Secrets, Conspiracies, and Cover-Ups
by Kevin D. Randle
ISBN: 978-1-57859-564-8

Unexplained! Strange Sightings, Incredible Occurrences, and Puzzling Physical Phenomena, 3rd edition
by Jerome Clark
ISBN: 978-1-57859-344-6

The Vampire Almanac: The Complete History
by J. Gordon Melton, Ph.D.
ISBN: 978-1-57859-719-2

The Vampire Book: The Encyclopedia of the Undead, 3rd edition
by J. Gordon Melton, Ph.D.
ISBN: 978-1-57859-281-4

The Werewolf Book: The Encyclopedia of Shape-Shifting Beings, 2nd edition
by Brad Steiger
ISBN: 978-1-57859-367-5

Werewolf Stories: Shape-Shifters, Lycanthropes, and Man-Beasts
by Nick Redfern and Brad Steiger
ISBN: 978-1-57859-766-6

The Witch Book: The Encyclopedia of Witchcraft, Wicca, and Neo-Paganism
by Raymond Buckland
ISBN: 978-1-57859-791-8

The Witches Almanac Sorcerers, Witches and Magic from Ancient Rome to the Digital Age
by Charles Christian
ISBN: 978-1-57859-760-4

The Zombie Book: The Encyclopedia of the Living Dead
by Nick Redfern and Brad Steiger
ISBN: 978-1-57859-504-4

"Real Nightmares" E-Books by Brad Steiger

Please visit us at visibleinkpress.com

Dark Spirits: Monsters, Demons, and Devils

Visible Ink Press®
43311 Joy Rd., #414
Canton, MI 48187-2075

Visible Ink Press is a registered trademark of Visible Ink Press LLC.

Most Visible Ink Press books are available at special quantity discounts when purchased in bulk by corporations, organizations, or groups. Customized printings, special imprints, messages, and excerpts can be produced to meet your needs. For more information, contact Special Markets Director, Visible Ink Press, www.visibleinkpress.com, or 734-667-3211.

Managing Editor: Kevin S. Hile
Cover Design: John Gouin, Graphikitchen, LLC
Page Design: Mary Claire Krzewinski
Typesetting: Marco Divita
Proofreaders: Larry Baker and Christa Gainor
Indexer: Shoshana Hurwitz
Cover image: Shutterstock.

ISBNs
Paperback: 978-1-57859-847-2
Hardcover: 978-1-57859-874-8
eBook: 978-1-57859-875-5
Cataloging-in-Publication data is on file at the Library of Congress.
Printed in the United States of America.

10 9 8 7 6 5 4 3 2 1

DEDICATION

For Jeff Belanger

CONTENTS

Contents

PHOTO SOURCES

Alpsdake (Wikicommons): p. 2.

Tim Bertelink: p. 165.

Simon Burchell: p. 187.

Cayobo (Wikicommons): p. 68.

Digital.library.ucla.edu: p. 170.

Richard Estep: pp. 15, 17, 29, 36, 38, 39, 84, 86, 88, 92, 94, 103, 104, 106, 111, 112, 113, 114, 115, 132, 134, 149, 151, 153, 154, 168. 198, 199, 200, 201. 202, 203, 204, 205. 206, 207 (top and bottom), 208, 209, 211.

Geograph.org.uk: p. 126.

Hess Brother's Department Store: p. 74.

Jahelle (Wikicommons): p. 66.

Michael A. Kozlowski: p. 90.

Library of Congress: p. 4.

Library.uta.edu: p. 161.

Los Angeles Police Department: p. 5.

Megamoto85 (Wikicommons): p. 142.

MrHarman (Wikicommons): p. 189.

Musée d'Orsay: p. 72.

Musée Rolin: p. 196.

National Archives and Records Administration: p. 19.

National Institutes of Health: p. 47.

Nuno Nogueira: p. 120.

Paul from USA (Wikicommons): p. 180.

Popular Science: p. 119.

Ron from Denton, Texas (Wikicommons): p. 182.

Seulatr (Wikicommons): p. 98.

Shutterstock: pp. 7, 9, 12, 21, 24, 30, 31, 33, 56, 59, 75, 79, 125, 129, 139, 156, 162, 174, 177, 194, 216 (modified by Kevin Hile).

SMG2019 (Wikicommons): p. 171.

Suffolk County Police Department: p. 96.

SUM1 (Wikicommons): p. 52.

U.S. Air Force: p. 160.

U.S. Navy: pp. 23, 144.

Public domain: pp. 44, 45, 46, 50, 110, 123, 128, 176, 192.

FOREWORD

With every ghost story I uncover or new spiritual encounter I witness or hear about, I'm reminded that these events are one of the few things that I believe separate us humans from the other mammals and creatures that we share the earth with. Not because they also don't experience paranormal events in some way, but because none of them have the ability to tell their stories. They're our instinct-driven cohabitants who seek shelter and food cyclically. That alone is against our very human nature. We have a need to fulfill a purpose, and we also have a constant longing to garner answers from unnaturally occurring matters that we don't quite understand. Similarly, we will always chase the context of those matters as voraciously as a lion pursues prey. So, then again, maybe we aren't so different from animals after all. Our prey is perhaps just a little bit different.

One of the first questions we wrestle with is one we may never have an answer for on this side of life: what were we made for? Yes, we have science and math and equations that show us the foundation of the inner workings of the world, but what they can't seem to explain is the pseudo nature of that science and how to quantify the anomalies that exist outside of their given parameters. The paranormal then becomes a rivaling concept to human logic that we can't shake—maybe for good reason. It compels us to acknowledge our lack of understanding of the world, and, if we happen to be someone who is intrinsically curious, why things are as they are. This sets us on a journey that many don't come back from.

From this point forward, it's no longer fair for us to leave stones uncovered, places unexplored, and histories untold. Through the pursuit of the paranormal, we ourselves evolve into the same tools we use to investigate the unknown because we expand on the myths, the legends, and the ghosts and communicate those stories in hopes of learning a little more about who we are. As humans, we walk hand in hand with our connection to the energy of this earth, and it manifests itself in one way or another in ways that make the hair stand up on the back of our necks. Sometimes through terror, sometimes through history, we can feel like we are entering a portal through time. This is the data that we hope to have stored away to share and to explain the mysteries that surround us.

The paranormal has played a tremendously large role in the human experiment for as long as we have walked the earth. It has always been the bridge between people and the earth and the reason why many have found meaning to the complexities of our world, simplifying it and being comfortable living in it. The unique combination of our own mortality, the chaos of life, and our place in the afterlife brings a vital importance to the position the paranormal holds in our lives. We live in a big universe that we can't comprehend at times; we feel insignificant in it at times, and our ghost stories, mysteries, and urban legends coincidentally bring a structure and validation to us that builds on what we know of the world and who we might be in the world, and not necessarily the other way around.

However, our deep thoughts and quest for answers aren't the only reason why we're fascinated by the paranormal. Fear, despite the negative connotations associated with this feeling, draws us to explore what we don't understand. It's the reason why the horror genre of art and entertainment has continued to thrive. It's why haunted houses, urban exploration, and ghost investigations have slowly but surely seeped into the general population and not just the people who have dedicated their lives to it. It plays into why this book is now in your hands. Regardless of what brings us to believe or acknowledge the paranormal, we leave with something that comes with any singular event that people can latch onto collectively: community.

For millennia, the paranormal has brought together full communities on the backs of superstitions and lore. It's been the way we explain the unexplainable and come to terms with the things we can't control. It's influenced the life and legacies of countless people who may have thought their lives insignificant or had no intentions of being tied to the paranormal endlessly once they reached their time. These ideas have also fostered horrific and deadly movements like the Salem witch trials that continued to have ripple effects on misunderstood women centuries later, the vampire panic that took the lives of hundreds of women because of supernatural hysteria being blamed for the rapid spread of tuberculosis, the vitriolic rejection of traditional medicine work, voodoo, and hoodoo practiced by minority cultures in the United States, and even the Satanic panic, which instilled unfettered fear into the hearts of many towards entire groups of people as the world quickly changed to accommodate new ideas and technology.

In spite of this, as a community, we still fight to make the paranormal fit into our world. Without the paranormal, whole accounts of history found in the annals of urban legends and stories may have been lost and never heard of again. It's caused us to dig a little deeper into the truths of our world and to learn about the figures who played a role in shaping our culture, for better or for worse, whether that role was big or small. It is through the paranormal that we have had the opportunity to preserve incredible and sometimes tragic pieces of our past that we can celebrate or grow from as humans. Ghost stories are more than just tales that we share at sleepovers or beside campfires. In them are critical pieces of context that ironically begin to become lessons for us to apply to our own lives.

We need that context. Simply put, not everyone has had a scary or life-changing experience, but nearly everyone has heard of someone else's. By sharing these stories, whether they're from a first-person encounter or they're a retelling of a secondhand account, we all want to feel safe in communicating strange tales that cause anyone to empathize with the respective parties involved. We want to have neighbors and friends around us who buy in to the notion that there is more going on in the universe than we understand and that it's okay to believe that without having our conclusions supported with anything other than the substantial accumulation of lore.

When compared to science, the paranormal has so few answers to give. There are rarely formulas that work the same each time we use them, and we can't use the scientific method to gauge whether we received the same results as the last time. We can even put ourselves in positions to experience the paranormal and still never encounter such phenomena.

The paranormal allows us to walk in the footsteps of those who were here before us without having to meet them and converse with them first. It allows us to feel what others have felt without us having to relive those same emotions and events. It allows us to do something incredible that only traipsing around in buildings and living spaces, new and old, can give us—a way to connect to our own humanity through the very humans who used to be here.

People will always find a way to connect to each other. To go a step further, even the entities we believe aren't human are included in that belief as well. There is something unique about humanity that evokes a deep attachment to otherworldly things. Why is it that everything that appears to be on the other side of life is so desperate to make contact with us? I believe it's because whatever and whoever the spirits and people are, they can count on us to pursue them or tell their stories or be their tangible earth tie while we go about our fleeting lives here.

My hope is that as you take in this incredible book by this incredible author you can learn to walk a mile in the shoes of the people that you read about. They are mothers, sons, fathers, daughters, workers, and people who tried to live here on this earth as we do today. It's critical that we remember who they are and that they are more than just props for our entertainment and the satisfaction of our paranormal fix. We are fortunate to have stories to tell that still live on forever in oral and written transcriptions. Let them fill you with empathy for the paths that these people walked.

Rightfully, there should be a thrill when it comes to the paranormal. It taps into senses that we either don't use often or are relatively muted. Ghost stories open the door for us to venture into the obscure, strange, and sometimes forgotten. So much of our anthropology and folklore has dabbled in spirituality, ghosts, creatures, and magic. As society continues to accept newer ideas, these concepts won't feel as niche. and those who have accepted this will be leading the charge to educate others as well.

But in the excitement of these recollections, let's remember not to forget the purpose of these stories of ghosts and hauntings and the experiences we've had. Storytelling is how these tales come alive within us, creating an immersive experience that we'll keep with us and even be able to share as we interact with someone just as interested in them as we are. They should push us to ask for even more stories and motivate us to share them.

Stories in the realm of the paranormal offer a link between the natural and supernatural, fantasy and reality, fiction and nonfiction, the world we live in and the one we presumably are headed towards. They have the capability to build whole new worlds and excite anticipation for the endless possibilities for the future. It is undeniable that this feeling will be the undercurrent of this book written by a master storyteller and compassionate and kind author.

The paranormal demands emotional intelligence, as it handles large quantities of information that can feel overwhelming. It's powerful on its own, and the human element that comes from storytelling requires authentic insight to make it memorable and add meaning to it beyond being just a compelling narrative. When reading this, ask yourself, "If this were me, who would I have been at that moment?" and do some introspection into how you value your life, the lives that have already been lived, and the way you interact with the humanity around you. If you can center your compassion and understanding with the help of these pages, this will be a book you will consistently come back to, one that will remain on your shelf for decades to come.

Joshua Dairen, Paranormal Researcher/Historian

INTRODUCTION

Who among us isn't fascinated by the darkness?

Often, it's a benign place, caused by nothing more than the absence of light…

But not always.

Sometimes, things lurk in the shadows. Strange things. Frightening things. Things that defy easy explanation.

I began my career as a paranormal investigator in 1995, associating myself with a field research team in the British East Midlands. In those days before the arrival of paranormal reality television, there were surprisingly few groups to whom the public could turn when they were faced with things going bump in the night. (Fast forward 35 years and ghost hunters and paranormal enthusiasts now number in the tens, if not hundreds of thousands).

My passion for all things paranormal began at a much younger age. My stepfather and his siblings grew up during World War II. While their father, my grandfather, was deployed to fight in Burma, my grandmother was left to raise the family as best she could and to keep the home fires burning. This she did with remarkable grace and fortitude, but help came from a surprising source: the spirit of an elderly woman who, it would transpire, had been the former resident of their modest Yorkshire home. None of the young children in the family questioned the presence of the kindly lady who came into their bedroom each evening to make sure that they were all tucked up in bed and ready to go to sleep. It was only later, following my grandfather's return from the war, that the apparition ceased to appear. With the family reunited, her work was done. The mission to watch over the children now fulfilled, she presumably moved on to whatever it is that awaits us once this physical life is over.

By the time I inherited the same bedroom in the 1970s, I had heard those ghost stories repeatedly. As a boy of seven or eight years of age, I would lie there in bed at night, the covers pulled up to my chin, listening to each creak of a floorboard as the old house settled down after the warmth of the day. In my young imagination, every unidentified sound was potentially a phantom footstep, a precursor of the old lady's ghost making a return visit to once again keep an eye on the children of the family. The anticipation I felt was tempered by the racing heart and dry mouth that accompanied my fear—a fear of the unknown that seeped into my blood and stayed there, combining with that innate fascination that all of us possess to some degree for what lies in the darkness.

There was little in the way of paranormal-themed television to help sate my curiosity. YouTube and social media platforms were decades in the future. In order to learn more, I turned to the library, and to books like the one you now hold in your hands. It was among their pages that I learned about classic hauntings, spirits and specters with colorful and sometimes tragic backstories. Some of them were kind and friendly just like the ghost who watched over my family.

Others were very much not.

Contrary to popular belief—a belief stoked by content creators and media outlets—the realm of the paranormal and the weird is not entirely composed of negativity and nastiness; yet that dark side certainly exists, and we ignore it to our own detriment.

This book aims to shine a spotlight onto some of the darker shadows. I must confess right from the outset that, as a paranormal investigator specializing in claims of ghostly activity, much of what you'll find within these chapters will cover dark and negative hauntings.

Some of the accounts come directly from my own files, cases that I have investigated in person, putting my boots on the ground, visiting the location and interviewing the witnesses myself. We'll journey to Denver Botanic Gardens, where thousands of sets of human remains lie beneath the earth, some saying that their restless spirits are drawn to the living when they visit the gardens. In Louisville, Kentucky, we'll walk the halls of the infamous Waverly Hills Sanatorium, where thousands died of tuberculosis … and some have remained behind decades after their deaths. We'll also venture into the Rocky Mountains in search of monsters such as the Slide-Rock Bolter, a gigantic worm that lumberjacks claimed would slide down mountainsides and gobble up its victims whole.

Other parts of the book focus upon strange encounters, places and creatures with which I have no personal experience but that have fascinated me for years. Is there really a lake monster prowling in the waters beneath Loch Ness, and if so, is it a dinosaur, a trans-dimensional being, or even a ghost?

What really happened to Betty and Barney Hill, a couple who believed they were abducted from their car on a lonely New Hampshire road in 1961? Were they taken by aliens, and if so, for what purpose?

Just what exactly are the "shadow people," mysterious apparitions that have been encountered by members of the public and paranormal investigators alike for many years? To some, they are sinister and malevolent, bringers of fear and harm. Others see them as protectors and guardians. One thing is for certain: Whatever they are, sightings of them are growing in number, and some of them are quite disturbing in tone.

Within this book, we'll look for vampires in Transylvania and England (both old and new); examine claims of demonic possession; cast a close eye on the darker side of Ouija boards and other methods of spirit communication; ask whether curses and hexes really do work; explore the link between serial killers and the occult; and go in search of monsters, aliens, and a panoply of weird phenomena.

Dark Spirits doesn't set out to be an exhaustive deep dive into any one single subject. My hope is that you, the reader, will find each section sufficiently intriguing and informative to venture forth and learn more about the most interesting cases. To that end, a recommended reading list has been included at the end of the book.

Welcome to the realm of the paranormal.

Richard Estep
Longmont, Colorado
March 2024

DARK CORNERS OF THE WORLD

FINAL DESTINATION: AOKIGAHARA

To the people of Japan, Aokigahara is known as a dark and haunted place. Some take that word—*haunted*—more literally than others. The reason for this lies in Aokigahara's nickname: the Suicide Forest.

Each year, more than 30 people on average, most of them Japanese, venture into the Suicide Forest with the express intention of never coming out again. Some estimates place that number three times higher, or even more. Not only do they refrain from publishing the information, but it is difficult for the Japanese government to obtain accurate figures on the annual death rate at Aokigahara; the forest guards its secrets zealously, and it is not unusual for the bodies of those who take their own lives beneath the trees to remain undiscovered for months or even years in the *jukai*, or "sea of trees."

Parts of the forest really do look like a sea of trees, with gnarled roots and branches intertwining and a leafy canopy so thick that it keeps out much of the daylight. This same density acts to dampen acoustics. Those who visit Aokigahara and return are commonly struck by the unnatural hush that pervades everything there. The atmosphere is sometimes likened to that of a church or a holy temple, one of solemnity and reverence for those who have lost their lives.

Upon walking deeper into the forest, once one has gotten past the outer fringes, evidence of its former occupants—although they typically occupied it for just a few hours at most—can be found everywhere. Shoes of all sizes and colors lie scattered among the foliage. In the undergrowth, clothes are strewn, sometimes haphazardly, other times arranged in neat little piles. Some of those who ended their lives in Aokigahara did so in the same fastidious manner in which they lived them.

Closer inspection may reveal the bones of the men and women who once wore those clothes. Here, a femur. There, a tibia and fibula. Perhaps a skull or a ribcage. The dead of Aokigahara are not buried. They lie where they died, usually upon the ground, but sometimes hanging from the boughs if that happened to be their chosen method of suicide.

The bodies are in varying states of decomposition. Teams are sometimes dispatched into the forest to find and recover as many sets of human remains as they can. No matter how hard they try, it is impossible for them to locate them all.

In recent years, the forest has become a macabre tourist attraction, a place to which the ghoulish are drawn for reasons best known only to themselves. Aokigahara is an increasingly popular destination for Western visitors due to the media attention it has gotten, both in the press and in at least two movies at the time of writing, *The Sea of Trees* (2015) and *The Forest* (2016).

Aiokigahara is a forest about 12 square miles (30 square kilometers) in size northwest of Mt. Fuji. Called the "Sea of Trees," the porous lava rock on the forest floor absorbs sound, making the place eerily quiet. Since the 1960s, it has oddly become a popular place for suicides.

Undeniably, Aokigahara is a haunting place. Some who believe it to be haunted by the spirits of those who died among the trees point to not only the deaths themselves but also the strong emotions of despair and hopelessness that led to them. For where one finds strong emotions, it is said, one also finds ghosts.

Despite the best efforts of the Japanese authorities, the pilgrimages into Aokigahara continue. They have done so since the 1950s. There are signs posted at regular intervals, entreating the pilgrims not to take their own lives. Paths out of the forest are clearly marked in the hope that some will think twice and turn back before the end. Volunteers seek out those who appear to be set on taking their lives and try to talk them out of it.

Thankfully, some visitors to Aokigahara do indeed accept those lifelines. Others do not. According to Japanese tradition, their ghosts are named *yurei*. Many cultures around the world equate suicide with a belief in restless spirits. One of the more disconcerting characteristics of yurei is their vengeful, vindictive nature. They are believed to seek out the living and terrorize them, their goal being one of retribution. Yurei are motivated by anger and rage. Belief in them goes back centuries, and even today they are both feared and respected.

Do ghosts, angry or otherwise, truly haunt the Suicide Forest—or are the stories simply folklore? Hikers regularly traverse the forest, passing through without apparent problems. Although camping overnight is permissible, only a hardy soul would spend the night there. (It is also strongly discouraged by the authorities.) Ghosts or not, the most important thing to remember is the many lives that have been lost there. Aokigahara should be treated with the respect and the solemnity that it deserves.

HORROR AT THE HOTEL CECIL

It seems as if every hotel has its ghost story. The more colorful, not to mention violent, its history, the more prevalent those stories tend to be. I was fortunate enough to spend several years leading ghost tours at the infamous Stanley Hotel in Estes Park, Colorado—inspiration for Stephen King's famous novel *The Shining*. Unlike its fictional counterpart, the Overlook, the Stanley has a very pleasant past, with little in the way of violence or tragedy to mar it. The haunting is primarily a playful and happy one, fed by the tens of thousands of visitors who flock there each to year to enjoy the clean Rocky Mountain air, take in the breathtaking views—and of course, hear about the ghosts.

The Stanley Hotel in Estes Park, Colorado, still benefits from tourism generated from the 1980 film *The Shining* for which it served as the inspiration for the setting of the horror movie.

At the opposite end of the scale is the Hotel Cecil. Located on the West Coast of the United States, the Cecil started out its life as a grand old dame of Los Angeles hotels. Built in the early 1920s for around one million dollars—a princely sum at the time—the 14-story Cecil was open for the holiday season of 1924. Not for nothing was this decade called the Roaring Twenties, and the owners of this 700-room behemoth set out to catch the eye of the well-heeled, catering to their refined tastes, while also presenting less ostentatious offerings for customers with a more modest budget.

When times were good, the Cecil did well. Unfortunately, the good times never last, as the arrival of the Great Depression proved. As work and money became scarce, the de-gentrification of the city blocks around the hotel progressed for several generations until finally the area was given a name synonymous with poverty and squalor: Skid Row.

All hotels have deaths. With a constant stream of humanity moving in and checking out, it is inevitable that nature will sometimes take its course. Many of those deaths are entirely natural. Others are decidedly not, and because of the volume and nature of the deaths that took place there, the Cecil began to acquire a reputation for being cursed.

Suicide became a regular occurrence at the hotel. Some were sufficiently grotesque or puzzling to make it into the newspapers. In 1932, a 25-year-old man shot himself in the head with a pistol. His body was discovered by a member of the housekeeping staff. He only lived two miles away from the Cecil and had apparently checked into the hotel for the sole purpose of killing himself.

In 1934, a former U.S. Army sergeant checked into the Cecil, cut his own throat with a straight razor, and swiftly bled to death.

The most common method of suicide was jumping from one of the upper floors. Some jumpers hit the rooftops of neighboring buildings, while others died on the sidewalk below. The year 1944 saw one of the most disturbing deaths when a pregnant 19-year-old delivered her baby in a hotel bathroom and hurled the newborn out of a window. She would later tell detectives that the baby had been stillborn, though the coroner found that to be questionable.

Other guests chose less brutal but no less terminal methods of taking their own lives. These included drug overdoses and self-poisoning. Some drank themselves to death. The Cecil became known as a place to go when a person hit their lowest ebb and could see no other way out.

On occasion, it was also a place for murder. On June 4, 1964, a 65-year-old homeless lady known as "Pigeon" Goldie Osgood was raped and then brutally killed in one of the Cecil's rooms. She earned the nickname because of her love for feeding the pigeons, and by all accounts she was a kind and compassionate soul. Her murderer was never caught. A few years later, a male hotel guest was given Goldie's old room, unbeknownst to him. He awoke in the middle of the night in a state of paralysis, unable to move a muscle. A sense of growing pressure in his chest quickly progressed to the feeling of being strangled by phantom hands. It's hard to imagine anything more frightening than awakening in a dark, unfamiliar room being choked. Mercifully, the gentleman was able to get away and flee. It was only after gabbling his story to the desk clerk that he was told of the room's dark history—and the fact that Goldie Osgood had been strangled to death.

Richard "The Night Stalker" Ramirez was a serial killer and rapist found guilty of killing 14 people. He died in prison awaiting execution.

The Cecil's most notorious resident was none other than serial killer and multiple rapist Richard Ramirez, aka the Night Stalker. Ramirez held a reign of terror in the Los Angeles area between 1984 and 1985, breaking into residences at night and sexually assaulting and murdering the occupants. Ramirez kept a room at the top of the Cecil, where he played loud rock music late into the night. There are also unsubstantiated stories of him carrying out occult rituals on the hotel roof. It is true that Ramirez had an interest in the occult, believing that Satan would protect him from capture during his killing spree. He was ultimately proven to be incorrect, as LAPD officers had to save Ramirez from being beaten to a pulp by a crowd of citizens who recognized his face from a newspaper front page.

Somewhat shorter was the residency of Austrian serial killer Johann "Jack" Unterweger, who came to the United States in 1991 after being released from prison, where he had served time for murdering a sex worker. On his arrival in Los Angeles, he immediately set about abducting and killing more sex workers. The Cecil was his home base, and although there is no evidence to suggest that either he or Ramirez brought their victims to the hotel (let alone killed them there), stories abound of their rooms having a dark, oppressive atmosphere.

Few had heard of the Hotel Cecil until the tragic death of Canadian tourist Elisa Lam in 2013. After checking in to a fifth-floor room on January 28, the 21-year-old intended to spend time seeing the sights in Los Angeles. Instead, she disappeared. After she was reported missing, the police launched a search of the Cecil but found nothing. Unfortunately, they neglected to check the water tanks on the hotel's roof.

Even before her disappearance, there was cause for concern. In the days before her death, Elisa had begun acting strangely, according to those she shared a room with. A series of public outbursts, including one at the taping of a TV show, had raised a few eyebrows. Then footage from the Cecil's internal CCTV camera system turned up, showing Elisa behaving in a very strange manner. She appeared to be either reacting and talking to somebody who wasn't there, or possibly to a person who was slightly out of the frame.

Elisa Lam's body was not discovered until 19 days after she was reported missing. She was found to be floating in one of the rooftop cisterns. Searchers were tipped off when a guest at the Cecil called reception to complain about the taste of the tap water.

No sooner was Elisa Lam's body recovered than the theories regarding her manner of death started to appear. They ranged from the common sense (a psychotic break or other behavioral crisis) through the macabre (she was drugged and then murdered) to the darkly paranormal (the malevolent phantoms of the Hotel Cecil lured her to her death).

Following its closure, the Cecil sat empty. It was then put into a state of renovation, with the aim of giving the old place a new lease of life. But no matter what is done to the structure in terms of modifying and redecorating it, it seems likely that the ghost stories will continue to resurface. In 2023, I interviewed Patti Negri, a witch, psychic medium, and recurring guest on the television show *Ghost Adventures*, about her experiences within the walls of the hotel.

In her view, the Cecil is experiencing the darkest of dark hauntings; in fact, Negri had no compunction whatsoever about labeling it "demonic," a term that generates controversy among members of the paranormal community. In her view, the dark force has swirled around the hotel for years, preying on the minds of some susceptible individuals who have boarded there. "That place makes you want to kill yourself," she recalled.

Patti Negri is a Hollywood psychic and author who is well known for her frequent appearances on the TV show *Ghost Adventures* on the Travel Channel.

Negri herself experienced a prolonged psychic attack while walking the halls of the Cecil, particularly in one very specific room: that of "Pigeon" Goldie Osgood. The more time she spent in the hotel, the stronger became the compulsion for Negri to take her own life—by hurling herself out of a window. It was, she says, only an intervention by *Ghost Adventures* host Zak Bagans that snapped her out of it, just in the nick of time.

Negri visited the Hotel Cecil in 2020, when it had no residents and was still sitting empty. Based on the overwhelming level of negativity she encountered, one can only wonder what future occupants of Skid Row's most infamous landmark will experience.

A DEAL WITH THE DEVIL: DOZMARY POOL

On Bodmin Moor in Cornwall, branching off from the A30, just a stone's throw from the famous Jamaica Inn, runs an unassuming back road. The person traveling on foot must remain aware at all times, keeping a watchful eye out for traffic. There is no pavement or sidewalk, just a grass verge on either side. After a time, the road dips downward and climbs again, curving around to the right, and there, at the far end of the road, lies Dozmary Pool.

The pool is now a shadow of its former self, with a much lower surface level than it once had. A bleak and desolate place, Dozmary Pool nonetheless has its own manner of windswept beauty that must be seen and experienced to be believed.

How did the pool get its name? Nobody knows for sure, although a macabre story claims that a local girl nicknamed "Dozy Mary" (presumably because of her lack of intelligence) was found dead there.

Cornwall is rich with Arthurian legend and folklore. Legend holds that Dozmary Pool is the place in which the young Arthur, then nothing more than a squire, was given the magical sword Excalibur by the Lady of the Lake.

Scholars believe that the Battle of Camlann may have taken place in Cornwall. This was the climactic battle between King Arthur and his nephew, Mordred, at Slaughter Bridge, ten miles from Dozmary Pool near what is now the town of Camelford. Arthur defeated Mordred but was mortally wounded in the process. Following his death, the knight Sir Bedivere took the sword from the lifeless hand of his king, rode to Dozmary Pool, and returned it whence it came. The Lady of the Lake stretched up a hand to catch the weapon by its hilt and pulled it back beneath the surface of the water, never to be seen again.

The pool was said to be bottomless back then, though it certainly is not now. In 2017, a young girl named Matilda Jones made a surprising find in the shallow waters at the edge of the pool—a sword. Nobody is quite sure how the sword got there, but its age can only be measured in years, not centuries. That seems rather a pity, because if this truly *was* the legendary Excalibur, then seven-year-old Matilda would have been entitled to call herself the one true monarch of Britain!

There is another candidate for the last resting place of Excalibur— Loe Pool, which lies about an hour and a half's drive to the southwest of Dozmary.

Historians have learned that Dozmary Pool's significance in the history books goes back to long before the Dark Ages. Flint tools and arrowheads have been found on the lakebed. As one of the largest sources of fish and fresh water in Cornwall, it would have been a focal point for the earliest hunter-gatherer tribes.

Ah, but what of the ghosts? Although there are no contemporary hauntings associated with it, Dozmary Pool is said to be haunted by a spirit named Jan Tregeagle—the ghost of a corrupt magistrate who, after his death sometime in the 1600s, made a deal with the devil and was forced into haunting the pool until he finished emptying it with a seashell. This is likely to be decidedly trickier than it sounds, because the shell has a hole in it! Legend has it that Tregeagle can still be heard shrieking across the moor on dark and windy nights.

Jan Tregeagle is one of the most popular figures in Cornish folklore, and the stories of his escapades continue to fascinate today, perhaps because they form a timeless morality tale that is best told in front of a roaring fire in a Cornish pub. After his death, Tregeagle supposedly came back from the pit of hell to testify in court that he had faked a legal document and bilked an innocent man out of a sum of money.

What with hell being a rather unpleasant place, the newly penitent spirit of Jan Tregeagle begged and pleaded not to go back there. Although there was nothing the judge could do about it, the local priest had an idea. If he made the itinerant spirit perform a series of Sisyphean tasks in the name of the Lord, work that could never be finished no matter how hard he tried, then the devil would never be able to claim

Dozmary Pool is a small lake near Bolventor on Bodmin Moor in Cornwall, England. Legend has it that this is where the Lady of the Lake gave King Arthur the sword Excalibur.

his due. With his only alternative being damnation, Tregeagle agreed to undertake whatever tasks the holy man assigned him.

Emptying Dozmary Pool with a leaky seashell was only the first item on Jan's to-do list. He was also tasked with weaving a long rope—no problem, one might think, except for the fact that this must be done on the beach at Gwenor Cove, and the rope formed only from sand. No matter how quickly Jan wove sand, the tide always came in and undid all his work.

Dispatched to Land's End for his next labor, he was forced to sweep Porthcurno Cove into the sea at Mill Bay. He is said to still be working on this eternal chore and can be heard screaming in rage and frustration, especially when a storm sweeps in from the ocean to make his burden more miserable still.

THE DEAD OF DENVER BOTANIC GARDENS

A number of wonderful ghost stories have made it to the silver screen. Without a doubt, my favorite of them all is *Poltergeist* (and I'm talking about the 1982 original, not the 2015 remake). Steven Spielberg and Tobe Hooper's classic chiller brought the supernatural to America's suburbs, taking the familiar, everyday world and injecting ghosts.

The suburban neighborhood in which the film is set turns out to have been built on top of a cemetery. As the movie builds toward its big finish and coffins explode from the ground all around the Freeling family residence, family man Steven Freeling grabs his weaselly boss and growls: "You son of a bitch! You moved the cemetery, but you left the bodies, didn't you? You son of a bitch, you left the bodies, and you only moved the headstones! You only moved the headstones! Why? WHY?!?"

As a plot device, it's brilliant. To save money on construction, a building company removes the headstones from a graveyard, smooths the ground over, and then begins building on top of it. This isn't just the stuff of Hollywood imaginings, however; it really did happen.

Denver's Mount Prospect Cemetery (also known as Prospect Hill Cemetery) hosted its first burial in 1859. Its location had been carefully chosen; it had to be within easy traveling distance of the city but, at the same time, not so close that it impeded Denver's growth. The cemetery grew but never realized its true potential. For one thing, because there was very little water in the vicinity, it was difficult to irrigate the grass, which meant that the graveyard contained as much dirt, weeds, and dust as it did greenery.

There was also no real organization to the way it was laid out. Catholics were buried next to Protestants, whose graves abutted those of Jews. At first, it was an ugly mishmash, and as the city grew, people wanted something better. Although Mount Prospect was better organized by the end of the Civil War in 1865, with separate areas for different religious factions, deceased Union soldiers, and a Potter's Field for the poverty-stricken, a competing cemetery was established in 1876. Named the Riverside Cemetery, this was where the rich and connected were buried.

After 1893, there were no further burials in Mount Prospect. Instead, it was decided that the cemetery would be converted into a park for the enjoyment of the public. The only problem was: what was to be done with the bodies? Thousands of men, women, and children were buried there. The services of a private contractor were engaged to exhume them and relocate them to Riverside. To say that this was not done in the most respectful manner possible would be an understatement. Two, three, sometimes four or more bodies were broken up and jammed together in the same casket. This mistreatment of human remains became something of a scandal, and the contractor was ultimately dismissed. Ghost stories began to circulate, and people avoided the area surrounding the cemetery at night in case they encountered the spirits of the restless dead.

A small number of Denverites made sure that their dead family members were relocated, but that still left thousands of bodies moldering beneath what would soon become Cheesman Park.

Families of those buried at Mount Prospect were given a few weeks' notice to arrange the movement of their loved ones' remains to a new resting place. After that, the headstones would be removed (and almost certainly destroyed), and the process of converting the area into a park would begin. A small number of Denverites made sure that their dead family members were relocated, but that still left thousands of bodies moldering beneath what would soon become Cheesman Park.

In 1926, an elegant mansion was built on top of Calvary Hill, formerly the Catholic section of Mount Prospect. The Waring House, as it came to be known, is currently the administrative center for Denver Botanic Gardens, which now backs onto the house itself. Considering the ground on which it was built, it should come as no surprise at all that the Waring House is said to be *very* haunted indeed.

A number of staff members refuse to work late, especially after night has fallen. Some have heard their names called, while others have heard voices telling them to get out. Lights switch themselves off and on, and doors are known to open and close by themselves. Footsteps walk across the floors of empty rooms. There have been sightings of shadow figures. It is a classic case of a haunting if ever I saw one, and when I was offered the opportunity to spend several nights there, I jumped at the chance.

For the most part, the people who work at the Waring House have a good sense of humor where the paranormal activity is concerned. A sign is posted on the basement door reminding staff to keep it closed "because it keeps the ghosts in."

The building is reputedly haunted by the spirit of a mischievous young boy, a prankster who loves to play tricks on staff and visitors alike. My colleague, Catlyn, may well have encountered him herself when she was paying a visit to the ground-floor restroom. The rest of our

Denver Botanic Gardens is a beautiful, relaxing place ... that is built right where there was once a graveyard and, consequently, appears to get visited by ghosts.

team had gathered in the main hall, and every one of us was accounted for when we heard the sound of the restroom door handle jiggling.

We just looked at one another and shrugged, assuming that the door, which was old and sturdy, was probably prone to sticking in the frame. All it would take to open it would be a sharp tug. When Catlyn finally emerged, she was not amused at what she thought was a practical joke on our part. Despite our team having a "no pranking on investigations" policy, she believed that one of us was deliberately holding the door shut, preventing her from getting out.

"That wasn't just a sticky door," she insisted. "Somebody was pulling hard on the other side, keeping me from opening it. For a moment, I couldn't get out."

We were gifted with both electronic voice phenomena (EVPs) and direct voice phenomena (DVPs), the most memorable of which was obtained in the basement. The basement is certainly the most eerie part of the building (aren't they always?), and it becomes even more so when you realize that directly beneath your feet are coffins containing the remains of people who died in the nineteenth century. When we asked the question, "Where are we?" we received the rather disconcerting answer: "In a mass grave."

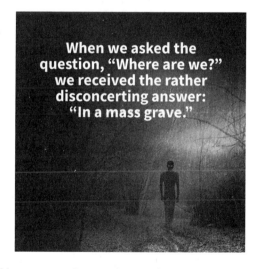

When we asked the question, "Where are we?" we received the rather disconcerting answer: "In a mass grave."

There were also a number of profane EVPs, which was only to be expected. After all, how happy would *you* be if your place of eternal rest was disturbed by construction workers and a manor house built on top of it? I can't speak for anybody else, but I'd be angry, and I'd do everything possible to make that anger known to the living.

Not only are the staff at Denver Botanic Gardens used to sharing their workplace with ghosts, but each October they embrace the subject fully by running tours known as Ghosts in the Gardens. It's an opportunity for visitors to learn about the haunted history of the gardens, and I heartily recommend signing up. If you should happen to use the restroom in the Waring House ... watch out for that door.

THE LAST BREATH:
WAVERLY HILLS SANATORIUM

Of the countless haunted locations that paranormal investigators flock to each year, few are as instantly recognizable—and purely iconic—as the Waverly Hills Sanatorium in Louisville, Kentucky.

Thanks largely to TV shows and bloggers who didn't do much in the way of actual research, the sanatorium is said to have been the scene of tens of thousands of deaths. It is not uncommon to find claims that anywhere between 50,000 to 65,000 people died at Waverly Hills. Both numbers are massively inflated. Author Troy Taylor cites the far more reasonable estimate of 6,000 deaths, based upon the documentation—in this case, legal death certificates—that were filed. Researcher Shannon Bradley Byers agrees. Byers has reviewed many of the Waverly Hills death certificates herself and has made it her mission to dispel as many of the myths and sheer bunk surrounding the sanatorium as she possibly can. This is a thankless task; far too many paranormal enthusiasts and those with a casual interest are willing to swallow the myth, rather than the reality, because it makes for a more exciting and spine-chilling story.

According to some accounts, a nurse hanged herself on the fifth floor after finding out she was pregnant, and the father was one of the married doctors at Waverly Hills. There are also claims of a nurse jumping from the roof to her death. There's not a shred of evidence to support either of these claims.

Why, then, is the Waverly Hills haunting such a fascinating case? Simply put, the place has to be experienced to be believed.

I spoke to several fellow paranormal investigators, people I trust who are not given to exaggeration, and all of them claimed to have witnessed some truly remarkable paranormal activity in the old sanatorium. This included multiple shadow figures (including one seen crawling along the *ceiling*), direct voice phenomena, and several Class A electronic voice phenomena, or EVPs. I was hearing the same stories over and over again from different friends and colleagues, so finally I just had to go and see for myself.

Although it is possible to take a reasonably priced tour, Waverly Hills, it must be said, is not a cheap place to rent. Nevertheless, my friends and I pooled our money and took over the sanatorium for a night in the summer of 2016. Arriving at sunset, we waited impatiently

The historic (and haunted) Waverly Hills Sanatorium once delivered state-of-the-art care to tuberculosis patients.

for somebody to come and unlock the main gate. Having seen, heard, and read so much about it over the years, every one of us was fired up to experience it for ourselves.

As you drive slowly along the tree-lined track, the sanatorium suddenly appears in front of you. It looks magnificent at the end of the day as the last rays of sunlight are starting to fade. Waverly Hills looks a little imposing, with the two side wings branching off from the central building looking as though they might be arms reaching out to engulf you, but I was expecting it to seem sinister and ominous. Inside, however, as I made my way through the hallways, stepping in and out of the rooms that once housed tuberculosis patients, all I felt was a sense of peace and tranquility.

Photographs of former patients had been left in one or two of the rooms, accompanied by the occasional bunch of flowers. Walking along the balcony at the front of the sanatorium, it was possible to stand where the patients used to be wheeled out of their rooms, still in bed, to lie in the sunshine and breathe in a little fresh air, no matter how bad the weather.

Fresh air was at one time believed to be the most effective treatment for pulmonary tuberculosis. It was certainly better than certain other methods of treating the disease, some of which bordered on the cruel and inhumane. Some sufferers had sandbags placed upon their chest. More weight was added to the sandbags each day, the theory being that as the bags got heavier, the patient's lungs would work harder to breathe in the same way that a weightlifter's arms strengthen after each workout—an effort to train the lung muscle, as it were.

Worse still were the experimental thoracic surgeries, which involved cutting open a critically ill patient's chest and artificially inflating the lung. More than one patient died on the operating table as a direct consequence of this procedure, which was never proven to have any clinical benefit whatsoever.

Yet it would be a mistake to think of Waverly Hills Sanatorium as a place of torture and misery, no matter how much some TV shows would like you to. Many of the photographs dating back to its period as a tuberculosis treatment center show people smiling and apparently enjoying themselves. The staff members and medical professionals worked long and hard in their fight against an awful disease, and while thousands of patients died, thousands more survived and got to go home again.

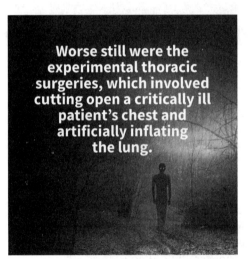

Worse still were the experimental thoracic surgeries, which involved cutting open a critically ill patient's chest and artificially inflating the lung.

On the roof, we found a swing set, benches, and children's toys. Pediatric patients often played up there, and the staff took breaks in the sunshine, enjoying a panoramic view of some beautiful, wooded countryside. Unbeknownst to me, while I was standing on the roof that night with two colleagues, enjoying the starry night sky and listening to the sounds of the night, my fellow investigators were having a bizarre experience down in the tunnel.

The tunnel slopes steeply downward from the sanatorium, and much has been made of it being a so-called "death tunnel" or "body chute." Stories abound that the death rate at Waverly Hills was so high that this tunnel was bored out as a means of quickly conveying bodies to the undertaker's hearse. As we have already seen, this isn't true. The tunnel existed primarily as a means of bringing food and stores inside and giving the staff members a sheltered way of getting into the building during inclement weather. However, bodies *were* taken down and delivered to the hearse from time to time, primarily because it was bad for morale for patients to see corpses being wheeled out across the front lawn. The tunnel provided a discreet method of removing them without disturbing anybody's day.

Unfortunately, this practice was halted abruptly after there was a terrible accident in the tunnel. A winch was used to lower bodies down a specially laid track. The cable snapped unexpectedly, sending a dead body hurtling down the track on a runaway cart. It had picked up so much speed by the time it reached the bottom of the tunnel that the cart blasted straight through the doors and flung the body out into the open air.

A small group of my colleagues was heading toward the tunnel entrance when they suddenly stopped in their tracks. They could hear a voice coming from somewhere within the tunnel. They could recognize the voice very distinctly: it was mine. Which was strange, because I was up on the roof at the opposite end of the building at the time. There was literally no way my voice could have carried that far, through several floors of an extremely solid building and down into a tunnel. When they went to check, the tunnel was completely deserted.

All of which begs the question: what on earth was going on down in that tunnel? Was something impersonating me, imitating my voice? I had been down in the tunnel earlier that night. Perhaps it was a replay of my own words, somehow paranormally replayed a few hours after I had said them. An even weirder possibility was that of a time slip, although I'll be the first to admit that such a theory is pretty far out there. We never did find a satisfactory explanation and just chalked it up as just another slice of the high strangeness that is Waverly Hills Sanatorium.

As the night wore on, my wife, Laura, hit upon the idea of spicing up the mood a little by playing some period-specific music. She's an aficionado of old tunes, and we soon had the smooth, dulcet tones of Cole Porter echoing through the darkness. It was our hope that the tunes would be pleasing to any spirits that may have been present.

The hallways and patient rooms once echoed with coughing and rasping breaths. They are now ominously silent.

Nothing spectacular happened to us that night. No shadow figures or light anomalies, no phantom knocking or unexplained cold spots; in fact, the night was hot and humid. But there was one other happening of note. As Laura was climbing one of the staircases to the second floor, a second set of footsteps followed her up. On reaching the landing, she turned around, and of course, nobody was there. The footsteps stopped seconds later, a few steps below her.

Perhaps somebody had liked the music after all.

GHOSTS ON THE LONDON UNDERGROUND

"The British are clever," an old joke goes, "because every city has got sewers, but only they thought up the idea of putting trains in them." They were referring, of course, to the London Underground, which has its origins in the early 1860s. To be precise, the first trains began rolling in 1863 on a single stretch of track. By the turn of the century, plans were well underway for the implementation of a sprawling network of interconnected tunnels and railroad tracks spanning the underbelly of the British Empire's capital like a great spider's web. In reality, the Underground system sounds more organized than it truly is; think of it as more akin to a patchwork quilt than a single blanket cut from the same cloth. To put it in American parlance, it's a bunch of smaller networks that were MacGyvered together, rather than the product of a single unified grand design.

Londoners have come to rely on the Underground as an integral part of their everyday lives. More than three million people, ranging from commuters to tourists, ride the rails every day. That's approximately 1.1 *billion* every year.

Small wonder some of them encounter ghosts.

Ever since its inception, the London Underground has had a connection with death. Tunneling beneath the streets of the city was thankless, dirty, and hazardous work. Men lost arms, legs, and even their lives while digging their way underneath London.

During World War II, thousands of families sought shelter from German air raids by descending into Underground stations to wait out the bombing. Unfortunately, the so-called tube stations were not always as safe as people hoped. On October 13, 1940, a Luftwaffe bomber struck the Bounds Green Station, killing 16 people and wounding many others. The station wasn't targeted deliberately: rather, a stray bomb hit a row of houses, which collapsed down into the tunnel where civilians were sheltering. The following night's air raid saw an even greater loss of life at the Balham Station, when the concussion from a bomb blast ruptured a water main. A torrent of mud, sludge, and water poured into the station, drowning or suffocating 68 people (the number is an approximation) and injuring 70 more. It took months for the overworked men of the London Fire Brigade to recover all of the bodies.

On the night of March 3, 1943, 173 people suffocated or were crushed to death while rushing down into Bethnal Green Station to take cover from an air raid. There was only one way in and out, a single entrance. The sound of anti-aircraft artillery firing nearby was mistaken for an exploding bomb, triggering a mass panic that quickly became a stampede. Sixty-two of those killed were children.

Londoners used the undergound as a shelter to hide in from the relentless air raids by the Nazis during World War II.

Bethnal Green Station is said to be haunted by the tragic events of that night. Stories circulate regarding the screams and cries of those poor souls who were crammed together in the darkness, still being heard decades afterward. This tends to happen most commonly at around 9 P.M., the time the incident took place. This has all the hallmarks of a residual haunting rather than an intelligent one; at least, we must hope that to be the case. It is less painful to accept the notion of the phantom screams being a sort of paranormal recording than it is to consider the possibility that some of those killed in the crush may still be around today.

Multiple train crashes throughout the history of the Underground have also claimed many innocent lives. On February 28, 1975, a train carrying 300 passengers didn't make its stop at Moorgate Station, instead slamming into the tunnel wall at 35 miles per hour. Moorgate was a so-called "dead end" or terminus station. It took six days and over 1,300 responders to rescue the 74 wounded and recover the bodies of the 43 passengers who were killed in the crash. The cause remains undetermined. Mechanical failure was ruled out, which meant that blame inevitably fell on the shoulders of the driver, the first man to be killed and the last to be recovered from the wreckage. A coroner's inquest found no evidence of his having suffered sudden illness in his final moments of life.

Curiously, the ghost sighting associated with Moorgate Station predates the crash by several weeks. In late 1974, as it still is today, most track maintenance was carried out late at night once the last trains had stopped running. Based on the fact that Underground maintenance commonly wore blue overalls, a work crew at Moorgate spotted what they assumed was one of their colleagues approaching them in the darkness. Then they got a closer look at him and saw that the workman appeared to be absolutely terrified, though of what, they could not say. All was quiet at the station that night, with no obvious cause for alarm. On the other hand, there was *significant* cause for alarm among the astonished work crew when they saw the apparition walk straight through a solid section of tunnel wall and disappear from sight.

The phantom was seen more than once and by multiple witnesses, and it was believed to be the apparition of a London Underground employee who was accidentally killed while performing his duties in the

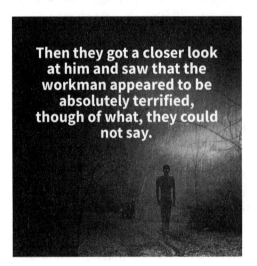

Then they got a closer look at him and saw that the workman appeared to be absolutely terrified, though of what, they could not say.

tunnel. It is tempting to draw a connection between the ghost sighting and the subsequent disaster. Some people formed the opinion that he was a harbinger of doom, presaging the tragedy that was about to take place at Moorgate. Others even theorized that the reason the driver of the ill-fated train failed to stop was because he saw the apparition himself, causing such a shock that he temporarily took leave of his senses. There is not a shred of evidence to support that contention, however, and based on the fact that he had recently twice failed to stop at other stations, it is not unreasonable to conclude that this was a case of distracted driving—with devastating consequences.

On November 18, 1987, an accidental fire at King's Cross Underground Station claimed the lives of 31 people, including a fire officer who was engaged in rescue efforts. The tragedy was caused by a discarded match. Beginning in the late 1980s, commuters traveling through King's Cross reported seeing the apparition of a young woman wearing contemporary clothing. She is always said to be in a state of great distress, sobbing unconsolably and pleading for help with open arms. Although her identity has never been conclusively established, it seems reasonable to conclude that the female apparition is connected with the fire in some way. It is worth remembering that this does not necessarily mean that she was killed in the tragedy. There are numerous cases on record documenting phantoms of the living, most prevalently in moments of great fear and stress; these are called crisis apparitions. Perhaps, rather than being the spirit of a dead person, this ghost is an after-echo imprinted on the environment of King's Cross Station at the time of the disaster, only to be replayed when the circumstances are right.

The same might also be said of the strong odor of smoke and burning reported by many people at King's Cross—a smell that seems to have no discernible source.

A few years back, I was fortunate enough to be invited to investigate part of the London Underground in person—specifically, one of the former electrical substations that used to help power the system. (By agreement, I will not identify the specific line or location.) Our host was a staff member who shared some of his own uncanny experiences while

London's famous King's Cross Station was the site of a 1987 fire that killed 31 people, and some travelers say that they have seen ghosts at the station since then.

DARK SPIRITS: MONSTERS, DEMONS, AND DEVILS

on the job. These included an escalator starting up all by itself, despite the fact that he had pulled its circuit breaker a short while before. The moving staircase was supposed to be completely devoid of power.

More alarming by far was what happened next. While making a cup of tea for himself and his colleague, the Underground veteran missed a sight that shocked the other man to his core. The room was awash with an icy cold. A man's disembodied head drifted through the wall, floated into the center of the room, stared at the two Underground employees briefly, and then vanished into thin air. The frazzled co-worker quit shortly afterward, and who could blame him?

The station I was investigating had plenty of reports of ghostly phenomena, including doors and drawers that would open and close of their own volition. The building was plagued with weird electrical issues. Disembodied voices were heard, usually at night. Because at least one death is associated with the location, staff tend to attribute much of the weirdness to the dead man's ghost and try their best never to be alone in the building after dark.

My own investigation into the location was inconclusive, as is so often the case with the haunting of the world's oldest underground railway network. The ghost sightings continue to arise and show no signs of slowing down.

INTO THIN AIR: THE BERMUDA TRIANGLE

If some of the stories are to be believed, then the waters between Miami, Florida; San Juan, Puerto Rico; and the island of Bermuda are among the most dangerous in the world. Not confined to the seas, the hazards extend to the skies above. The Bermuda Triangle has a reputation for swallowing boats, ships, and aircraft. Some disappear without a trace, never to be seen again. Where do they go? Is the Triangle *really* as deadly as we've been led to believe? And what is behind it all?

In 1880, the British training frigate HMS *Atalanta* vanished without a trace while sailing in the waters around Bermuda, bound for Great Britain. Weather conditions in the region were stormy and would have made for a difficult passage. All 281 of the *Atalanta*'s crew were lost with her. Because she was a training ship, many of those hands were raw recruits, with just a few experienced seamen and officers to oversee their education. The ship also rolled heavily and could easily have overbalanced in rough seas.

In March 1918, with World War I just entering its final stages, a large U.S. Navy transport ship set sail into the waters of the Bermuda Triangle. She was named the USS *Cyclops*. Loaded with manganese ore mined in Brazil, the *Cyclops* had made an impromptu stop in Barbados before making course for the port of Baltimore. She never arrived, having vanished without a trace somewhere out on the ocean. Although this was wartime, German U-boats were not to blame. None were operating in the region in which the *Cyclops* vanished along with her crew of 306 souls.

The USS *Cyclops* was a *Proteus*-class collier (cargo ship) heading for Baltimore with a load of manganese ore when it disappeared in March 1918. Was she a victim of a German U-boat or the Bermuda Triangle?

One hypothesis is that subterranean methane gas rose to the surface and was responsible for her sinking. Another is that the manganese cargo may have ignited and blown up the *Cyclops*, though no wreckage was ever found. Another possibility is that the ship broke in two amidships due to poor distribution of her cargo load and sank so quickly that all of her crew were pulled down into the ocean depths along with her.

Although the ship was big, she was designed to carry coal, not heavy ore. The *Cyclops* rode low in the water on her final voyage. A large wave could have swamped her deck. Rough seas could have damaged the ship's structure and led to her sinking—yet the final radio transmission received from the *Cyclops* said, "Weather well, all fair." However, the Bermuda Triangle is well known for having volatile weather conditions, which can flip from safe to deadly in a relatively short amount of time.

A flight of five U.S. Navy TBM Avenger torpedo bombers disappeared on December 5, 1945, while out on a training exercise from their home base, Naval Air Station Fort Lauderdale in Florida. Their designation was Flight 19. Later that afternoon, its commanding officer, Lt. Charles C. Taylor, broadcast a message stating that they had lost sight of land. Taylor was no wet-behind-the-ears rookie. On the contrary, he was an experienced veteran with thousands of hours of flight time under his belt. For him and his fellow pilots to become lost on a training exercise in home waters would be unusual. A few minutes later, another radio message was received by the base control tower, equally confused. The flight reported that they were running low on fuel and that as soon as a single one of the Avengers reached critical levels, all five would ditch into the ocean as close together as possible.

"Everything looks strange," one of the transmissions said. "Even the ocean looks wrong."

Four hours after Flight 19 had taken off, the radio transmissions stopped.

A rescue flight comprised of two Martin PBM Mariner flying boats was sortied that evening with orders to investigate and recover the downed airmen. These aircraft were so big, they came with a galley where food could be prepared to sustain the crew of 13. Contact was lost with one of the Mariners just a short time after takeoff, the lumbering plane vanishing off the radar screen. It was never seen again. The Navy had lost five of its aircraft, complete with all personnel—some 27 men in all, vanished without a trace.

For five days, the Navy and Coast Guard threw all the resources they could spare into searching the ocean for survivors or debris. They found neither. Finally, the military admitted defeat and called off the search, formally declaring the airmen missing. It is a mystery that has never been solved.

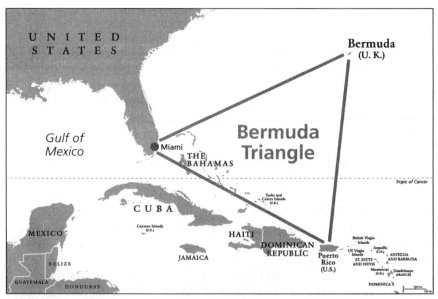

The expanse between Miami, Bermuda, and Puerto Rico that is known as the Bermuda Triangle has been plagued by mysterious disappearances of ships and airplanes.

Weather conditions at the beginning of Flight 19's planned route were fair that day. Visibility was good along the Florida coast, although the sea conditions were a little rough. Yet as the day wore on, conditions deteriorated, with the air becoming turbulent and the cloud cover descending. The ocean became violent. Sailors reported seeing a single plane catching fire and crashing into the ocean, along with a massive explosion. In all likelihood, this was the missing Mariner flying boat.

The disappearance of Flight 19 is even stranger. The most conventional explanation is that the flight became disoriented, unsure of its position (as confirmed by its increasingly nervous radio traffic), and finally ran out of fuel over the open ocean. By nightfall, the seas had become treacherous, making the survival of the aviators highly unlikely even if they were able to ditch successfully.

There are other theories, ranging from abduction by UFOs operating from undersea bases (Steven Spielberg popularized this notion by inserting it into his movie *Close Encounters of the Third Kind*) to the aircraft having entered another dimension or an alternate reality. Some believe that huge waterspouts blasting up above the surface of the ocean knocked the Avengers out of the sky, while others hypothesize that the planes entered a rift or portal that sent them backward or forward in time.

Unless what remains of the missing Avengers are ever found, the answer will never be known for sure.

Although ships, boats, and planes have been reported lost in the Bermuda Triangle for hundreds of years and no doubt will continue to be so in the future, examining the data reveals that transiting these waters is statistically no more dangerous than journeying through any other part of the Atlantic Ocean. Despite being prone to violent weather, including hurricanes, the Bermuda Triangle is filled with ships and aircraft every day. In seagoing and aviation terms, it's the equivalent of a major highway. It would be remarkable if there weren't accidents, sinkings, and crashes.

Where did the commonly held belief that the Bermuda Triangle is so deadly originate? The term "Bermuda Triangle" dates back to February 1964, courtesy of Vincent Gaddis, who wrote an article for *Argosy* magazine titled "The Deadly Bermuda Triangle." In it, Gaddis laid the foundations by listing numerous ships and aircraft that had disappeared under potentially mysterious circumstances while passing through the area. He did not posit a weird explanation for those disappearances—that would come ten years later.

Much of the responsibility for popularizing the Triangle and cementing its dark reputation can be laid at the door of author Charles Berlitz, whose 1974 book *The Bermuda Triangle* really took the ball and ran with it. During the 1970s, readers were eager for tales of mystery and the supernatural. Berlitz's book became a smash hit, selling tens of millions of copies worldwide and forever planting the term "Bermuda Triangle" in the popular consciousness. Some of his research was questionable, as was his hypothesis that the lost city of Atlantis might lie at the heart of the Bermuda Triangle and be behind the disappearances.

Yet there are those who still believe there is something paranormal at work in those stormy waters. They point to the mysterious disappearances of the USS *Cyclops*, Flight 19, and others, reminding us that when it comes to the great expanses of ocean that cover most of the globe, we don't have all the answers ... and perhaps we never will.

THE DEVIL WITHIN

Since ancient times, human beings have believed in the existence of demons. Although the Western world tends to associate them with the Christian belief system, such beliefs span the globe, being found in a multitude of cultures over thousands of years. There's an inherent logic to the line of thinking that holds that if one believes in a god or gods in some form, then there must be both positive and negative aspects—good *and* evil, light and dark, two opposing and balancing forces.

From the djinn of Middle Eastern cultures to the fallen angels of some Christian beliefs, humanity has for millennia looked to these supernatural entities as an explanation for some of the darker aspects of the world. The blame for floods, earthquakes, famine, and pestilence have been laid at their feet. An accompanying belief has long held that demons have the capacity to enter the physical body of a suitably vulnerable human being and take over, possessing their (usually unwilling) victim to achieve their own infernal agenda. History is replete with such cases, many of which make for grim reading when studied.

The primary weapon used against demonic possession is the ritual of exorcism, in which a holy personage—usually working with a support team of varying sizes—attempts to expel the possessing entity. This is not without its risks. It is fair to say that the ritual of exorcism, especially when it takes place over an extended period, is fraught with risks—including the potential death of the person being exorcised. Despite this fact, in the twenty-first century, claims of possession are on the rise, and the demand for exorcism has never been greater, according to the Catholic Church.

THE *EXORCIST* BOY: RONALD HUNKELER

If one single case can be said to encapsulate our present-day perception of exorcism, it is that of a teenage boy named Ronald "Ronnie" Hunkeler. The 13-year-old lived with his parents in Maryland when strange phenomena began taking place around him in January of 1949. Scratching sounds in the walls, at first believed to be rats, turned out to have no such obvious explanation. The puzzled exterminator left empty-handed. Items large and small were seen to move by themselves, including heavy pieces of furniture. The intensity and frequency of these bizarre phenomena ramped up when Ronald's aunt died.

The Hunkelers were a Lutheran family. Taking their concerns to the church brought them no solution. Ronald spent a night in the home of his minister, only to have the bed vibrate and shake as though being manipulated by unseen hands. This ended any theories that the Hunkelers were living in a haunted house. Based on the phenomena having followed him to another location, it was beginning to look like the focus of whatever was happening was their son.

Matters soon escalated to the next level. Ronald began to act out of character, his mood swings happening more often and his behavior growing increasingly bizarre. Just as any good parents would, Mr. and Mrs. Hunkeler took Ronald to doctors to rule out medical and psychological causes for the disturbances in their home and their son. He came back with a clean bill of health, leaving his mother and father with more questions than answers.

How to explain the poltergeist-like phenomena taking place around young Ronald or, worse still, the cuts and welts that began mysteriously appearing on his skin? The Hunkelers began to believe that he might be demonically possessed. The Lutheran faith places far less emphasis on demons and possession than does the Catholic Church, to which the Hunkelers turned for help next.

Ronald was taken to Bel Nor, Missouri, a suburb of St. Louis, to stay in his uncle's home while representatives of the Catholic Church assessed the need for an exorcism. What the priests saw convinced them of the necessity, and permission to carry out the ritual was formally requested from the bishop. Permission was granted. Two Jesuit priests took the lead. Father William Bowdern and Father Raymond Bishop, assisted by Walter Halloran, could not have known at the outset that they were in for the spiritual fight of their lives.

This anonymous-looking house in a St. Louis suburb was the scene of the world's most famous exorcism.

The relatively normal teenager turned into a growling, clawing monster after dark, swearing and cursing at the priests who stood watch over him and performed the rite of exorcism. In addition to raving blasphemies and profanity, Ronald hit and kicked anyone who came within range. For safety's sake, he was restrained to the bed as the exorcism went on night after night. As the days turned into weeks, both he and the priests felt themselves becoming worn down, both physically and emotionally. Angry red welts developed on the possessed boy's skin, spelling out words such as *NO*. The poltergeist activity grew even more severe, with items such as books flying across the room, far from Ronald's physical reach.

Anybody who has seen the movie *The Exorcist*, which was greatly influenced by the Hunkeler case, can easily picture the scene. Although exaggerated for dramatic effect, writer William Peter Blatty and director William Friedkin effectively conveyed the grinding, frenetic feel of Ronald's prolonged exorcism. Ronald—or whatever possessed him—fought hard, and on one of the occasions when he was his usual self, he said that he kept dreaming about being in battle with a dark and evil demonic spirit.

Moving him to the Alexian Brothers Hospital on the nearby university campus was a sound move. It had resources and personnel available that couldn't be brought to bear in an ordinary residence. Ronald was kept in a secure room and watched at all times. This was where the final battle would take place. The teenager underwent a Catholic baptism, and the priests launched a final push to expel the demonic influence from within him.

Ronald would later claim to have seen a vision of St. Michael intervening on his behalf, stepping in to send the demons and evil spirits straight back to hell. It was a suitably epic ending to what had been a grueling ordeal and one that would be debated hotly for decades afterward. A story based on the event was popularized in Blatty's bestselling 1971 novel *The Exorcist*, and movie audiences fainted and vomited in the aisles when the film adaptation was released two years later. The production was said to be cursed, plagued with an unusually high number of deaths, injuries, illnesses, and other misfortunes (though statistically, the claims are questionable). The *Exorcist* franchise made a fortune for Warner Bros., putting demons and possession center stage in the public consciousness.

As for Ronald Hunkeler, rather than cashing in on his status as "the Exorcist boy," he chose instead to keep the events of his childhood absolutely secret. He got married, had children, and worked as an engineer for NASA. Hunkeler hated the thought of being associated with the St. Louis exorcism, particularly when its dramatized version was playing on cinema screens across the world. Whether he really was demonically possessed, was faking the whole thing, or was in the grip of mental illness is impossible to say. Writer and researcher Troy Taylor, author of the book *The Devil Came to St. Louis: Uncensored True Story of the 1949 Exorcism*, has pointed out that the Hunkeler case bears many of the hallmarks of a poltergeist outbreak, including the very rapid onset and equally swift cessation of phenomena. If the eyewitness accounts are to be believed, then *something* uncanny happened to Ronald Hunkeler in the spring of 1949. We can only wonder whether he spent the remainder of his life concerned that whatever it was might rear its head again at any time. He died on May 10, 2020.

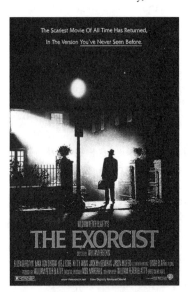

The movie adaptation of William Peter Blatty's *The Exorcist* was a blockbuster that introduced many non-Catholic Americans to the ritual of exorcism.

AN UNNECESSARY DEATH: ANNELIESE MICHEL

Anna Elisabeth Michel was born in Bavaria on September 21, 1952. To friends and family alike, she was known as Anneliese. Her parents were devout Catholics and raised their children in strict adherence to that faith. At the age of 16, she began to suffer from seizures, which terrified her parents and siblings. Hospitalization resulted in a diagnosis of epilepsy, which doctors attempted to treat with anticonvulsants. Unbeknownst to them, epileptics are between eight and ten times more likely to suffer from psychosis than are those who don't have the condition. They can suffer from severe delusions and become partly or even completely dissociated from reality as the mental health disorder progresses.

Anneliese prayed regularly but became concerned when she began hearing voices in her head responding to her prayers. Next came what were probably visual hallucinations, demonic faces growling and snarling at her when she least expected it. To the deeply religious Anneliese and her parents, the problem was obvious: she was possessed by demons and evil spirits—including Adolf Hitler and Judas Iscariot.

One of the symptoms of possession that representatives of the church look for is a strong aversion to religious iconography. Anneliese, who had taken such great comfort in her faith, now wouldn't go anywhere near a rosary or a Bible, let alone a church. Her behavior became increasingly unbalanced, and she sometimes acted more like an animal than the 23-year-old woman she was. The obvious answer was exorcism. Although we might think of an exorcism as a ritual undertaken in a single session or possibly a handful, Anneliese Michel's was a protracted ordeal that lasted for ten months, beginning in September 1975 until her eventual death in July the following year.

There would be a total of 67 sessions, each one presided over by priests who were determined to cast the demon out of the innocent young woman. Throughout the ten-month period, Anneliese ate or drank so little that she barely reached subsistence level. Malnutrition and dehydration became increasingly severe, bringing with them significant weight loss. By the summer of 1976, the once fresh-faced, healthy Anneliese appeared skeletal, barely a shadow of her former self. The priests pushed

Anneliese developed an aversion to religious objects such as Bibles and rosary beads. She also could not bear to enter a church.

on, yet try as they might, the demon they believed possessed Anneliese only fought harder, hurling abuse at the exorcists who earnestly tried to save her. It's difficult to comprehend the suffering that the poor woman experienced in the days leading up to her death as she grew weaker and ravaged by hunger. By the time of her death on July 1, her now acidotic 70-pound body was literally eating itself alive, the cells desperate for nourishment and hydration despite her lack of eating or drinking.

Even after her funeral, Josef and Anna Michel still clung to the idea that their daughter was possessed by a demon. In February 1978, after a nun claimed that Anneliese's body would not decay, they had the grave opened and her remains exhumed. Contrary to the nun's vision, decomposition was in line with a body that had spent a year and a half in the ground.

> It was alleged that Anneliese was ... the victim of illness, compounded by the strong religious factors that sent her down the path of exorcism instead of more stringent medical care.

One month later, criminal charges were leveled against both the exorcists and Anneliese's parents, alleging that their neglect was solely responsible for her death. They had chosen to stop medical and psychological treatment and instead commended their daughter into the hands of the church. The intervention of medical professionals would have saved her life, had they allowed it.

When the case went to trial, prosecutors outright rejected claims that Anneliese had been possessed by demons—a concept that few judges are willing to allow in their courtroom. It was alleged that Anneliese was instead the victim of illness, compounded by the strong religious factors that sent her down the path of exorcism instead of more stringent medical care. Although guilty verdicts were handed out to all four of the defendants, none of them was sentenced to prison time. The stiffest penalty imposed was shared payment of court costs.

With the benefit of hindsight, most contemporary students of the case believe that Anneliese Michel's tragic death was entirely preventable, a case of mistreated illness rather than genuine demonic possession. Yet there are also those who insist that the conditions of depression, epilepsy, and psychosis may have rendered her vulnerable to possession by opportunistic dark entities. Ultimately, whichever position an individual lands on will likely be colored by their own religious beliefs—or the lack thereof.

DEVILRY IN GARY?
THE AMMONS DEMON HOUSE

Zak Bagans, the star and driving force behind the TV show *Ghost Adventures*, called it "the Demon House." The small, ordinary-looking house on Carolina Street in Gary, Indiana, was said by some to be the scene of one of the twenty-first century's most disturbing demonic hauntings. In the winter of 2011, Latoya Ammons and her family moved into their new home. Almost immediately, they claimed that strange things began to happen, beginning with flies clustering inside their porch. There are those who believe that the presence of swarms of flies will accompany a demonic infestation, a belief that has been firmly cemented in the mass consciousness since the movie *The Amityville Horror* featured it in 1979. This may stem from the naming of the demon Beelzebub as "Lord of the Flies." Like many people, the family believed the infestation of flies in their new home to be something abnormal for the time of year—December was too cold for them to still be active, it was

Not only is Zak Bagans the man behind the television show *Ghost Adventures* but he also owns Zak Bagans Haunted Museum in Las Vegas, Nevada.

thought. In actuality, flies do seek warmth and shelter during the winter months, looking for out-of-the-way spots for their eggs.

More unnerving still were the phantom footsteps that were heard inside empty parts of the home, sometimes accompanied by the sounds of doors opening and closing. The apparition of an adult male was seen, presumably the source of the footsteps. Matters took a turn for the terrifying when Latoya and her mother witnessed one of the children, a 12-year-old girl, levitating above her bed while she was sleeping.

Desperate for help, the family reached out to self-professed psychic mediums, who told them that the source of the activity was demonic infestation … with not just one or two, but *hundreds* of demons crammed inside the modestly sized house. Understandably, the family was now living in abject fear. As Christians, they tried to combat the dark forces lurking within their home with prayer and the power of faith—to no avail. If anything, this only seemed to anger the unwanted presence even more as the malign influence turned its attention toward the children in the house, seeming to possess each of them on multiple occasions. The children growled and appeared almost feral before snapping back to their normal selves.

In many cases of supposed possession, the root cause of the symptoms turns out to be of a medical or psychological nature. Even though she believed they were being assailed by demons, Latoya Ammons sought medical help for her children. At the medical clinic, they began acting as if they were possessed, culminating in one of Latoya's two boys being thrown through the air by some invisible force. Police officers and paramedics responded to the scene, transporting the children to the hospital by ambulance. While there, the eldest boy, a nine-year-old, turned aggressive and began attacking his family members.

One of the most controversial and remarkable aspects of the Ammons case is said to have happened next. According to the official intake report, in the presence of a psychiatric counselor and an Indiana Department of Child Services family case manager, the same boy "walked up the wall as if he was walking on the floor and did a flip over the grandmother." If this is indeed what happened, then either the child in question showed the agility of a highly trained gymnast, or the laws of physics as we currently understand them were somehow violated. The same applies to the claim that his sister levitated above her bed.

Unfortunately, there is no objective evidence to back up those claims—no video footage or photographs. Although there were eyewitnesses present at the time, the eye is easily fooled, especially in highly stressful and emotionally charged situations. Time and time again, it has been proven that we don't always see what we *think* we see.

The house was subsequently blessed, and Ms. Ammons underwent multiple exorcisms. Two years later, in 2014, Zak Bagans purchased the house for $35,000. Although the Ammons family moved out, one has to wonder whether the demons that were said to have plagued them (but no other tenants of the property) remained behind. Bagans shot a documentary film based on his acquisition. Titled *Demon House*, it was released in 2018. Viewer reception was split between shocked awe and disbelieving ridicule. Bagans had the house destroyed after principal photography was complete, retaining just the basement steps, which are on display at his museum in Las Vegas. Unfortunately, this means that nobody else will be able to research the

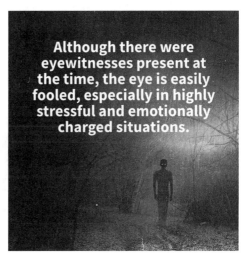

Although there were eyewitnesses present at the time, the eye is easily fooled, especially in highly stressful and emotionally charged situations.

house in the hopes of providing further answers. It's saddening to think of the potential the house on Carolina Street may have had as a 24/7/365 ongoing paranormal research lab—assuming that the claims of demonic activity were true, that is.

Zak Bagans claimed that *Demon House* was a cursed production, with a string of misfortunes both major and minor afflicting numerous people who were involved with the film. This has been said of other demon-centric movies, most notably *The Exorcist* and *The Omen*. For fans of Bagans and his work, this will not be difficult to believe. For others, such as skeptics Kenny Biddle and Joe Nickell, the Ammons case holds little if any water.

A PLACE OF DARK SECRETS:
THE MONROE HOUSE

"Occult Rituals and Human Remains Hidden Inside Indiana's 'Demon House.'"

With a colorful history and claims of violent paranormal activity, the Monroe House is a place of many secrets.

The title of the article, written by *Week in Weird*'s Dana Newkirk in 2016, made me sit up and pay attention. Of course, that's exactly what headlines are supposed to do: many of them are deliberately sensationalized to hook the reader and get them to click, swipe, or read further. How much truth was there to this one?

As things turned out, there was quite a bit. The more research I did into the haunting of the Monroe House, the murkier and yet more fascinating it turned out to be.

The property, located in Hartford City, Indiana, had a history that was as colorful as it was complex. Over the years, it has primarily been a private residence, with many different families calling it home. Often, one family would live up on the second story while another occupied the ground floor. The house is big enough to accommodate so many people quite comfortably.

When investigating the history of an allegedly haunted location, I always make a habit of delving into the property records. One of the things that immediately raises a red flag is when a place changes hands multiple times over a relatively short period of time. Such was the case with the Monroe House, which went through three owners in less than three years before finally being purchased by Eddie and Pam Norris, the current owners.

The Norrises realized that the house needed some money, time, and attention put into it and saw the place as a good investment—a house that they could fix up and flip, rather than as a potential home for themselves.

Unfortunately, Eddie and Pam didn't know about the rumors surrounding the house until they had signed on the dotted line. The first inkling that something was wrong came when Eddie was working late up on the second floor one night, doing a little construction. Usually, he was out of the place by nightfall, turning the late shift over to his brother, who carried on after dark. On this particular night, thanks to the radio station that was keeping him company by playing some great music, he had lost all track of the time.

Glancing up for a second, Eddie suddenly caught sight of a person at the end of the hallway. The figure, which he naturally assumed was his brother coming to take over, suddenly turned and walked into a room that Eddie knew to be empty and totally dark. Confused as to why his brother would do something like that, Eddie went after him. Standing in the doorway of the room, which was brightly illuminated by the moonlight streaming in from the window outside, he was shocked to find it completely empty.

It didn't take long for fear to kick in. Eddie knew with absolute certainty that whoever he had seen could not have been a living person. Although the sound of the radio could conceivably have drowned out the sound of footsteps, he was sure that nobody could have gotten out of that room without going past him. He had the only exit door in full sight the entire time he was approaching the room. The window was closed and latched, and besides, he would have heard it being opened if the mysterious intruder had gotten out that way.

Suddenly afraid of whatever it was that walked the hallways of his own house, Eddie did something that he is still embarrassed about to this day: he opened that window, climbed out, and dropped down from the second floor into the yard outside. "It was the only way out, because there's no way I was going to walk down those stairs in order to get back out," Eddie told me during an interview we conducted in the living room of the Monroe House in 2019.

Two of the items within the paranormal field that generate the most fear—dolls and talking boards!

The paranormal activity only intensified after that. Now it began taking place during broad daylight. One day, as he was once again doing a little construction work, Eddie heard the sound of footsteps running from room to room up on the second floor. They were light and fast, the sort of noise a child would make if they were playing. Concerned that a local neighborhood kid might have broken into the house on a dare, he made sure that the doors were all locked and then went from room to room, floor to floor, looking for any sign of an intruder. He found nothing. The footsteps were always one step ahead of him, and he was never able to determine their source.

The word around the neighborhood was that No. 218 was haunted. People spoke of the lights switching themselves off and on late at night when the building was locked up and should have been empty. Others claimed to have seen shadowy figures staring back at them from the windows on the second floor. Ghost stories and urban legends swirled around the house, making it all but impossible to separate fact from fiction and truths from half-truths.

Things took a definite turn for the macabre when an unexpected discovery was made in the earth of a crawlspace beneath the house: bones. Bones that were quickly determined to be human in origin.

Now the question was, who did they belong to—and what were their remains doing underneath the Monroe House?

Hoping to find some answers, Eddie invited in some paranormal research teams. The results were unexpected, to say the least. Some of the teams didn't even make it through the entire night. The house seemed to have a way of pitting them against one another, playing havoc with their emotions and inducing fits of anger with no apparent cause. Members of one team actually threw down physically, going at one another with their fists in a totally unprovoked fight.

A number of visitors claimed to have had a run of very bad luck after visiting the Monroe House. Some teams broke up and went their separate ways. Several visitors, including a member of Eddie and Pam's immediate family, reported experiencing paranormal activity back at home, as if something had attached itself to them and followed them back from the house.

One story that has been repeatedly attached to the Monroe House is that of occult rituals supposedly having been performed there some decades ago. A former tenant claims that he and several unidentified others deliberately conducted ceremonies in the house, attempting to conjure up dark entities. According to his claim, they succeeded, which explains why so much of the activity taking place there is negative in nature.

If these claims are true—and we only have the anecdotal claims to go on—then it would make the Monroe House a very dangerous place indeed. Small wonder that the house has changed ownership so many times.

I visited the house myself in 2019, staying for four days and nights along with a small team of hand-picked fellow investigators. It took us the better part of an entire day on the road to travel from Colorado to Indiana, but to say that the Monroe House did not disappoint us would be an understatement.

Something feels "off" about the house, for want of a better word, from the moment you first set foot inside. Some of the strange noises heard within its walls can be attributed to the vagaries of an old structure expanding and contracting as day turns to night, but by no means all.

The house owner covering the crawlspace in which human remains were discovered beneath the property.

I was sitting on one end of a couch in the living room while a colleague, Linda, sat at the opposite end. Suddenly, we heard the plaintive sob of a woman crying in distress.

Although the house didn't yield a great many electronic voice phenomena for us, our Spirit Box sessions were more rewarding. At one point, my team had two separate Estes Method sessions going on in the same second-floor room. For those who might be unfamiliar with this technique, the so-called Estes Method involves using a radio-sweeping device hooked into a pair of high-quality headphones. One experimenter sits quietly with the headphones in place, blindfolded to reduce external sensory stimuli, while their companions take turns asking questions. The headphones are connected directly into the Spirit Box, so only the person wearing them can hear whatever words come out of the device.

Traditionally, Estes Method sessions involve one listener and multiple questioners. At the Monroe House, we decided to mix it up, so we had two listeners paired off with two questioners. Despite the fact that it was impossible for the two listeners to hear one another, imagine our surprise when they suddenly began to speak back and forth with each other, falling into a conversation that made complete sense. It was the strangest thing and became slightly disturbing when one of the Spirit Boxes began putting out phrases with decidedly threatening overtones.

The highlight of our stay took place on the final night, when we were all packing up our equipment and getting ready to hit the road. I was sitting on one end of a couch in the living room while a colleague, Linda, sat at the opposite end. Suddenly, we heard the plaintive sob of a woman crying in distress. Linda and I stared at one another, dumbfounded. Had we really just heard what we thought we had heard?

Fortunately, I had left a digital voice recorder running, and when I played the audio file back, we were relieved to discover that the cry had been picked up very clearly. This wasn't an EVP—Linda and I had both heard it with our own ears at the time, which made it more of a direct voice phenomenon.

A number of visiting sensitives say that they have picked up on the presence of what appear to be two different spirits, a male and a female entity. The male is said to be the more dominant of the pair and is seeking to keep the female spirit suppressed in some way. Some investigators have theorized that there may be a connection between these two entities and the human remains that lie buried in the crawlspace.

To this day, those bones have yet to be identified. Could they perhaps belong to the crying woman?

Only time will tell. For now, at least, the Monroe House continues to jealously guard its dark secrets.

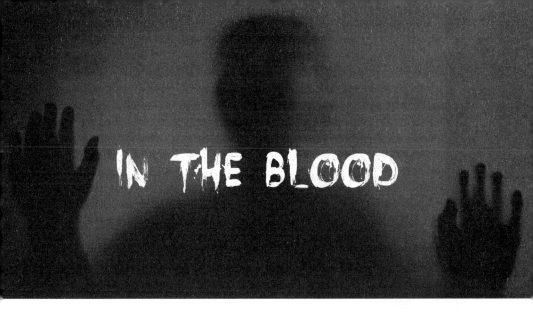

IN THE BLOOD

Tales of vampires and vampirism have been with us for centuries in one form or another—time-honored legends of predatory creatures that rise from their graves in the dead of night to hunt for victims on whose blood they could feed. From the early days of motion pictures such as *Nosferatu* through the many screen incarnations of the most famous vampire of them all—Count Dracula—and the cool, hip, and sexy vamps of twenty-first-century Hollywood, movie audiences have had a love affair with the bloodsucker that shows no sign of letting up.

Although similar accounts date back to the days of antiquity, the popular conception of the vampire as we know it today has its roots in Eastern Europe of the Middle Ages, when it was commonly believed that the bodies of the recently deceased could return as vampires if they had been bitten by one. Once such stories took hold, villages and sometimes entire regions could find themselves in the grip of fear. This led them to dig up the bodies of the recently deceased. When it appeared that the hair and fingernails had grown after death, or the mouth was found to contain blood, the vampire explanation was bolstered. In reality, the hair and nails only appear longer because the soft tissue in which they are embedded has shrunk and retracted. A similar process can take place in the mouth, where the gums shrink and give the teeth a more pronounced appearance. We know today that this is an entirely natural postmortem development, but for the superstitious rural folk of the fifteenth century, the sight was understandably quite terrifying.

On those occasions when a body was unearthed and found to be in a lesser state of decomposition, such as in periods of colder weather,

An 1864 illustration depicts medieval villagers burning vampire bones in an effort to defeat the blood-thirsty demon from rising again.

the belief that vampirism was at work became even more deeply entrenched. As gas moves within the corpse, it can cause unexpected movements and sounds, similar to belching, flatulence, and even moaning. If you're a fifteenth-century villager with little knowledge of the science of death, it's understandable that you might think the body of your dead mother might be coming back from the grave as a vampire.

Various techniques were developed to deal with the pesky blood-sucking creatures of the night. The decapitation of the corpse prior to interment was one, as was the stereotypical pounding of a wooden stake through the heart to prevent the owner's unwelcome resurrection. For good measure, the limbs and other anatomical regions were sometimes staked as well. Rather than being buried in cemeteries, suspected vampires and their victims were often interred at crossroads, with the intent of confusing their sense of direction if the undead creature ever climbed out of the ground again—a precaution that was also applied to those who took their own lives.

To modern eyes, this all looks like superstition. Yet it has its own consistency and logic if viewed through the same prism as past generations. Belief in them was so strong and widespread that vampires became entrenched in human folklore, where they remain to this day.

SON OF THE DRAGON: DRACULA

If one name is synonymous with that of the vampire, it's Count Dracula. The titular protagonist of Bram Stoker's novel was partly inspired by Vlad III Tepes of Wallachia, better known as Vlad the Impaler due to his habit of impaling enemy captives on tall wooden stakes. His father, Vlad II, was known as Vlad *Dracul* ("Dragon"), which meant that Vlad inherited the title Son of the Dragon—or *Draculea*. It's only the work of removing a single letter to bring us to Dracula.

Vlad III had no tolerance for dissent. Those who opposed him had a tendency to end up dead, usually in the most gruesome manner possible, and often with a side order of torture beforehand. Men, women, children, and the elderly all died violently at his hand or by his direct order. In addition to ruling Wallachia, a region of modern-day Romania, with an iron fist during the mid-1400s, Vlad III took an even harder line with his enemies, principally the Ottomans. In addition to impaling prisoners of war, Vlad also placed their families on stakes alongside them, lining the roads for miles with long columns of impaled victims, who were either dead or dying in agony. The man himself liked nothing better than to eat his dinner amongst them, unmoved by their piteous screams and sobs. Some stories even have Vlad using his bread to soak up their blood.

Vlad III's sobriquet of "The Impaler" was a well-earned name. His heinous treatment of his enemies made him reviled throughout the region.

As the old saying goes, live by the sword, die by the sword. When he and his bodyguard were caught in an Ottoman ambush, Vlad was overwhelmed and killed. His head was cut off and sent to the Ottoman capital of Constantinople to be put on display.

It is easy to see how the Son of the Dragon would serve as a suitable foundation for the world's most famous fictional vampire: Vlad the Impaler undeniably had a taste for blood, even if it was more figurative than literal. To this day, the Transylvanian fortress Bran Castle is popularly known as "Dracula's Castle," and it draws throngs of tourists, especially in the run-up to Halloween. Needless to say, it's reputed to be haunted by the tortured spirits of those who died at the hands of the Impaler.

BATHED IN BLOOD: ELIZABETH BÁTHORY

Countess Elizabeth Báthory might have been born 130 years after Vlad III Tepes, but she shared the Wallachian aristocrat's lust for pain and blood. Rather than targeting rivals, opponents, and military enemies, the Hungarian countess reserved her own murderous attentions strictly for young women. If even half the accounts of her depredations are accurate, then Báthory qualifies as having been Hungary's most prolific serial killer. More than 600 deaths have been laid at her door.

It is difficult to determine exactly how much of Báthory's story is fact and how much is legend. According to contemporary accounts, the

Countess Elizabeth Báthory de Ecsed was a Hungarian noblewoman who purportedly tortured and murdered hundreds of people and was accused of drinking and bathing in their blood. Some historians, though, aver the accusations—most coming after her death—were rumors meant to destroy her family's reputation.

noblewoman killed women to drain their blood, then both drank and bathed in it, in an attempt to maintain her own beauty and longevity. She began by killing servant girls who were in her employ, reasoning that it was easier to cover up the death of a commoner than that of another noble. After literally getting away with murder over and over again, the story goes, she then turned her attentions to females closer to herself in the social pecking order. This overconfidence would prove to be her undoing. Rumors of the disappearances and grisly murders taking place at Báthory's home finally reached the ears of the king, who ordered an immediate investigation.

After being found guilty, Elizabeth Báthory was imprisoned in her home under armed guard for the rest of her life. The court was not so lenient to her servants, who were executed for their role in procuring victims for their mistress.

Some scholars believe the charges against the countess were overblown, pointing out that little in the way of documentary evidence pointing to her guilt has survived. Although her servants confessed prior to being put to death, their confessions were extracted under the most horrific of torture. Under such conditions, a person will say literally anything to make the agony stop. Whether Countess Elizabeth Báthory truly was guilty of torturing and killing hundreds of women or was the victim of a deliberate hoax designed to benefit her accusers and convicted on little more than hearsay is impossible to say for certain.

In the wake of her death, folklore began to paint Báthory as the female equivalent of Dracula. This rumor was fueled primarily by the claims that she was obsessed with the blood of her victims, and it is important to note that they may or may not have had any substance.

VAMPIRES IN THE NEW WORLD

Much like UFOs and witchcraft, vampires have been the cause of mass hysteria outbreaks throughout history. Throughout the relatively young history of New England, there were multiple instances of "vampire flaps" that threw society into a panic.

One example took place in rural Connecticut during the 1850s. Immediately prior to their deaths, several adult male members of the unfortunate Ray family began to show signs of what was taken to be vampirism. They became pale and began to lose weight. With the Ray men dying at an average rate of one per year, all in the same ugly manner, it seemed clear that the curse of the vampire had descended upon them. There was only one way to stop it: exhume the bodies of the walking dead men and kill them once more, only this time, with fire.

Two Ray brothers named Lemuel and Elisha were duly disinterred from their graves. The bodies had already begun to decompose while they were in the ground—a fact that should have argued against them having been vampires. Undeterred, their fearful neighbors threw the corpses on top of a bonfire and burned them anyway. It was hoped that this would put an end to the string of ugly deaths that was taking place.

What came to be known as the case of the Jewitt City Vampires was researched and documented extensively by folklorist and author Michael Bell, who, in his work *Food for the Dead: On the Trail of New England's Vampires*, highlights the real culprit behind the deaths that plagued the Ray family.

Tuberculosis wasn't formally diagnosed and categorized until March 24, 1882, thanks to the efforts of Dr. Robert Koch. Koch identified the disease's cause: a bacteria named *Mycobacterium tuberculosis*. Until then, the condition had been known as "consumption" because of the way those who contracted it wasted away until they were a shadow of their former selves, almost as if they were being consumed from within.

The disease killed tens of millions throughout the eighteenth and nineteenth centuries, and the United States was not immune to its predations. One common side effect of tuberculosis is the coughing up of frank red blood as the sufferer's irritable airway attempts to expel bleeding up from the lungs. Such expulsions could stain the tongue, teeth, and lips blood red. After death, seepage of blood up

Dr. Robert Koch brought scientific reasoning for the cause of consumption (tuberculosis) by discovering the cause as a bacteria, not vampires.

from the lower airway and out through the mouth could easily be mistaken for the result of vampiric behavior. Even once knowledge of the disease became common, it would not be adequately treatable for more than half a century afterward.

Bacteria, not bloodsuckers, had cursed the Ray family. Nor were they alone. Michael Bell's research has identified numerous other cases of New England families in which deaths were attributed to vampire attacks. The corpses were often treated harshly, the dead bodies being decapitated and beaten repeatedly until the bones were broken, presumably with the intent of keeping the soon-to-be-vampire trapped in its coffin for all eternity.

Tuberculosis was the culprit in numerous vampire cases, such as the case of the Brown family of Exeter, Rhode Island. Throughout the 1880s and into the early 1890s, members of the family continued to die, wasting away and coughing up blood in the process. The cause of death was usually listed as "consumption," a very reasonable diagnosis given the symptoms and circumstances. Tuberculosis was rampant in New England, leaving few towns and cities untouched. Death followed in its wake. Matriarch Mary Brown died of the disease, along with her two daughters, Mercy Lena and Mary Olive, who went by Olive. Their younger brother, Edwin, also contracted the condition in 1889. Like many Americans of the time, Edwin traveled west to Colorado Springs, where the more agreeable climate sometimes helped send the disease into remission—or, at the very least, alleviated some of the uglier symptoms.

Rumors circulated to the effect that either his mother or one of his sisters was rising from their grave at night and was responsible for his fast-dwindling health.

Although seemingly on the mend, once Edwin returned to Exeter, his tuberculosis flared up again. Symptoms of tuberculosis included night sweats, fever, and chills, which he suffered after going to bed. Edwin also began to have nightmares in which he was tormented by a mysterious and terrifying woman. Rumors circulated to the effect that either his mother or one of his sisters was rising from their grave at night and was responsible for his fast-dwindling health.

There was only one way to tell for sure. Townsfolk opened up the graves of Mary, Mercy, and Olive. The bodies were exhumed. Those of Mary and Olive had decomposed all the way down to their skeletons, just as expected. Mercy's, on the other hand, had not. Her body had only been in the ground for two months; she had died in January and was exhumed in March. Those are some very cold months in New England, and the ground temperature would almost certainly have been low enough to slow down the rate of decomposition. To all intents and purposes, her corpse had been kept inside nature's refrigerator.

Despite this logical explanation, the relatively unchanged state of Mercy's body, coupled with the finding of blood within it, caused superstition and hysteria to override common sense. The exhumers cut out the heart and burned it. The ashes were given to Edwin Brown in the hope that they would somehow heal him.

They did not. Edwin soon joined his mother and sisters in death, despite having ingested the charred remnants of Mercy's heart. Tuberculosis continued to kill its way through the Brown family afterward. Some believe that the sad case of Mercy Brown and her family helped inspire Bram Stoker's seminal novel *Dracula*.

TODOR GLAVA: THE COLORADO VAMPIRE

In 1918, tuberculosis was overshadowed by another pestilential scourge: the so-called Purple Death, the great influenza pandemic. World War I ended that same year, killing an estimated 20 million people and wounding close to that same number. Approximately 20 million more would also die of the flu as it ravaged nation after nation, spreading like wildfire—and that number of deaths may well be on the low side, with some sources placing it in the range of 40 to 50 million.

The great outbreak was inaccurately dubbed the Spanish flu. Even today, more than a century later, many believe this was because that particularly deadly strain originated in Spain. In reality, nobody knows exactly where the first cases appeared, but the Spanish press was among the very first media outlets to report on the effects of the disease. Many other countries were limited by journalistic restrictions for war-related security reasons. Spain wasn't censoring its flu coverage, and so a legend was born.

It is entirely possible that the disease originated in North America. Certainly, the United States was hit hard by the 1918 flu pandemic. More than half a million Americans would die, and many others fell ill but did recover. Soldiers returning from European battlefields sometimes brought the disease with them. Troop ships were particularly effective incubators.

The state of Colorado was not spared. One casualty of the Spanish flu was a miner named Theodore "Todor" Glava, who emigrated from Romania to the United States and, like so many who came to the New World in search of a better life, found himself doing hard, dirty, and dangerous work to get by. Lafayette was a gold-mining town, and it is where Todor Glava lived and ultimately died. The known details of his life are sparse and often obscured by the legends that sprang up around him after his death. Indeed, his simple gravestone declares "Todor Glava Born In Translvania" (mis-spelling intentionally uncorrected) and dates his death as December 1918. Whether he was truly born in Transylvania or not, this perception probably fueled the claim that he was a vampire.

Glava's grave can be found in the poorest section of a cemetery in Lafayette. Legend has it that after his burial, the townspeople dug up the

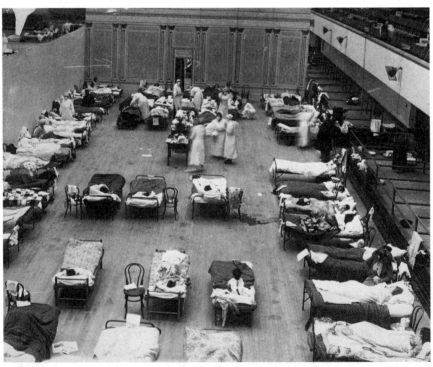

Much like the COVID-19 pandemic, the Spanish Flu plague that crossed the globe from 1918 to 1920 strained medical staff and supplies to their limits.

coffin, opened the lid, and drove a stake through his chest to make sure that this suspected vampire would never rise from his grave and come after them. (Embellishing this story further, it is also said that the tree that grows at the site sprung up from the wooden stake in Glava's heart.) There's little proof to back those stories up, and yet still they persist.

Ghost stories also surround his grave site, sightings of a mysterious figure lurking in the shadows, that have been passed on from one generation to the next.

It's likely that Glava was nothing more than a fish out of water, someone who looked, spoke, and acted a little different than many of the other townsfolk. This, perhaps taken in conjunction with his country of origin and the pale complexion many miners attain after spending so much time underground, may explain why he would one day come to be known as the Lafayette Vampire. Today, his grave is one of the best tended in the cemetery. Visitors leave offerings such as coins and flowers, gestures of remembrance for a man who seems to have been deeply misunderstood and maligned.

HORROR IN HIGHGATE

Leaving New England and the New World behind entirely and journeying across the Atlantic to old England, there is also no shortage of vampire lore to be found. One of the earliest accounts dates to the twelfth century and was recorded by the scribe William of Newburgh, author of *Historia rerum Anglicarum*. Newburgh wrote of a vampire at Northumberland's Alnwick Castle, one of England's oldest northern fortresses. The vampire in question would emerge from its grave once night had fallen to venture in search of prey. The local populace lived in fear, refusing to leave their homes after dark lest they fall foul of the vampire's thirst for blood.

Even with these precautions, nobody was truly safe. Finally deciding that enough was enough, they banded together, armed themselves, and set out to hunt the undead thing down. Presumably waiting for the safety of daylight to do it, they exhumed the vampire from its grave. The slumbering creature's body was bloated and swollen, filled with the blood of its recent victims. The locals put an end to the Alnwick Vampire by cutting out its heart and burning the body to a crisp.

Arguably the most infamous British vampire case involves London's historic Highgate Cemetery. Dating back to 1839, Highgate was

Alnwick Castle (considered a "country home" by British royalty, it seems) is the home of the 12th Duke of Northumberland and his family, who only occupy a small part of the stone building while keeping the rest open to the public.

the place to be buried; the names on its crypts and gravestones are a veritable Who's Who of the famous and infamous. Although at first glance Highgate appears to be the product of a bygone age, people are still buried there today.

Karl Marx is buried in Highgate, as is the eminent scientist Michael Faraday, the pioneer of electromagnetic science. Douglas Adams, author of the immensely popular *Hitchhiker's Guide to the Galaxy* stories, is buried there. So is the pop star George Michael, who went on to great success as a solo artist after building a career as half of the pop duo Wham. At the end of his life, Michael had made his home in Highgate, so it is only fitting that he chose to be buried in the cemetery that bears the same name.

Highgate Cemetery became the focus of national attention during the late 1960s and early 1970s when stories circulated about a vampire lurking in one of the crypts. According to eyewitnesses, the creature in question was a tall, black-clad figure that was said to have "hypnotic red eyes."

The remains of brutalized cats and foxes were found in the vicinity, providing more grist for the vampire mill. Once television news caught wind of the situation, the floodgates were opened. Hordes of self-professed vampire hunters came out of the woodwork and began staking out the cemetery at night—no pun intended.

Things took a turn for the worse when one of the coffins was opened and the body of a woman long since dead was set on fire. For good measure—presumably the hapless corpse was that of the vampire—the miscreants cut off its head.

Of the many individuals who were fascinated with the claims of vampiric attacks on the residents of Highgate, arguably the best known were David Farrant and Sean Manchester. Both men were colorful and flamboyant individuals, and they soon developed an intense rivalry over their respective hunts for the Highgate Vampire. Farrant was eventually arrested in the cemetery, and although he was subsequently acquitted of "vampire hunting" charges in court, he would later serve prison time for other nocturnal activities at Highgate. He steadfastly maintained his innocence.

Farrant went on to express his belief that whatever lay at the heart of the reports, it was almost certainly not a vampire. Indeed, Farrant did not believe in the existence of vampires. His hypothesis centered on the fact that Highgate had become a favorite location for occultists to perform rituals, some of which were very dark in nature. He proposed that the use of dark magic may have conjured up or invited in an evil entity that was being misidentified as a vampire. He may well have had a point. Vampires were a hot commodity in the 1970s, just as they are in the 2020s, with a steady stream of low-budget horror films on the subject gracing movie screens at that time.

Sean Manchester, on the other hand, not only professed the belief that the entity that was seen in Highgate and nearby Swains Lane was a vampire, but he also claimed to have tracked its location to the cellar of a house on the edge of Highgate (as opposed to a crypt at the cemetery) and driven a stake through its heart in the traditional manner. Following the impalement, Manchester and his assistants supposedly dragged the coffin outdoors to bask in the rays of the rising sun. The vampire's body liquefied in moments. The remnants were then set on fire.

Obviously, both Farrant and Manchester cannot be correct. Both have their supporters and their detractors. (David Farrant sadly died in 2019.) However, a third possibility is that the vampire stories were simply that—stories, fueled by overactive imaginations, media publicity, and various personality factors on the part of multiple participants. Whichever explanation is the truth, one cannot deny that the image of a vampire stalking the gothic tombs and crypts of historic Highgate is a striking one. Sightings of the so-called Highgate Vampire seem to have ceased, but who knows what the future may hold for London's best loved cemetery … and the creature said to have stalked it?

THE DARK SIDE OF THE BOARD

TALKING TO THE DEAD?

There can be few objects as feared, controversial, and yet simultaneously ridiculed as the talking board—more commonly known as the Ouija board. Some see it as little more than a harmless piece of wood or cardboard, embossed with letters, numbers, and decorations—a prop on which the overly imaginative and credulous can play out their fantasies of communicating with the dead and beings from other realms.

At the other end of the spectrum are those who believe that the board can open doorways that are best left closed a route for evil entities and demons to enter our own plane of existence, allowing them to run riot and in some cases even take possession of the bodies of the living.

Marketed as a toy and sold by the millions each year, is the talking board in fact a portal to dark realms?

Talking boards as we know them today date back to the late 1800s. It is a common misconception that the name of the board—Ouija—derives from the French and German words for *yes*. In fact, talking boards were being made and sold commercially by the Kennard Novelty Company in 1890, and a less generic name was needed for branding purposes. A participant named Helen Peters sensibly asked the board itself what it should most appropriately be called, and the five-letter answer to her question adorns every Ouija board made to this day. Although the Ouija board went on to be patented by Elijah Bond, Peters

Ouija boards aren't nearly the popular fad they once were, but if you wish to gather a few friends around to talk to demons and the dead, they are still available on the internet and at gaming stores.

is an unsung hero of the Ouija story, and her name deserves much broader recognition than history has given her thus far.

Stories of dark encounters have been around for as long as the Ouija board has existed. For much of its early life, it was seen as a thing of mystery and fun rather than fear. Ouija and its non-branded competitors were popular dating aids, with special romantic versions produced to bring potential lovers together in a lighthearted and frivolous way. Other versions played up the board's reputation for being an oracle, such as the 1940s-era boards containing prewritten questions asking whether Hitler was going to surrender in the near future. For a population beset with the grief and uncertainty brought about by World War II, it is understandable that they would turn to something like the talking board in an attempt to answer burning questions and allay their fears.

What changed the mass perception of the board toward being a tool of darkness? One key factor was the release of *The Exorcist*, a bestselling novel by William Peter Blatty that was subsequently adapted for the big screen and directed by William Friedkin. After the central character, a little girl named Regan, plays with a Ouija board and communicates with an entity calling itself Captain Howdy, all hell breaks loose—literally. She becomes possessed by an ancient demon named Pazuzu, and the resulting exorcism shocked and nauseated movies audiences around the globe.

MURDER OR SELF DEFENSE?

The subject of demonic possession is raised elsewhere in this book. Equally if not more disturbing are Ouija-related murders. Talking boards have played a role in several real-life horrors, such as the March 17, 1923, murder of Robert Murdock in Biggs, California. He had been married to his wife, Mae (some sources call her May). While we can only speculate as to the happiness (or lack thereof) in their union, it is undeniable that, seemingly out of the blue, she shot her husband four times with a revolver. Three shots entered his torso, while the fourth hit his chin.

Murdock did not die instantly. Taken to the hospital, he survived for two weeks. Before expiring, he identified his wife as the one who had pulled the trigger, and he added that in his opinion, she was insane. Clinical professionals testified before the court. Some agreed with his amateur diagnosis, whereas others did not. Yet the specific trigger that had set Mae Murdock off was none other than her Ouija board.

History demonstrates that "the devil made me do it" is a generally ineffective defense for any crime, particularly murder. Judges and juries simply do not find it convincing. The same proved to be true with Mae Murdock's claim that the Ouija board had incited her to kill her husband—in self-defense. The board had revealed that Robert was plotting to murder her, she insisted, so she had no choice but to strike first.

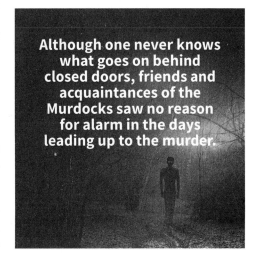

Although one never knows what goes on behind closed doors, friends and acquaintances of the Murdocks saw no reason for alarm in the days leading up to the murder.

What was Robert Murdock's motive for planning to murder his wife of 26 years? The answer could be found in Mae's diary, in which she recorded the secrets that the Ouija board had shared with her.

Mae had gotten too old for his tastes and he had begun sleeping with other women. He planned to use an axe to kill her, Mae had journaled, and she would later tell the court that they had not had a true quarrel during their marriage—which seems difficult to believe.

The Murdock case isn't cut and dried. If Mae had developed mental illness that grew in severity until she exhibited a psychotic break, there were few obvious red flags to be found. Although one never knows what goes on behind closed doors, friends and acquaintances of the Murdocks saw no reason for alarm in the days leading up to the murder. Yet she had gone so far as to file a police report claiming that Robert was having an affair with another woman. A patrol officer followed up on the allegation and found it to be baseless.

Upon taking the stand, Mae confessed to the shooting but denied remembering it, which meant that she did not accept responsibility for killing her husband. All she recalled was Robert chasing her in the moments leading up to the incident. Mae testified that the ghost of her dead mother had visited her during her time in prison.

Although Mae had unquestionably shot her husband with intent to kill, she was surprisingly found guilty of manslaughter rather than the more serious crime of murder. After serving four years in prison, she regained her freedom and promptly disappeared into obscurity. It's unknown whether she ever touched a Ouija board again, though we can only hope she did not.

The question remains: Can the murder of Robert Murdock be explained as a case of mental illness, or were malign influences associated with the Ouija board really to blame?

MURDER IN BUFFALO

Another Ouija-related murder took place on the afternoon of March 6, 1930, in Buffalo, New York. Fifty-one-year-old Clothilde Marchand was found dead on the staircase landing of her home. Examination of her body and the scene of her death soon revealed evidence of foul play, including injuries on her body that were inconsistent with a stumble and fall down the stairs. She bore obvious signs of blunt force trauma. Clothilde Marchand's mouth and throat contained a wedge of paper that had been doused in chloroform.

Her body was discovered by her 12-year-old son, Henri Jr., who had spent the day at school. In such cases, suspicion invariably falls on the spouse of the deceased before all others. What motive could artist Henri Marchand have had for wanting his wife dead?

As it transpired, there was an age-old reason. Marchand had taken a lover named Lila Jimerson. She and her friend Nancy Bowen were members of the Seneca tribe. Bowen's husband had recently died. Believing his death to have been murder, Bowen wanted to know the identity of the perpetrator. With her friend Jimerson's assistance, she asked the Ouija board to name the guilty party.

Which it did: one Clothilde Marchand. Already suspecting that her husband had been murdered by a witch, Bowen allowed herself to be convinced that Clothilde had been the witch in question. Manipulated by Jimerson into murdering Jimerson's love rival, Bowen went into the Marchand residence and bludgeoned Mrs. Marchand to death with a hammer. The murder probe uncovered damning evidence, including a bottle of chloroform and the fact that the murder weapon had been purchased by Lila Jimerson.

It's likely that Jimerson had been deliberately misleading Bowen during their Ouija sessions, using the board to prime the gullible and

A Ouija board used as a prop to manipulate murder? That was the case with the death of Clothilde Marchand, who was killed by Nancy Bowen, a gullible woman led to murder by her friend Lila Jimerson, the lover of Henry Marchand.

superstitious Bowen to commit murder. Unable to understand English, she relied upon Jimerson to interpret the communications emerging from the board.

A series of letters, ostensibly from a psychic medium named Mrs. Dooley but probably penned by Jimerson herself, instructed Bowen to kill what they referred to as "the white witch." The letters claimed that the medium was communicating with the spirit of her dead husband, who wanted Clothilde dead as retribution for killing him. If she failed to do so quickly, the letters warned, Bowen would die herself, along with several other members of her family.

Suspicion also fell on Henri Marchand as the driving force urging the murder of his wife. Jimerson said as much to investigators. The accusation was never proven, however, and remains a matter of conjecture. Jimerson received not one but two trials. The first ended as a mistrial. She was suffering from tuberculosis, and after collapsing in the courtroom, a new trial was initiated. At its conclusion, she was found not guilty.

Nancy Bowen pled guilty to the lesser charge of manslaughter and, having already served a year's worth of jail time, was allowed to go free. Although Clothilde Marchand was clearly the victim of a heinous crime, a case can be made that Bowen was a victim of a different sort. She had been set up to carry the can for Clothilde's murder, a murder that benefited either Lila Jimerson, Henri Marchand, or both of them, depending on which of their testimonies you believe. The Ouija board was used as a means of exploiting an uneducated and grief-stricken woman. The evil spirit (or spirits) that were truly responsible for the death of Clothilde Marchand were very real—and completely flesh and blood.

THE OUIJA BOARD SLAYER: MATTIE TURLEY

The death of Clothilde Marchand is far from the only case in which a Ouija board was blamed for inciting murder. On November 18, 1933, a 15-year-old Arizona girl named Mattie Turley tried to kill her father, Ernest, by shooting him in the back. Mattie waited until her dad's back was turned and then unloaded both barrels of a shotgun into him. Mr. Turley fell to the ground, mortally wounded, and would die six weeks later, despite the best efforts of physicians to save him.

Cases in which teenagers have such hatred for a parent that they wish them dead are by no means unusual. What was strange about the Turley situation is that Mattie claimed the Ouija board told her to do it.

Yet that wasn't the story she told at first; Mattie said the shotgun went off accidentally when she tripped. The position of the pellets embedded in Ernest's back and thorax argued otherwise; they had not been fired at an angle consistent with her having fallen down.

It had been a premeditated attack.

When the press covered the killing, much was made of the fact that Mattie's mother, Dorothea, had been a beauty queen. Once her daughter's story changed, Dorothea began to be perceived as a seductress. Mattie said that her mother had taken a lover, a cowboy named Kent Pearce. Torn between the two men, Dorothea took to the Ouija board to ask which of them she should choose. As she and Mattie worked the planchette, it spelled out clearly that Ernest Turley had to die. More specifically, the board said that Mattie must be the one to shoot him, and that although he would not be killed instantly, everything would turn out for the best in the end. Once her husband was out of the way, Dorothea would be free to marry Pearce.

Before he died, Ernest Turley told investigators that his wife and daughter had been unduly influenced by the Ouija board for many years prior to that fateful day.

Mattie was understandably worried that she would get in trouble with the police if she shot her own father dead. The board assured her that there would be no problems, however. There would even be life insurance money to be collected. Believing she was acting in her mother's best interest, the teenager finally plucked up the courage to go through with it.

Before he died, Ernest Turley told investigators that his wife and daughter had been unduly influenced by the Ouija board for many years prior to that fateful day. Whatever it told them to do, they did, as Dorothea insisted on following its instructions. The will of the board often conflicted with Ernest's, causing friction within the household.

For her part, Dorothea Turley denied the whole thing, insisting she was not in love with Pearce and had certainly not encouraged her daughter to shoot her husband. According to her, Mattie had been given the shotgun by her father and told to wait for a skunk that had taken up residence beneath the house to show its face. He had told her to kill the animal as soon as it appeared. Dorothea repeated Mattie's initial story to the police: that her daughter had stumbled, and the weapon had discharged accidentally. According to Dorothea, Mattie's Ouija-related confession was the product of her having been relentlessly badgered over the course of several days, until she finally broke down and told officers what she thought they wanted to hear.

Dubbed the "Ouija Board Slayer" by the press, Mattie Turley was found guilty of killing her father and was made a ward of the state of Arizona as a consequence. She was remanded to the custody of a state facility until she turned 18, when she was given parole. Her mother was also convicted of intent to murder, but the conviction was overturned at the conclusion of a retrial by the Supreme Court of Arizona after she spent two years in prison.

This sorry state of affairs naturally begs the question: did the Ouija board *really* convince Mattie and Dorothea Turley to commit murder? If so, the communicator in question must have been a malicious and ill-intentioned spirit. On the other hand, if Dorothea really was cold-hearted enough to have her daughter kill her own father in cold blood, she could certainly have been callous enough to nudge the planchette with her own fingertips to produce the answers that supported the narrative she was constructing.

In the end, it comes down to this: either an evil spirit or an evil human being was responsible for the death of Ernest Turley. In all likelihood, we will never know for sure which one it was, but in either case, the culprit was a truly dark soul.

TRIAL BY JURY: THE FULLER MURDERS

In the cases we have looked at so far, using a Ouija board landed the participants in court on murder charges. In an equally unusual but very different case, a jury used a Ouija board to try to get to the truth of criminal allegations—with less-than-pleasant consequences.

In 1993, insurance broker Stephen Young was convicted by a British jury of murdering a married couple named Harry and Nicola Fuller. The crime took place in the Fullers' home. On February 10, 1993, the couple were taken by surprise and quickly shot dead by their assailant. Harry Fuller died of a single gunshot fired from close range as his killer entered the house. Nicola Fuller was shot repeatedly. After making it to the telephone and initiating a 999 call to the police, she died of a bullet to the head.

The presumed motive was financial; the Fullers were wealthy, and Stephen Young was deeply in debt. He could be placed at the scene of the crime but insisted when questioned by police that he had nothing to do with the murders. Although he had no prior record of violence, the fact that Young had deposited a large amount of cash into his bank account on the day after the murders was extremely suspicious. He knew of the Fullers' reputation for wealth and was posing as a potential customer for Harry's car dealership, setting up a meeting at their house to discuss business—or so Mr. Fuller thought.

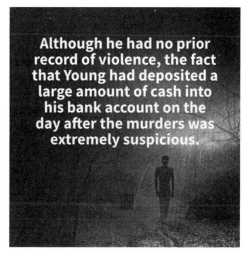

Although he had no prior record of violence, the fact that Young had deposited a large amount of cash into his bank account on the day after the murders was extremely suspicious.

Unlike the majority of Britons, Stephen Young had access to firearms, both legally and illegally obtained. Bankrupt and on the brink of losing everything, it made sense for him to carry out a cold-blooded high stakes double murder in a last-ditch attempt to pay off his creditors.

Young was found guilty by the jury, which came as little surprise. Things took a bizarre turn after his conviction when it emerged that four of the jurors had started drinking one night during the trial. They were staying at a hotel, lodging at the government's expense. Making up their own talking board using paper and a wine glass to serve as a planchette, the jurors tried to communicate with the spirits of the Fullers and asked them to name their killer.

The communicator claimed to be none other than Harry Fuller himself. The glass spelled out the name of Stephen Young, followed by the word *shot*. As the session came to an end, the board instructed them to *vote guilty tomorrow.*

When news of the drunken session came to light, the Fullers' next of kin were justifiably horrified to hear that Young's conviction was over-turned on appeal. A new trial was ordered for Young on the grounds that the four jurors may have been biased by the pronouncement of the talk-

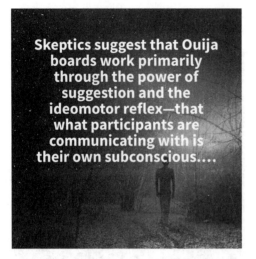

Skeptics suggest that Ouija boards work primarily through the power of suggestion and the ideomotor reflex—that what participants are communicating with is their own subconscious....

ing board. Despite their insistence that the board had not influenced the jury's final decision, this was clearly the only reasonable decision the legal system could have made.

Skeptics suggest that Ouija boards work primarily through the power of suggestion and the ideomotor reflex—that what participants are communicating with is their own subconscious, manifesting through tiny muscular movements in the fingers. Believers maintain that the talking board allows the spirits of the dead and other intelligent entities to interact with the living, conveying messages, thoughts, and sometimes instructions ... such as *vote guilty tomorrow*.

When it came to the brutal murders of Harry and Nicola Fuller, use of the makeshift Ouija board did far more harm than good. In addition to further traumatizing the Fullers' family members during the five-week retrial, there was the possibility that the man who had already been found guilty of killing their loved ones would now be set free. Whether he was innocent or guilty, that was for the jury to decide—and every defendant is entitled to a jury that is as unbiased as possible when determining their fate. In that regard, Stephen Young was dealt an injustice as soon as the first word was spelled out on the talking board.

If Stephen Young thought that his luck had changed for the better, he was mistaken. The second jury reached exactly the same conclusion as the first. He was sent back to prison for the long haul, where he continued to maintain his innocence and to lodge appeals. His case is used as a cautionary example in law schools around the world, considered to be a classic example of what can happen when juries misbehave.

CURSED

Throughout history, most cultures have believed in curses—the idea that a dark and harmful influence can be placed on another person, an object, or a place. This even extends to specific enterprises, including the making of motion pictures such as *The Exorcist* or *The Twilight Zone*. Curses are usually placed deliberately, with the full intention of causing harm. There is a school of thought that holds that cursing a specific individual can be every bit as dangerous to the person inflicting the curse as it can be to the intended recipient.

There are many different ways of casting a curse. Virtually all of them involve summoning a torrent of negative energy—anger, hatred, resentment, a lust for revenge—and turning it into a weapon. Not all curses are targeted at a single human being. Some are broader in scope, and these tend to be associated with places or items … such as the curse of King Tutankhamun.

Tutankhamun ruled ancient Egypt between 1333 and 1323 B.C.E. and died at the age of 19. He was entombed among his peers in the Valley of the Kings. Fast-forward over 3,000 years to November of 1922, when a British archaeologist named Howard Carter was engaged in an expedition to uncover historical artifacts in the valley. It was he who found the tomb of Tutankhamun secreted behind a hidden entrance. The youthful king's mummified remains were surrounded with a trove of priceless treasures.

Carter's expedition had been funded by the Earl of Carnarvon, George Herbert, a man with a fascination for ancient Egypt and deep

King Tutankhamun's tomb contained a fortune in ancient treasures, including this golden sarcophagus inside of which were two more nested sarcophagi.

pockets to match. The two men were agog at what they had found. Newspaper headlines trumpeted word of their great find. It would take a decade to remove and catalog the contents of the tomb. During that time, illness and death visited some of those who had been there at its opening—and even those who hadn't.

The deaths started soon after the find. Arguably the most famous was that of the Earl of Carnarvon, who died the following year at the relatively young age of 56. After a car crash in his thirties, Herbert suffered a series of complications that included regular infections and illnesses. It was a deep-reaching infection that finally ended his life, spreading pneumonia throughout his lungs and stressing his already overburdened immune system. The source of infection was believed to be a mosquito bite; Carnarvon was in Cairo at the time of his death.

One month later, financier George Jay Gould died of pneumonia. He had also been invited to visit the tomb. Egyptologist Hugh Evelyn-White fatally shot himself. The notion that the burial chamber was cursed soon gained traction. In 1924, Sir Archibald Reid, an expert in the field of medical radiology, was asked to X-ray Tutankhamun's mummified body in Egypt, but he died just days before he got the chance to do so.

The list of those supposedly cursed by connection with King Tutankhamun's tomb included archaeologists and manual laborers alike and was expanded to include individuals who had not even set foot in the tomb or the presence of the mummy. Although scientists dismissed the idea of a curse, that didn't stop the newspapers of the day from using it to generate sales copy.

Howard Carter himself met a sad end; he died in 1939, aged 64, while living alone in a flat. The cause of death was Hodgkin's lymphoma, a relatively rare form of cancer that is more common in women than in men. Proponents of the curse hypothesis point to his death as being yet another example of its long reach, yet Carter himself believed it was nothing more than mere superstition—or as he liked to call it, "Tommyrot."

ROBERT THE DOLL

Much like hauntings, curses come in broadly three forms: cursed people, cursed places, and cursed objects. Astute observers will note that there's a fine line and much overlap between curses and hauntings. A case in point is that of Robert the Doll, a child's toy the existence of which dates back to the early 1900s. Although the doll is now showing signs of wear and tear, it is difficult to see how, even when Robert was brand new, he wouldn't have scared any owner, whether adult or child, half to death. A featureless fabric face is punctuated with two glazed black eyes, every bit as soulless as those of a shark. Robert was made in Germany by Steiff, the toy company we have to thank for the notion of teddy bears. Somehow, the white sailor outfit Robert wears only adds to the sinister air the doll cultivates. (Sorry, Robert—no offense!)

Originally the property of a little boy who lived in Key West, Florida, named Robert Eugene Otto (known by his middle name), Robert quickly transitioned from being a boyhood companion to a scapegoat for any mischief Eugene got into—a handy get-out-of-jail-free card. ("Robert did it!" became a familiar refrain.) When Eugene and Robert were alone together, others in the house would swear they could hear the sounds of two distinct and separate voices talking to one another in the room they shared.

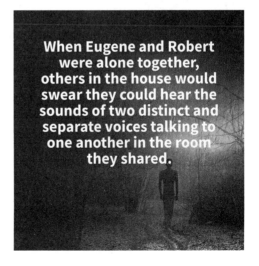

When Eugene and Robert were alone together, others in the house would swear they could hear the sounds of two distinct and separate voices talking to one another in the room they shared.

Eugene treated Robert as if he were a living, breathing flesh-and-blood pal. The two were inseparable. In and of itself, that isn't necessarily of grave concern. Yet children are supposed to grow up and put away childhood things. Not so when it came to Robert. Even after he reached adulthood, Eugene kept his stuffed straw buddy around. While Eugene painted in one of the upstairs rooms of his home in Key West, Robert the Doll sat in the window, giving him a good view of the world outside. Stories began to circulate about passersby seeing the doll move past the window, seemingly of his own volition. Disembodied giggling and the sounds of phantom footsteps were heard in Robert's presence, even when the room containing him was completely empty.

To that point, it seemed as if Robert was simply a haunted object. The poltergeist activity that regularly took place around him certainly seemed to suggest this. Yet there was a darker side to this particular haunting, one that persists to this day. After he passed out of Eugene's hands, Robert the Doll remained in Key West. His current home is the Fort East Martello Museum, sitting on a chair within a glass display case—whether for his own protection or that of others is up for debate.

For it is believed that Robert the Doll is cursed. The museum has received many stories from those who have mocked him, only to pay the price later. Some fell ill with mysterious ailments. Others sustained injuries from freak accidents. Bankruptcies and breakups have all been blamed on Robert. Cars break down. Homes flood. Pets die. David Sloan, author and researcher, has extensively chronicled the dark consequences that can result from disrespecting Robert.

Robert the Doll can be viewed on display at the Fort East Martello Museum in Key West, Florida.

One is advised to approach Robert's case with care and a suitable amount of deference. Certain rules come into play when one enters the doll's presence. He is to be addressed as "Robert," not "Rob," "Robbie," "Bob," "Bobby," or any other permutation of the name. Thousands of tourists flock to see Robert the Doll each year, many of whom want to pose for a picture with him. Before doing so, the wise visitors will consider introducing themselves. Some ask Robert politely for permission to take his picture, though in an interview with a writer for the Key West *Florida Weekly*, author David Sloan advised against it. "I don't advise asking permission because it empowers the entities" that, he said, he believes are attached to Robert the Doll and are responsible for much of the mischief and misfortune that's attributed to him.

Robert the Doll frequently receives numerous letters of apology from visitors across the globe. They are usually written by those who scoffed at Robert and his powers or made fun of him. Some writers beg his forgiveness and entreat Robert to lift the curse they believe he has put on them. Not all of the letters are regretful in tone, however; Robert also receives his share of fan mail, and you can write to him at Robert the Doll, 3501 S. Roosevelt Blvd., Key West, FL 33040.

Potential writers are advised to choose their words *very* carefully.

THE CURSE OF THE CRYING BOY

From cursed dolls to cursed paintings, we move on to the strange case of the Crying Boy. In the 1980s, stories began to spread across the British press concerning a painting that depicted a young boy who was crying. It was claimed that numerous houses and apartments had caught fire under mysterious circumstances. Once firefighters brought each blaze under control and salvaged what they cut from the smoke and fire-damaged properties, it was noticed that one of the few items to survive was one of these paintings.

The Crying Boy painting was all the rage at that time. There were a number of different versions of the same theme, painted by different artists who were not connected with one another. Cheap to buy and readily available, some people believed the pictures brought a touch of class to their home. In reality, the paintings give off a distinctly creepy vibe, which was adroitly exploited by the tabloid newspaper *The Sun*. The paper ran a series of articles on what it took to calling "the Curse of the Crying Boy," quoting firefighters who said they had seen the painting survive serious blazes on multiple different occasions.

And thus, a curse was born. Then, as now, people loved a good scary, supernatural story. Readers contacted *Sun* reporters to share their own experiences with the supposedly cursed painting, many of which were tenuous to say the least. Among households in which a Crying Boy picture hung on the walls, misfortunes ranging from major to minor were blamed upon it—particularly fires. Even the official position of the fire brigade—that there was no discernible link between the painting and the ignition source of any of the fires—did not reassure the worried British public. This may well be the first time that firefighters have been called upon to officially quash the notion of a curse.

Fanning the flames of the curse even further—all in the interest of a spicy headline—*The Sun* invited nervous readers to mail in copies of the painting for disposal. Once a large pile of Crying Boy pictures had been collected, reporters set fire to it while glamor models stood by. As thousands of paintings went up in smoke, photographers snapped away to capture the moment for posterity—and the next day's print edition.

As an exercise in generating publicity, the entire Crying Boy campaign was nothing short of pure genius, a piece of grand theater. For the British fire service, it was a monumental waste of their time and efforts, which could have been better spent elsewhere.

Several different urban legends purporting to explain the reason for the curse began to circulate. Some are still making the rounds today, but there's no evidence to support any of them. Yet somehow the lack of information regarding its origin story only makes the curse seem more mysterious, and therefore, more appealing. It is tempting to dismiss the whole thing as nothing more than a publicity stunt, but that ignores the possible effect that tightly focused mass thought might have. It has been widely noted that when curses work, it is primarily because those people at their center have come to believe in them. Thousands of people purchased or were gifted Crying Boy paintings in the 1980s. Once a mass-market newspaper, a supposedly respectable source (which history would prove to be anything but), began trumpeting claims of a curse, many of those painting owners believed it unquestionably.

> Once a mass-market newspaper, a supposedly respectable source ..., began trumpeting claims of a curse, many of those painting owners believed it unquestionably.

Belief is a powerful thing, as anybody who has benefited from the placebo effect can attest. With so many individuals buying into the curse of the Crying Boy, is it possible that the mass infusion of belief somehow activated or energized what then became an all-too-real curse?

Although not nearly as frequent as during its heyday, claims of cursed Crying Boys still arise today. Prints can be purchased from online retailers such as eBay. No matter what you might believe when it comes to the subject of curses, it is worth asking the question: would you be willing to let a Crying Boy painting hang on the wall in *your* home?

CURSED PRODUCTIONS:
MACBETH, SUPERMAN, AND *POLTERGEIST*

Perhaps second only to sailors, actors and performers are among the most superstitious people on the planet. The best-known example of this involves productions of William Shakespeare's *Macbeth*, or as actors tend to refer to it, "the Scottish play"—when they're inside a theater, that is. Neither should dialogue from *Macbeth* ever be spoken aloud, except when actually performing or rehearsing a production.

Macbeth dates to 1606, a time when a fear of witches ran rampant through the population of Britain. The fact that Shakespeare included them in his play made for great controversy (not to mention publicity), but legend holds that his writing was a little too close to the mark; the incantations and rituals performed and spoken by the three witches were sufficiently accurate that *real* witches cursed the play for all time.

If the curse story is true, then it certainly didn't hurt the play's success; in fact, quite the opposite seems to be true. *Macbeth* has always been one of Shakespeare's most popular plays and remains so more than 400 years after its debut. At the same time, there is no shortage of performers and production crew who have their own stories of misfortune associated with performances of the Scottish play.

One of the most extreme examples took place in 1849 in New York City and stemmed from the rivalry between two great stage actors of the time, William Macready and Edwin Forrest. Both men had large followings and the type of ego sometimes seen among leading thespians who found themselves competing head-to-head. There was also a certain amount of class warfare and xenophobia involved; Macready was Brit, and Forrest was American. Macready was the darling of the upper classes. Forrest's fanbase was largely blue collar. Although they shared a common love of Shakespearean theater, their respective audiences couldn't have been more different. The rivalry between them was not unlike that of a pair of top-ranked sports teams.

In William Shakespeare's tragedy *Macbeth*, a trio of witches predict the title character's fate with a nearly inscrutable prophecy. Some say actual witches felt the playwright hit too close to the mark and so they cursed productions of the play in perpetuity.

The enmity escalated to a fever pitch on May 10, when tens of thousands of Forrest's fans turned up outside the theater where Macready was all set to go on stage as Macbeth. They pelted the building with bricks. A full-fledged riot broke out. To quell the violence, armed militiamen were deployed to the scene. Attempting to restore order, the troops fired a single warning volley first. When that failed to deter the mob, they fired their weapons into the massed crowd, killing 22 and wounding approximately five times that many.

The events of May 10, 1849, became known as the Astor Place Riot, named after the Astor Opera House at which Macready was performing. The venue's name was permanently blackened, tarred by association with the riot. It eventually went out of business and became a library. Historians have come to see the Astor Place Riot as a battleground in the class war between the rich and poor, yet there are also those who believe the curse of *Macbeth* was at work that night, not least because Edwin Forrest was appearing in his own production of the Scottish play at that same time.

Another long-standing entertainment industry curse revolves around the character of Superman.

In 1938, comic book artists and writers Jerry Siegel and Joe Shuster created the Man of Steel from the planet Krypton. Superman is arguably the most recognizable superhero on Earth (somewhat ironic, as he doesn't come *from* Earth), and tens of millions of readers have thrilled to his adventures over the decades since Superman first appeared in the pages of *Action Comics #1*.

With his growing popularity, it was inevitable that Superman would make his way to the screen (although Batman beat him there in 1943). He was first portrayed by actor Kirk Alyn in the 1948 serial *Superman*. Kirk Alyn lived until the age of 88. If there really is a "curse of Superman," then it seems to have passed him by—although some claim the fact that his acting career never really took off (so to speak) after playing Superman is evidence that the curse began with him.

More tragic is the case of Alyn's successor, George Reeves, who donned the famous red cape and blue tights in 1951. Thanks to his chiseled good looks and clean-cut, all-American persona, Reeves became immensely popular as the Man of Steel, emulated by children everywhere. Television was growing increasingly popular, and Reeves fought villains on small screens across the country on a weekly basis. It all came to an end on June 15, 1959, when he was found dead at his home in Beverly Hills, killed by a single gunshot wound to the head. He was 45 years old and had already completed filming on the TV series at the time of his death.

Although ruled a suicide by the coroner, much was suspicious about Reeves's death.

Although ruled a suicide by the coroner, much was suspicious about Reeves's death. According to his fiancée, Lenore Lemmon, and their house guests, he had gone to his bedroom, and then they heard a shot fired from upstairs. Although his time as Superman was over, he and Lenore Lemmon were set to marry just two days later. Strangely, Lemmon was reported to have said that Reeves was "going upstairs to shoot himself."

His obituary in the *Los Angeles Times* on June 17, 1952, noted that Lemmon had given almost a blow-by-blow commentary: "See, he's opening the drawer to get the gun," she said after hearing a sound from the bedroom. After the gunshot reverberated through the house, this was followed by: "See there, I told you. He's shot himself."

Indeed, he had. The actor was found lying on his bed, completely naked. The weapon used was a Luger pistol, commonly used by the German military during World War II, and available readily and cheaply. It had fired a single 9mm round and was found on the bedroom floor close to Reeves's body. The shell casing was found on the mattress underneath the corpse. When the pistol grip was dusted by law enforcement officers, George Reeves's fingerprints were not found on it.

It's hard to see Lemmon's remarks as being anything other than callous and sinister. When asked about them by homicide detectives, the actress insisted that she had only been joking. If so, it was a rather sick joke.

Equally suspicious was the fact that it had taken more than half an hour for those present in the house at the time of his death to call the authorities. The fact that everybody was drunk may explain it, but many think that either one of them or an outsider actually murdered him. One possible suspect was a spurned ex-lover of Reeves's named

Actor George Reeves will always be remembered for his role as the first Superman to appear on television during the 1950s. He tragically committed suicide in 1959.

Toni Mannix. When he broke the affair off, she did not take kindly to being rejected and pursued the *Superman* star to the point of harassment. Based on the principle that "hell hath no fury like a woman scorned," one hypothesis holds that Toni hired a hit man to kill her former beau as a form of revenge. If this was true, it backfired. George's death sent her into a serious emotional tailspin.

Did Reeves have a motive to take his own life? Although he had earned national fame as Superman, he wasn't exactly sitting on a pile of cash. The show had been cheaply made, and little of the profit had trickled down his way. The actor also feared being typecast, which was not an unreasonable concern. The phone hadn't been ringing off the hook since he had hung up the cape. He had taken to drinking and drank heavily on the night of his death. Reeves was also taking pain killers in the wake of a car accident that had left him with a lingering injury. He was down, certainly, but not necessarily out.

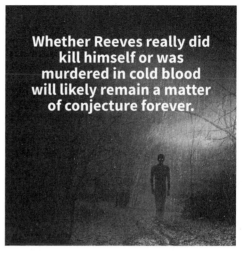

Whether Reeves really did kill himself or was murdered in cold blood will likely remain a matter of conjecture forever. What we can say for sure is that he died too young and under mysterious and tragic circumstances.

The actor most associated with the character of Superman is almost certainly New York–born Christopher Reeve. No relation to George Reeves, Christopher brought Superman back to the big screen in 1978 and returned to play him in three sequels. Reeve epitomized the character's Boy Scout nature, equally at home rescuing cats from trees and children from peril as he was battling supervillains and deranged supercomputers.

Disaster struck in 1995 when Reeve, a keen equestrian, was thrown from his horse, breaking his neck. Were it not for the timely intervention of paramedics, the actor would likely have died. High spinal cord injuries can result in a cessation of breathing from impingement on the nerve that carries signals to the respiratory muscles. Flown to the hospital by a medical helicopter, Reeve went into emergency surgery, which saved his life. Unfortunately, he remained paralyzed completely from the neck down.

Paralysis took a toll on Reeve's mental health, but he fought back like the superhero he portrayed on the big screen. Along with his wife, Dana, he set up the Christopher Reeve Foundation to fund research into finding a cure for spinal injury. Despite requiring a respirator to breathe, in 1997 he directed his first movie, and he even returned to acting.

Christopher Reeve, who starred as Superman in the movies *Superman, Superman II, Superman III,* and *Superman IV: The Quest for Peace,* was paralyzed in a horse riding accident and later died as a consequence of those injuries.

Christopher Reeve died on October 10, 2004. He was 52 years old. His wife, Dana, died shortly afterward of lung cancer at the age of 44. She was not a smoker.

Proponents of there being a Superman curse maintain that it is not restricted to the actors who played the title character. Two of Christopher Reeve's fellow performers also experienced a share of tragedy after filming *Superman*. Lee Quigley, a British actor who had played Superman as a baby, died at the age of 14 after overdosing on solvents. Actress Margot Kidder, who played opposite Reeve as reporter and love interest Lois Lane, suffered serious mental health issues that culminated in a nervous breakdown. She died in 2018, at the age of 69, of a drug and alcohol overdose that was ruled a suicide.

If one is willing to cast a wider net, the curse could also be said to apply to co-stars such as Marlon Brando and members of his family, Richard Pryor, creators Jerry Siegel and Joe Shuster, and many more. Casting a skeptical eye on the curse, it must be pointed out that it has taken thousands of people to bring the adventures of Krypton's last surviving son to life over the years. It would be remarkable if there *weren't* deaths, illnesses, accidents, and various misfortunes associated with them, as a statistical near certainty.

There are also a number of on-screen Supermen after Christopher Reeve who did not seem to be affected by the curse at all. The most recent actor to portray him, Henry Cavill, went on the public record stating that he did not believe in it. At the time of writing, with Cavill being a world-famous megastar who has also been considered a frontrunner for the role of James Bond, he seems to lead the very opposite of a cursed life.

Another unanswered question involves the source of any such curse. Unlike the witches who were said to have cursed *Macbeth*, nobody seems to have done the same to *Superman*. In stark contrast to *The Exorcist* and *The Omen*, the subject matter doesn't include demonic forces. Superman is about as wholesome as it gets.

The same cannot be said of Steven Spielberg and Tobe

Hooper's 1982 blockbuster *Poltergeist*. The movie tells the story of the Freeling family, a stereotypical American family who, unbeknownst to them, are living in a house that was built on top of an indigenous graveyard. Naturally their home turns out to be extremely haunted, and after a steady escalation of paranormal phenomena, their daughter, Carol Anne, is kidnapped by an immensely powerful dark and malevolent entity.

Poltergeist is by turns funny, poignant, and terrifying. Even more than 40 years after its release, the film maintains its ability to scare modern audiences in addition to entertaining them. Rightfully acknowledged as an all-time classic, *Poltergeist* also retains a place in the public consciousness for a darker reason: some believe it to be cursed.

It's undeniable that the cast of *Poltergeist* suffered a greater-than-average share of bad luck, the worst of which involved several deaths.

O'Rourke was the only cast member to star in all three of the *Poltergeist* films, and it was during the filming of the third installment, *Poltergeist III: The Other Side*, that she unexpectedly fell ill.

Following the film's completion, 22-year-old actress Dominique Dunn, who portrayed the family's teenage daughter Dana, was strangled into a state of unconsciousness by her then-boyfriend John Thomas Sweeney. A chef by trade, Sweeney had shown abusive tendencies that deeply worried Dunne's friends and family. On October 30, Sweeney showed up at her apartment and assaulted her, leaving Dunne in critical condition. He surrendered to the police without putting up a fight, telling them, "I killed my girlfriend."

Paramedics rushed the comatose Dominique Dunne to Cedars Sinai hospital, where she was placed on life support. She died five days later.

Although charged with murder, Sweeney was convicted of the lesser charge of manslaughter. He served just half his sentence and was released on parole three and a half years later. Based on his employment record as a chef working at high-end restaurants, Sweeney had no difficulty finding employment—until the Dunne family tracked him down and began protesting outside his workplace, telling diners that the hands that prepared their dinner had also murdered Dominique Dunne. Sweeney changed his name and left Los Angeles in a bid to start a new life, though he continued to work in the food services industry.

Equally tragic was the death of Heather O'Rourke, the child actress who played the Freeling family's youngest daughter, Carol Anne. O'Rourke was the only cast member to star in all three of the *Poltergeist* films, and it was during the filming of the third installment, *Poltergeist III: The Other Side*, that she unexpectedly fell ill. The 12-year-old actress began suffering abdominal cramps, which doctors attributed to inflammation caused by Crohn's disease. In reality, she had developed a bowel obstruction, a condition that proved to be fatal. She died on February 1, 1988, a shock to all who knew and loved her, including the legion of fans she had garnered through her film and TV work.

One of her co-stars from *Poltergeist II: The Other Side*, Julian Beck, also died shortly after completing his work on the film. The death of Beck, who played the villainous Reverend Kane to chilling effect, actually makes little sense in the context of a potential curse; the actor was suffering from terminal stomach cancer while shooting *Poltergeist II*, and his death was sadly a foregone conclusion.

Yet the curse stories continued to circulate, to such an extent that actor and real-life shaman Will Sampson was said to have performed a cleansing and exorcism ceremony on the movie set. Whether this had any effect on the run of bad luck that was said to have plagued the production is difficult to say, though it may well have helped the cast and crew feel better.

Why were *Poltergeist* and its sequels supposedly cursed? One popular explanation involves the sequence at the end of the first movie when coffins begin blasting out of the ground in and around the Freeling house and its swimming pool. Unbeknownst to actress JoBeth Williams, who played the matriarch Diane Freeling, the skeletons that shared the scene with her—including quite a bit of physical contact—were not replicas. They were actual human skeletons, sourced from a biological supply company. When the movie was shot, buying the real thing was a significantly cheaper option than paying a special effects team to make a batch of fake skeletons.

Who's to say that their restless spirits didn't play a role in the mishaps and misfortunes that took place during the film's production—and after?

Poltergeist was remade in 2015. If the curse was real, it does not seem to have affected the cast and crew of the remake. At least, not so far.

THE HEXED HEADS OF HEXHAM

Human beings have always known that there can be an inherent risk in digging up the past. Some things that lie buried were placed there for good reason, and woe betide the person who unearths them and, in doing so, wakes the mysterious energies associated with them from their slumber.

One particularly chilling example was the case of the Hexham Heads. Hexham is a historic town in the north of England, green and picturesque. It sits close to Hadrian's Wall, the fortification built in the name of the Roman emperor Hadrian to keep marauders from crossing the northern border of Britannia.

In 1971, two young brothers were at play in the garden of their home when they dug up something rather curious: two small pieces of stone, crudely carved into the shape of human heads. Bringing the heads indoors proved to be a mistake. Poltergeist activity flared up almost immediately. Items inside the family home spontaneously broke themselves. The heads, which had been placed on a shelf, had a habit of

Hexham is a small historic town in Northumberland, England, located near Hadrian's Wall. Artifacts are still found there on occasion, including the mysterious Hexham Heads.

swiveling about when nobody was looking. One night, the Robson boys' bedroom window broke without any apparent cause.

Yet the paranormal activity being experienced by the Robson family was overshadowed by the goings-on in the home of their neighbors, the Dodds. The Dodd children had begun complaining that an unseen something was prodding them and pulling their hair when they were trying to sleep. At first, it's tempting to write this off as either a hypnagogic or hypnopompic hallucination—the strange sensations we commonly experience when we're on the brink of either falling asleep or of waking up. The timing was suspicious, however, coming as it did so soon after the discovery of the heads in the ground next door. And what came next was terrifying.

This may evoke thoughts of the Goatman stories recounted earlier in this book. As terrifying as this sounds, however, author Stuart Ferrol offers a non-paranormal explanation in a superbly researched article on the case.

According to one Hexham resident, a local man was making his way drunkenly back from the pub that night when he took it upon himself to break into the slaughterhouse and steal the remains of a dead sheep's pelt, which he supposedly threw over his shoulders and wielded to terrify Mrs. Dodd. Ferrol finds this an unconvincing explanation, and I tend to agree. The idea that she was unable to tell the difference between a man wearing a sheep carcass and some kind of human/sheep hybrid is hard to believe.

The origin of the heads provided another mystery. Some, including Dr. Ross, believed them to have been Celtic, in which style they definitely seemed made.

It's hard to blame the Robsons for wanting to get the stone heads out of their house as quickly as possible. They gave them to archaeologist and author Dr. Anne Ross, an expert on the Celtic people and their art. As soon as the academic took them into her keeping, it was her family's turn to be haunted—this time, by a man-beast that was more wolflike then sheeplike. Although the story of the Hexham Heads has generated controversy over the years, by this stage there were two separate households reporting encounters with two separate (albeit similar) human/animal hybrids—and in both cases, this happened after the mysterious stone heads were brought into their homes.

The origin of the heads provided another mystery. Some, including Dr. Ross, believed them to have been Celtic, in which style they definitely seemed made. Matters were complicated when a local man named Des Craigie came forward and claimed to have made the heads himself as toys for his children. Craigie had lived at the Robsons' house before they had taken up residence. While the Hexham heads were never conclusively dated, it seems beyond the bounds of coincidence that the bizarre and frightening paranormal activity only began after they were unearthed and brought indoors. The Robsons gave no indication of there having been any disturbances prior to that.

Little wonder that the heads soon developed a reputation for being cursed. Author Paul Screeton, who studied the case extensively, noted that when the heads were submitted for analysis, experts could not agree on their age or their origin. Dr. Ross passed the heads on, and they resided with several other individuals, and it must be noted that other than some relatively minor incidents that could be put down to mere happenstance, nothing paranormal followed them. Nobody else reported encountering human/sheep or human/wolf creatures in their homes or places of work.

Unfortunately, we are not likely to get answers to the many questions surrounding the Hexham Heads. They disappeared sometime in the late 1970s, never to be seen again. Perhaps they are sitting on a shelf in somebody's office or gathering dust in a garage somewhere. It is intriguing to wonder whether their current owner, whoever that may be, is plagued by paranormal activity themselves. We can only hope that someday, the heads will be rediscovered and subjected to rigorous scientific analysis. Until then, all we can do is watch ... and wait.

THE HAUNTING OF FOX HOLLOW FARM

Herbert Baumeister was a sick man.

He had always been strange, of that there was no doubt. What else are we to make of a man whose nickname was "Weird Herb"? But then, there's weird, and there's *weird*.

To all outside appearances, Herb and his wife, Julie, were living the American dream during the early 1990s. Owners of the Sav-A-Lot chain of thrift stores, the Baumeisters made enough money to allow them to purchase a beautiful house on a large plot of land in rural Indiana. The house was surrounded by trees and set far back from the road, approached by a long driveway.

Its name was Fox Hollow Farm.

The house had a stable block, spacious garage, acres of land on which the children could play, and even a basement swimming pool.

But Herb Baumeister had a dark secret. When his wife and children were away at the lake for the weekend, he adopted another persona: that of a man named Brian Smart. Using this new guise, Herb trawled the gay bars and clubs of Indianapolis, looking to pick up young men who wanted to party. He chose his targets carefully, selecting those who were unlikely to be missed if they were to disappear.

Fox Hollow Farm was once home to the serial killer Herb Baumeister. It is now a family home, but traces of its dark past still remain.

Luring the unsuspecting men back to Fox Hollow Farm with the promise of drink, drugs, and a good time, Herb took them downstairs to the swimming pool, where he would strangle them with a rubber hose. Herb then dragged the dead bodies into the woodland behind the farm, where he would cut them up, pour gasoline on the remains, and set them on fire.

The precise number of victims that Baumeister murdered will never be known, but it could be as many as 20. When the fact that he was leading a double life was finally uncovered, Herb made a dash for the Canadian border, then shot himself in the head on a scenic beach in Pinery Provincial Park, located on Lake Huron.

Despite the best efforts of a small army of forensic researchers and their assistants and the retrieval of literally thousands of bones and bone fragments on the grounds of Fox Hollow Farm, some of the victims remain unidentified. Baumeister didn't even bother to bury them in shallow graves, which meant that they were exposed to the elements for months or, in some cases, years. Foxes and other critters took parts of the remains and spread them far and wide, meaning that some will never be found.

Most places in which serial murders have taken place are demolished. Not so with Fox Hollow. The Graves family purchased the estate after it had been vacant for several years. Wanting a place to raise their children and one that was suitable for horses, they were not put off by its macabre history. Yet it wasn't long after they took up residence that strange things started to happen.

The power cable from Mrs. Graves's vacuum cleaner was yanked out of the socket. She came home one night and saw what she thought was a trespasser at the back of the property, a young man wearing a red shirt strolling through the woods. She was just about to challenge him when she realized that he had no legs. As she watched, the apparition disappeared in front of her eyes.

> Wanting a place to raise their children and one that was suitable for horses, they were not put off by its macabre history. Yet it wasn't long after they took up residence that strange things started to happen.

The next person to encounter the apparition was the Graves's lodger, who saw the same young man while walking his dog in the woods one night. He began to have nightmares in which he was running for his life through the trees, fleeing from someone who wanted him dead. He was renting the apartment that was attached to the main farm building. Somebody began hammering on the door in the early hours of the morning, pounding violently on the knocker. When it was opened up, there was nobody outside.

Things turned violent in the swimming pool one day when the lodger felt unseen fingers tightening around his throat. Suddenly, he was yanked beneath the surface of the water and held there. He was being attacked by something that he couldn't see. Fortunately, he was able to break free and rush out of the pool before he was seriously hurt.

Another ominous incident took place when a friend of the family brought his young daughter over to visit. The child could not possibly have known of the events that had taken place at Fox Hollow. As she was passing the open door of the pump room located a few feet away

The basement swimming pool into which Baumeister lured his unsuspecting victims.

from the swimming pool, the little girl shushed her father and told him to be quiet because "the men are sleeping in there." Because it is a cold and dark place, it is believed that Herb Baumeister may have kept the bodies of some victims in the pump room before taking them out into the woods.

I was fortunate enough to be given permission for an investigation of Fox Hollow Farm and made two separate journeys to Indiana to spend a few days getting acquainted with the place. The Graves family were extremely friendly and welcoming, sharing their experiences in a matter-of-fact way that I found to be convincing. After hearing about the paranormal activity that they and numerous visitors reported experiencing there, one thing was very apparent: the haunting really seemed to kick into high gear with the arrival of the lodger named Joe. My theory for this was that Joe was about the same age as many of Herb Baumeister's victims, and his presence may have acted as a stimulus or catalyst of some kind.

Joe was kind enough to take some time out of his schedule and join us at Fox Hollow. Over the course of an evening that lent some credence to my theory, activity spiked inside the house, particularly in the pump room, where I felt disembodied fingers brush the bare skin of my arm and a female investigator was poked in the back.

During the course of our stay, the farm continued to surprise us. We recorded electronic voice phenomena (EVP) at one of the body-burning sites in the woods (a gravelly old man's voice growling, "Get away from there"), and when I took a swim in the pool, a younger male voice could clearly be heard whispering the name "Laura." That happens to be my wife's name and served as a chilling reminder that sometimes, being a paranormal researcher can become uncomfortably personal.

There are several different theories as to who (or what) haunts Fox Hollow Farm. The most unpleasant, to my mind, is the possibility that some of Herbert Baumeister's victims are still resident there. The fact that both Joe and Mrs. Graves recognized the man in the red shirt as being one of them tends to support that theory. I call it the most unpleasant because those poor young men suffered enough at the end of their lives, and I do not like the possibility that they may not be at rest.

It is also a popularly held belief among those familiar with the case that Herb Baumeister himself may be active at Fox Hollow, though whether he is permanently in residence there or only drops in occasionally is a subject of some debate. On the other hand, some visiting psychics have claimed that the root of the haunting is a non-human entity of some kind that was supposedly drawn to the place because of all the negativity that surrounded it during the time of the murders. This entity, which has been nicknamed "the Frog," is said to impersonate Baumeister and behave aggressively toward visitors, with the intent of evoking fear.

This entity, which has been nicknamed "the Frog," is said to impersonate Baumeister and behave aggressively toward visitors, with the intent of evoking fear.

Despite the amount of time that I spent there, I am still none the wiser as to which of these theories is correct—if, indeed, any of them are. It has been two years since I last visited, and in that time, the haunting appears to have quieted down. The Graves family are happy in their home and want nothing more than to live in harmony alongside the spirits with whom they share Fox Hollow Farm.

I politely ask you, dear reader, to please respect their right to privacy.

THE GATEWAY TO HELL:
BOBBY MACKEY'S MUSIC WORLD

Every paranormal investigator has a bucket list of places they'd give their right arm to spend the night at. Sitting at the very top of mine was Bobby Mackey's Music World, a honky-tonk club in the small town of Wilder, Kentucky. Back in 2016, I finally got the chance to cross it off the list. For one night, and one night only, Bobby Mackey's would be mine to explore.

The place has a fearsome reputation, and to be entirely truthful, I was a little bit apprehensive when I pulled into the parking lot of this iconic building. It was a hot and humid summer's eve. My small team and I had arrived before our appointed time, giving us the chance to explore the surrounding area.

Bobby Mackey's Music World sits on a stretch of land above the Licking River. I climbed slowly down the steep riverbank to the edge of the water. In 1892, a little further up the river, there had been a bridge collapse that killed at least 40 men. Partway down I found the circular entrance to the tunnel that led underneath the club. It was dank and cold inside.

Much has been made by certain TV shows of the fact that in 1896, a woman named Pearl Bryan was murdered and decapitated in the vicinity. Pearl's head was cut off while she was still alive, according to analysis of blood splatter at the murder scene, and legend has it that her head was thrown down into a well on the property where the honky-tonk now stands. Her ghost is associated with Bobby Mackey's Music World, but in reality, as historian Shannon Bradley Byers points out in her treatise *Paranormal Fakelore, Nevermore*, Pearl's death occurred miles away, and there is no evidence whatsoever to suggest that Pearl's head was brought anywhere near the place. Neither do the lurid stories of devil worship on the site have any proven basis in fact. Tales often grow in the telling, and never has this been truer than in the case of Bobby Mackey's.

The stage of the United States's most infamous haunted road house, Bobby Mackey's Music World.

When it comes to this location, it is difficult, if not next to impossible, to separate fact from fantasy with respect to some of the stories and legends associated with it. One persistent myth claims that the site was once the location of a slaughterhouse, when in fact, the building that actually stood on that spot was a distillery. That makes a lot of sense, considering its easy access to the river.

During the twentieth century, the building was a bar/club and casino, often under the rule of organized crime, and it is from this latter role that one of the more believable stories comes. There are claims that those who had tried to cheat the house while gambling were beaten to a pulp, down in the cellar, to be taught a lesson. It is entirely possible that this took place after hours so that nobody could hear their screams.

As far as I have been able to determine, the ghost stories associated with this location first arose after it was acquired by a country singer named Bobby Mackey. Many of the accounts came from a gentleman named Carl Lawson, who lived upstairs on the second floor. Carl fulfilled the duties of handyman and janitor at the club.

Lawson claimed to have found a journal in the well down in the basement—a journal that belonged to a former dancer named Johanna. Dan Smith, author of *Ghosts of Bobby Mackey's Music World*, reproduces some of the contents of this journal. The entries supposedly claimed that Johanna fatally poisoned her father and then herself, her father having been a Satanist who conducted rituals in the area and had opened "a portal to hell" through

> The entries supposedly claimed that Johanna fatally poisoned her father and then herself, her father having been a Satanist who conducted rituals in the area and had opened "a portal to hell" through the very same well.

the very same well. Johanna believed her father had murdered her lover, a young man named Robbie, and she hoped that in death, she was going to join her sweetheart.

In an ending twist worthy of a Dennis Wheatley novel, the dying Johanna encountered the spirit of one of Pearl Bryan's murderers, who took responsibility for throwing her decapitated head down the well in an act of satanic worship. Dan Smith sounds appropriately skeptical of this tale, as indeed am I. He also rightly points out that generally, people dying of a poison overdose rarely tend to write down their thoughts during the final few minutes.

Carl Lawson continued to live and work at Bobby Mackey's, and so great was the ghosts' apparent influence on him that he ultimately submitted to an exorcism to rid himself of them. Mr. Lawson has now sadly passed away, and I certainly do not mean to speak ill of him. Nobody will ever truly know what he endured while living at Bobby Mackey's Music World, but one thing does seem clear: in some way, shape, or form, he was most definitely haunted. I truly hope that he now rests in peace.

One of the first things that caught my eye when I walked inside the club was the sign, prominently displayed, that stated that the building was purported to be haunted, and that management refused to accept any liability for harm done by the ghosts. I had a hard time deciding whether it was a legitimate disclaimer or something done to add a little spice to the legend. Maybe a bit of both.

The club wasn't open to the public on that particular night, so our tour guide, Angie, showed us around. She had a wealth of knowledge about the history and haunting and shared her personal experiences there, which included having the doors slamming open and closed by themselves. We were warned that although we could use any equipment and techniques we liked during the course of our investigation, it was a

A sign at the entrance to Bob Mackey's warns patrons that the establishment is haunted and that the establishment cannot be held accountable for any supernatural incidents.

really, *really* bad idea to provoke—especially if that provocation involved religious iconography such as Bibles and crucifixes.

There are stories—quite a few stories, actually—of visitors to Bobby Mackey's being physically harmed by something malevolent there. These accounts include people being pushed forcefully across the room, slammed into the wall, pinned, scratched, and otherwise traumatized. The likelihood of this happening is said to increase exponentially for those who go in and provoke.

On the other hand, many of the people who visit Bobby Mackey's Music World experience absolutely nothing otherworldly at all. After spending the entire night there, I was sad to have become a member of the second group. I sat alone in what is said to be Johanna's dressing room and spent a lot of time in the vicinity of the well down in the basement. I found no evidence of it being paranormally active. In fact, I had a hard time staying awake.

To coin a phrase, it turned out to be a quiet night in hell.

We recorded no EVPs, felt no inexplicable cold drafts, and experienced no physical contact with anything unseen. Despite the many stories of demonic entities manifesting to terrorize the living, it was so quiet that I could quite easily have unrolled a sleeping bag and fallen asleep on the main stage. Upstairs, in Carl Lawson's living quarters, were overflowing ashtrays and memorabilia of days long gone, but nothing ghostly that night.

Does Bobby Mackey's Music World deserve its reputation as a haunted hot spot? That's not for me to say. I'm certainly fond of the place. It has history, and it has character. It may very well be haunted. Considering its link to the mob and the bridge collapse nearby, I would find that very easy to believe. Just because a place is haunted doesn't mean it is *always* haunted. We could simply have been there on the wrong night.

There is a mass of eyewitness testimony from staff and visitors claiming that ghosts and spirits of some kind *do* tread the boards at

Bobby Mackey's. I'm saddened that they never came out to meet me, and someday, I would very much like to go back there and try again.

KILLER CLOWN: JOHN WAYNE GACY

When insurance agent Robbin Terry brought home a unique piece of furniture, he had no idea of the mayhem it would cause. Robbin and his wife, Norma, live in a former movie theater in the small town of Auburn, Illinois. It's a quiet place, for the most part, with a sedate pace of living that most of the residents appreciate.

The R Theater, as the Terrys' home is known today, is a wonderful place. I fell in love with it just a few minutes after crossing over the threshold for the first time. Norma is an avowed bibliophile. Not only do the shelves practically groan with books, but they are also stacked in piles on many stairs throughout the residence. Some have been read; others are to be read. I was gratified to see a number of my own titles gracing the stacks of Norma's library.

The R Theater in Auburn, Illinois, haunted by the ghost of serial killer John Wayne Gacy.

Robbin, on the other hand, will be the first to tell you that he isn't a reader by natural inclination. Two of his great passions are Scooby Doo and the paranormal. Proof of the former comes in the form of the Mystery Machine, a fully functional replica of the van used by the cowardly pooch and his four human sidekicks to take them ghost hunting. This was made as a promotional prop by Hanna Barbera studios and now takes pride of place in Robbin's vast collection of all things Scooby, which fills much of the R Theater's vast parking garage. (The remainder is occupied by Robbin's collection of classic vehicles.)

When it comes to his other great passion, the paranormal, Robbin is equally committed. He is the owner of Ashmore Estates, a commercial haunted house that began its life in 1916 as an almshouse. His collection of talking boards and other paranormal esoterica would make most enthusiasts salivate with excitement.

Yet something else occupies the R Theater—something, or rather, someone, with a very unsavory reputation.

It all began in the usual way. Footsteps in empty rooms and along quiet hallways and corridors. Household objects disappearing, only to turn up again days or sometimes weeks later in completely unexpected places. Cold spots in an otherwise temperate building. Many of the early signs of an incipient haunting, and more, clued the Terrys in that something decidedly strange was going on inside their beloved home.

Fortunately, Robbin does not lack connections within the paranormal community. All he had to do was pick up the phone for investigators he trusted to come and pay the R Theater a visit. It wasn't long before two of the sensitives, working independently, told him that a male entity by the name of John Wayne had taken up residence alongside himself and Norma.

Robbin's first thought was a cheery, "Oh wow, the Duke himself, John Wayne, is haunting our movie theater! Cool!"

Except this wasn't the much-loved legendary screen cowboy John Wayne. This was John Wayne *Gacy*, the infamous serial killer, who had murdered more than 33 men and buried the majority in the crawlspace underneath his house.

Gacy was known to frequent a multitude of places in the Chicago area and its surroundings, but what would bring him to a defunct movie theater in sleepy little Auburn?

The armoire which once contained Gacy's crude paintings.

In a word: furniture.

Before all of the high strangeness had kicked off in his home, Robbin had brought in a carved wooden armoire given to him by a friend. That friend had been one of several attorneys who had represented John Wayne Gacy. The armoire had been used to store some of Gacy's paintings, the crude daubing of clowns he had made while sitting on death row. Although the locked cabinet no longer contained any of the dead serial killer's art, the psychics who examined it theorized that some part of Gacy remained attached to the armoire even now, years after his execution by lethal injection.

When I heard about this, via my Texan friends Brad and Barry Klinge, I was intrigued and wanted to know more. They connected me with Robbin Terry, who graciously allowed me to bring a small team into his home for a few days to investigate.

Readers wanting to know more about that particular investigation are directed to my book *Gacy's Ghost*, which details everything that happened. I brought in a number of sensitives myself, independently of one another, in an attempt to figure out what was going on. They were in agreement that Gacy's spirit does haunt the R Theater, though whether he resides there permanently or simply drops in from time to time was a matter of some debate.

For my part, I'm not entirely sure. Talking board interactions such as the one we had on the R's main stage were very suggestive:

"He's coming!"

"Who's coming?"

"John."

"Where's he coming from?"

"From hell."

All of which implies that the spirit of this ghastly man is on his way back from the fires of eternal damnation (if one believes in such a thing, it's hard to think of a more suitable candidate than Gacy) to tread the boards at the R Theater. But we must also consider an alternative explanation: that there's something else at the R, something that likes to imitate John Wayne Gacy for its own amusement.

The imitator is something we see quite often in the paranormal realm. Simply put, this appears to be an intelligence of some kind that likes to disguise itself as someone or something other than itself. At the R, I've often wondered whether there's an opportunistic entity that gets its kicks pretending to be the notorious serial killer to frighten people. (If so, it's not a very effective tactic. Both Robbin and Norma keep whatever it is firmly in its place and refuse to be cowed or intimidated in their own home.)

Still, the Terrys are no fools. Whatever it is that truly haunts their home, be it the ghost of John Wayne Gacy or something pretending to be him, they avoid stirring the pot. Robbin does not allow teams to come into his residence with the intent of poking the bear; attempting to communicate with Gacy at the R Theater is verboten.

Sometimes, when you show an interest in the darkness, it takes an interest right back.

THAT NIGHT IN AMITYVILLE

To readers in North America, the iconic example of a dark, malevolent haunting would be the so-called Amityville horror. Even now, more than 45 years after the Hollywood adaptation of Jay Anson's best-selling novel first hit theaters and terrified a generation of moviegoers, the alleged haunting of the house in Amityville continues to generate controversy. Few people would fail to recognize the iconic image of the house at 112 Ocean Avenue, Amityville, Long Island, with the distinctive eye-like windows peering balefully down from the upper floor.

In the wake of a tragic and vicious case of familicide, fact and fiction collided. The murders that took place in the early morning hours of November 13, 1974, were the culmination of a feud between the overbearing head of the family, 43-year-old Ronald DeFeo Sr., and his 23-year-old son, Ronald Jr., who went by "Ronnie" or "Butch." Both men had a violent temper. The two had been at one another's throats for years, culminating in Butch pointing a loaded gun at his father's face and pulling the trigger—only for the weapon to misfire.

As the increasingly resentful Butch DeFeo grew from a teenager into an angry and troubled young man, he also began drinking and using drugs and stealing money, and he became known as a habitual liar—a trait that is important to bear in mind when considering his claims of what happened on the night of the DeFeo family murders. Both of Butch's parents, Ronald and Louise, were shot dead while they lay in bed. All four of his siblings—sisters Dawn (18) and Alison (13) and brothers Marc (11) and John (9)—were shot dead with the same high-powered rifle that was used to murder their parents. The only survivor was Butch. After the sun came up, with the dead bodies of his family lying in their beds on different floors of the house, he went to work as usual, already cooking up plans to get away with murder. He knew nothing about the deaths, Butch insisted. His father had some shady connections with organized crime, and it had been a mob hit.

He failed. It didn't take detectives long to see through his cover story and arrest him for murder. He had the motive to kill his parents—Butch loathed his father and disparaged his mother. Yet his reasons for murdering his siblings were harder to explain. In an attempt to shift some of the blame onto his sister, Butch claimed that Dawn had killed the three younger siblings while he was out, and that he shot her when he found out what she had done.

Ronald "Butch" DeFeo was quickly arrested after shooting his parents and all four of his siblings dead on that horrible night in 1974.

In court, Butch's attorney, William Weber, tried using an insanity plea to secure his client's freedom. It didn't work. The jury found him guilty on all six counts, and he was sentenced to six life sentences for the crime of slaughtering his family—and there the story should have ended, as a tragic example of family annihilation. Unfortunately, there was money to be made off the back of it, based mainly on the horrifying experiences the next tenants of the house on Ocean Avenue would claim to suffer.

In late 1975, one year after the brutal deaths of the DeFeo family, the house on Ocean Avenue was purchased by George and Kathy Lutz, who promptly moved in with their children to what they thought would be the home of their dreams.

What happened over the next 28 days is still a matter of interpretation and fierce debate, with the Lutzes, along with Ed and Lorraine Warren (later of *The Conjuring* fame) and their supporters, squaring off against skeptics such as Dr. Stephen Kaplan and his wife, Roxanne. The Kaplans would go on to publish a book debunking the alleged haunting (*The Amityville Horror Conspiracy*) to serve as a counterpoint to author Jay Anson's bestseller *The Amityville Horror*, which was written with the cooperation of George and Kathy Lutz.

> The sheer range of reported phenomena runs the entire gamut of paranormal events, from demonic possession and poltergeist activity to the unexplained opening of doors and phantom footsteps....

Crucially, Anson's book purports to be an honest accounting of the Lutzes' monthlong residency in the house. The sheer range of reported phenomena runs the entire gamut of paranormal events, from demonic possession and poltergeist activity to the unexplained opening of doors and phantom footsteps of a more "traditional" haunting. A smattering of those claims are the following:

- A demonic face with glowing red eyes was seen peering in through a window, accompanied by cloven hoof prints found in snow outside the house.

- Doors slammed open and shut in empty rooms.

- The walls, ceiling, and even toilets oozed viscous slime.

- Hordes of flies, which are considered by some to be a sign of demonic infestation, swarmed inside the house.

- Kathy's face aged rapidly and transformed into that of a toothless old hag. She also levitated above her mattress while in bed one evening.

- A priest that the Lutzes claimed was brought into the house to bless it was supposedly growled at to "get out!" It would subsequently be alleged that this visit never happened, yet it remains an iconic moment in the movie adaptation.

- As time went on, George Lutz began to behave strangely, his wife said. He took on an increasingly aggressive and belligerent affect, as though he was being possessed by some malevolent influence.

The house where the murders and subsequent hauntings occurred has had its postal address changed to make it harder for tourists to find.

From the outset, the Lutzes sought publicity—something that would raise the suspicions of many a paranormal investigator. When money is involved—and in the case of *The Amityville Horror*, it came to be *big* money—there also comes the tendency to question the motives of those involved. As skeptics began to pick the claims apart, pointing out the numerous inconsistencies in the Lutzes' testimony and in Anson's book, the couple doubled down, insisting that their story was true.

Was Amityville a hoax or a genuine haunting? It is suggestive that none of the subsequent owners of the house on Ocean Avenue ever reported any paranormal activity there. The explanation tendered by believers is that the activity focused not on just the house but on the Lutz family, and that the dark and vindictive spirits that supposedly plagued them during their stay moved out along with them.

A careful analysis of their claims, made by skeptical investigators such as Stephen Kaplan, Joe Nickell, and author Ric Osuna, has identified enough holes and outright confabulations in the Lutzes' story that if the claims of a haunting were ever tried in a court of law, it would almost certainly be thrown out.

Ed and Lorraine Warren came down unequivocally on the side of the house being haunted by demonic forces and said as much after participating in a seance inside the home that was attended by members of the TV news media. They maintained that without a definitive exorcism, the house would be too hostile an environment for anybody to live in.

From his prison cell, Butch DeFeo scoffed at claims of paranormal activity playing a role in the slayings. In a letter to local news reporter Marvin Scott, who had covered the case extensively, he insisted that there was only ever one demon at work in Amityville: a demon named Butch DeFeo Jr. He took the real story with him to his grave when he died in the winter of 2021, but his claim that there was no haunting was backed up by his defense attorney, William Weber, who openly confessed to having been in cahoots with George and Kathy Lutz all along, cooking up the entire story one night while the three of them were drinking wine.

Today, the former DeFeo residence has been renumbered from 112 to 108 Ocean Avenue (a fact that is readily available at numerous websites). On Google Maps' Street View, the house is intentionally blurred out. Previous owners removed the iconic eye-like upper windows in an attempt to throw curious members of the public off the scent; indeed, unwanted and unwelcome trespassers have been the only thing to curse those who have lived in the house since the Lutzes fled. Although the people of Amityville realize that their town will forever be associated with the Amityville horror, they can only hope that someday, the story of what happened on Ocean Avenue—and more important, the memory of the murdered DeFeo family—will finally be permitted to rest in peace.

HUNTING WITCHES

In twenty-first-century parlance, few terms are more overused to the point of being meaningless than "witch hunt." Claiming to be the victim of one has become a convenient way for public figures to deflect any criticism of and accountability for their behaviors when they are questioned or accused.

Five hundred years ago, on the other hand, those two words held a literal meaning that led to the brutal torture and often the execution of innocent women and men.

Although the name of Salem, Massachusetts, is synonymous with the 1692–1693 witch trials, a century before that Britain was beset with exactly the same blight following the ascent of Queen Elizabeth I to the throne of England in 1558. Harsh physical punishments against those convicted of witchcraft, up to and including execution, were codified into English law.

It became open season on witches.

Superstition was widespread, particularly in rural areas of the country, but those who lived in major population centers believed in witchcraft too. Tales of women dancing naked around fires, cavorting with demons, and flying through the air were widespread. In smaller communities, such beliefs were paired with simmering feuds between individuals and families. During a witch hunt, accusing one's enemy of aligning with dark powers could be an effective way of settling the score, but in more than one such case, such an accusation turned out to be a double-edged sword. The accuser could quickly find themselves also accused in turn.

Because the devil and his diabolical minions were believed to have wide-ranging powers, which they sometimes granted to witches to carry out evil acts on their behalf, there was a tendency to attribute anything that was not readily understood to witchcraft. This ranged from physical maladies and ailments such as strokes, seizures, and birth defects, to blighted crops, violent weather, and natural disasters. Demons and witches served as convenient scapegoats for those aspects of nature that the science of the time could not yet explain.

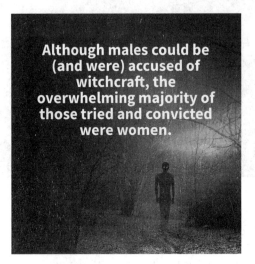

Although males could be (and were) accused of witchcraft, the overwhelming majority of those tried and convicted were women.

Although males could be (and were) accused of witchcraft, the overwhelming majority of those tried and convicted were women. Most were poor and, tellingly, unmarried or widowed. Even after hundreds of years, the classic perception of the withered old crone living in a hovel in the woods, accompanied by familiars such as cats and practicing magic, remains with us today. This is exactly the mental image the word "witch" conjures in the minds of many people, particularly around the time of Halloween. More sinister by far is the fact that females were not only far more likely to find themselves accused during a witch hunt than their male counterparts, but due to the social inequalities of the time, they also had less power and influence with which to defend themselves. Despite the fact that a woman was on the throne of England, patriarchal injustice was given free rein.

SATAN IN ST. OSYTH

Of the many haunted locations I have investigated, one of the strangest has to be a small private residence in the English village of St. Osyth, Essex. The majority of visitors who pass through notice nothing especially unusual about the anonymous-looking property, which sits unobtrusively at the end of a terraced row.

Yet the Cage, as it is called, has a bizarre and convoluted history. Although accounts vary, it is believed to have once been a prison, and not just any old prison—it was used to jail those who had been accused of being witches.

There is a long and well-established tradition of witchcraft in the Essex area. In 1582 came the trial of the St. Osyth Witches, a group of 14 women who were accused of consorting with the devil and using what was believed to be the dark arts to harm, curse, and even kill their neighbors and rivals. Killing another person by means of witchcraft was a capital crime, and this was the charge leveled against ten of the accused.

One of the best-known of the St. Osyth witches was a lady by the name of Ursula Kemp (in some accounts, her last name is spelled Kempe). Ursula seems to have been a fairly harmless and ordinary woman,

Formerly a witches' prison, now a private residence, the Cage is said to be haunted by many spirits.

by all accounts, who took an interest in the use of herbs and plants to heal illnesses and treat injuries. She also had skills in midwifery, which would have made her the go-to wise woman of the vicinity whenever a childbirth was imminent.

Yet all it took to turn Ursula into a villainess in the eyes of her neighbors was a spurious accusation from somebody who knew Ursula and wanted to settle a score.

Ursula was experienced in the art of caring for children, which landed her the occasional job as a nursemaid. When a local woman named Grace Thurlowe employed Ursula's services as a healer, only to then renege on payment of the agreed-upon fee because her condition did not clear up, Ursula took umbrage and complained—loudly. The aggrieved client responded by accusing Ursula of practicing witchcraft.

A number of very serious charges were leveled at her when Ursula was tried in front of a kangaroo court at Chelmsford. Her young son was tricked into testifying against his own mother, citing her supposed activities as a witch. Trapped and with no other way out, Ursula confessed to a ridiculous litany of alleged crimes. She had under her control four different spectral minions, two of which obeyed her commands to go forth and murder whosoever Ursula wanted dead. The other two inflicted injury, disease, and misfortune on their assigned targets. It was effectively a demonic hit squad, operating under Ursula Kemp's beck and call.

Grace Thurlowe's infant child had fallen from its crib and died of a broken neck. Matters took a darker turn at the trial when Ursula Kemp confessed to this having been done at her bidding, with the crib being upturned by one of her spirit familiars. This was death by witchcraft, a hanging offense under the law of the land.

Ursula had made her outlandish confession in the hope that the magistrate, one Brian Darcy, would go easy on her. She was, after all, a mother with a young son to raise out of wedlock.

Although he promised leniency if she were to confess her crimes, Darcy actually offered nothing of the sort. Ursula Kemp was sentenced to death, not by burning at the stake (a practice not commonly used in the English witch trials, though there were exceptions) but by hanging. She went to the gallows at Chelmsford after having spent a period of incarceration inside the Cage.

Realizing there was no way out, Ursula Kemp wasn't going to take the fall alone. She accused several other St. Osyth women of being witches. Once arrested and charged, they in turn accused still others. By such means did mass "outbreaks" of witchcraft occur, as floundering individuals sought to spread the misery and take others down with them.

The old-world charm on display belies the dark history that the oldest part of this building has.

No matter how outlandish the tales of demons, familiars, and mysterious powers of the black arts were, most of them were accepted in the courtroom as being the truth.

Fast-forward five and a half centuries, give or take. The Cage had been essentially a square brick building no larger than a single room. A two-story house had been built around it, and from what I could discover, most of the tenants had lived there peacefully.

All of that changed when a single mother by the name of Vanessa took ownership of the house. After moving in with her baby son, she soon began to experience strange goings-on. Electrical devices such as the TV and stereo would switch themselves on in the middle of the night. Then the lights started doing the same thing.

The paranormal activity taking place inside the house grew increasingly hostile and frightening in nature.

Footsteps were heard walking across the floorboards of the rooms upstairs, rooms that Vanessa knew to be completely empty. She saw the apparition of a glowing woman one night, who she came to believe was the spirit of Ursula Kemp.

Vanessa knew that the house had a colorful history, parts of which were tragic. In addition to the incarceration of those poor unfortunates awaiting trial for charges of witchcraft, the Cage also saw the untimely death of an owner who had taken his own life by hanging himself from a beam at the top of the staircase.

As the months passed, Vanessa's dream home turned into something out of her worst nightmares. The paranormal activity taking place inside the house grew increasingly hostile and frightening in nature. A visitor to the Cage was pushed down the stairs by an unseen force. Vanessa herself was struck by an invisible hand as she was engaged in the upstairs bathroom.

Pools of a mysterious substance that looked a lot like blood appeared, seemingly out of thin air. The straw that finally broke the camel's back happened one day after Vanessa had put her young son down in his crib, located in one of the upstairs bedrooms. A short while afterward, she was horrified to discover the apparition of a man standing over her son, staring down at him. His intentions, Vanessa believed, were nothing but harmful.

Running at the apparition, she scooped up her son and fled the house. She could no longer live there, and although she retained ownership, Vanessa and her son did not spend another night sleeping inside the Cage.

I learned about the haunting from a TV documentary show, and Vanessa's story fascinated me from the outset. It sounded as if she had been put through her very own personal hell by the spirits of the Cage, and I wanted to know if they were still active even though she no longer lived there.

Although the stories she told about her time spent living there were somewhat fantastical, there are also multiple well-attested eyewitness accounts of paranormal activity from visitors. This even includes reporters from national newspapers, one of whom fled the house one night after seeing a set of chains that hung from one of the walls begin

Mirrors have long been used as a conduit to connect the worlds of the living and the dead.

to sway from side to side, seemingly of their own volition. On the other hand, the neighbor I spoke with dismissed any claims of activity taking place in their own house and really didn't buy into the ghost stories surrounding the Cage either.

A number of passing motorists had reported seeing the specter of a haggard old woman gazing forlornly out of the upstairs bedroom window on days when the Cage was unoccupied. At least one had mistaken it for a Halloween decoration, so ugly and decrepit was she.

In addition to the house's dark history, the track behind the Cage is known locally by the nickname of Coffin Alley, as it was the path undertakers once took to transport the dead to a nearby churchyard for burial. Such phantom processions have been seen there on occasion by eyewitnesses, most likely a residual echo of real funerals long past.

The Cage had no permanent tenant when I turned up there with three fellow investigators in tow. It was early spring, and the weather was freezing cold. We had been in the house for just a few short minutes before strange things started happening.

Vanessa met us a short distance away and drove us to the Cage. From the outside, it looked like any of a thousand other houses we'd passed on the way from London. Inside, it was dark and gloomy, as one might expect of a house without occupants. Vanessa gave us the grand tour. I watched her every bit as much as I watched the house itself. As a paramedic, I have a good eye for body language and a sense for when I'm being lied to. She wasn't raising any red flags. Vanessa seemed uncomfortable all the while we were inside the Cage, perpetually on edge. Based on her past experiences there, it was hard to blame her.

On the upstairs landing, close to the spot where the body of a former owner had been found hanging, my colleague, Stephen, and I were both running digital voice recorders. I asked Vanessa if there was a light switch somewhere nearby. Before she spoke, a croaking, raspy old woman's voice left us a remarkably clear EVP that distinctly said: *"Yes, in the bathroom."*

My fellow investigator, Lesley, was taking a smoke break outside the back door when it suddenly slammed itself in her face. There was no wind whatsoever to account for it.

Ouija boards were extraordinarily active inside the Cage during our investigation, introducing us to a number of colorful communicators, including one who claimed to be a former shepherd named Redfast. An odd name, one might think, except for the fact that Redfast was a very

> Ouija boards were extraordinarily active inside the Cage during our investigation, introducing us to a number of colorful communicators, including one who claimed to be a former shepherd named Redfast.

old nickname for somebody who was red-faced—somebody who enjoyed a drink, perhaps, or a shepherd who spent much of his time outdoors.

On our final night, my colleague Stephen—a priest and exorcist—conducted a ritual of blessing on the Cage, leaving several containers of blessed salt concealed in various parts of the structure. Despite his optimism, the reports of paranormal activity continued unabated long after we had flown back to the United States and written a book on the haunting (*Spirits of the Cage: True Accounts of Living in a Haunted Medieval Prison*).

It may simply be that whatever haunts the Cage is too strong to be removed so easily. At the time of writing, the Cage has a new owner, one seemingly undeterred by the claims of dark paranormal activity that had engulfed the property. Perhaps the arrival of new energy will bring with it a lightening of the haunting, maybe even a complete cessation.

Perhaps.

SPECTRAL EVIDENCE IN SALEM

The events in St. Osyth did not herald the end of witch hunts in England—far from it. Under the auspices of the self-styled Witchfinder General, the sadistic Matthew Hopkins, they continued through the seventeenth century. If those pilgrims who left English shores to start a fresh life in the New World believed they had left such horrors behind them, they were sorely mistaken—as the people of Salem, Massachusetts, would find, to their great cost.

In January of 1692, 110 years after the witchcraft hysteria infected St. Osyth, on the far side of the Atlantic, dark rumors began to spread throughout the puritanical settlement of Salem. The people of Salem were already disposed to believe that the devil was more than capable of walking among them, either in person or in the form of agents and collaborators. It began with strange behavior by young girls, nine-year-old Betty Parris and 11-year-old Abigail Williams. They acted in ways that some would say were consistent with a state of demonic possession but others would call childish horseplay or possibly even temporary mental illness. There's also a theory that they were unintentionally poisoned by eating bread contaminated with a naturally occurring fungus named ergot, which could be found in moldy bread and is capable of inducing hallucinations and aberrant behavior. It's difficult to square the ergot hypothesis with the fact that the two children were the only members of their respective families to display behavioral symptoms, despite everyone in their households sharing a common food source.

Betty was the daughter of Samuel Parris, the minister of Salem. Abigail was his niece. When the young cousins began howling and barking like animals, contorting their bodies and shrieking unconsolably, it made sense to the people of Salem that they might be attractive targets for Satan due to Samuel's position as a holy man. Once the word "witchcraft" had been uttered, the bigger question became: who, exactly, had bewitched them? Fingers quickly began pointing at the slave charged with their care, a Native American woman named Tituba. Frustrated at the lack of an explanation for the girls' bizarre behavior, Parris found the elderly woman to be a convenient scapegoat.

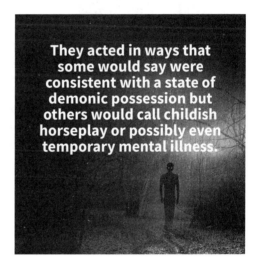

They acted in ways that some would say were consistent with a state of demonic possession but others would call childish horseplay or possibly even temporary mental illness.

For reasons that still remain unclear, Tituba confessed to being a servant of the devil and having signed a blood pact with him. (She would later withdraw her confession, claiming that Samuel Parris had beaten it out of her.) Her testimony, delivered before judges and an assembly of the people, was damning, a dark fairy tale in which Tituba claimed to have been threatened by the Dark One into doing his bidding or else be killed. Her imagination knew no bounds, and her accusers listened with increasing outrage as she told tales of demonic animal familiars and accused others of joining her in witchcraft.

It was from here that the flames begun by Abigail Williams and Betty Parris turned into a wildfire—one that would tear through Salem and its

Tituba was a slave from the West Indies who was accused of being a witch and telling depraved stories to Abigail Williams and Betty Parris to corrupt them.

surroundings, leaving devastation in its wake. Tituba was imprisoned for the duration of the witch trials but escaped execution at their culmination. As the accusations mounted, other Salemites were not so lucky. The same gender bias that ran through the English witchcraft trials was also prevalent in Salem, with 14 of those executed being female and the remaining six being men.

Calling them "trials" may actually be giving what passed for legal due process in 1692 an excess of legitimacy. The concept of so-called spectral evidence was still admissible. This centered upon the idea that witches were capable of a sort of astral travel, their spirits leaving the physical body at will and entering the dreams of those they wished to torment. In other words, if somebody dreamed that their neighbor entered their bedroom at night and inflicted pain and suffering on them while they slept, then those events had actually, physically happened.

The product of overly active imagination became accepted as fact. So did outright lies, as some individuals sought to gain an advantage over their neighbors before the same could be done to them. People were hanged on the basis of spectral evidence, which became increasingly compelling the more people came forward to say that they had been visited in the night by the accused parties.

The nightmare of the witch trials would not be over until May of 1693. In the aftermath, some of those involved would express remorse and repentance for their role in the executions of 20 innocent women and men—plus the deaths of at least five others who perished while awaiting trial in prison. Pardons were handed out, efforts at compensation were made, but the stain of what began the previous January could never be made clean again.

DARK HAUNTINGS IN SALEM

Present-day Salem is a town that still bases its entire identity upon one thing: the witch trials, their legacy, and all things witch re-

Hordes of tourists descend upon Salem each year, particularly in the fall months, in order to soak up the spooky ambience. Hopefully some also gain an appreciation for the true meaning of the tragedy that took place there.

lated. It is impossible to walk the streets at any time of the year without being reminded of that, but if one is unwise enough to visit in the fall (especially October), then it's impossible to avoid vast throngs of tourists wearing pointy black hats and kitschy witch attire. It is a sad way to commemorate the 20 innocent victims who lost their lives during the witch trials.

If the folklore is to be believed, then one of those victims may have exacted his revenge on the people of Salem: Giles Corey, who was ordered to be pressed to death with heavy stones. An obstinate man, Corey refused to plead guilty *or innocent*, preventing the possibility of a trial. This despite the excruciating pain and suffocation that the increasingly large mass of stone exerted on his chest and abdomen. When asked again to voice a plea partway through his execution, lying naked in the middle of an open field, he simply grunted: "More weight."

There was a method to Corey's madness. Entering a plea would have led to Corey's estate being taken from him postmortem. By dying

Rather than being hanged, the accused Giles Corey was crushed to death slowly with a heavy rock. He remained unrepentant until his last breath.

without declaring his innocence or confessing guilt, he ensured that his earthly possessions would then pass to his children. (Corey's wife, Martha, was hanged for witchcraft during the same trials.)

It was the responsibility of the sheriff to carry out the pressing, and it is toward him that Corey supposedly uttered his final curse—both toward the sheriff and the town of Salem itself. The sheriff was named George Corwin. When the pile of stones didn't achieve the desired effect of making Giles Corey utter a plea, Corwin stepped up onto the dying man's chest and added his own bodyweight to the pressure bearing down upon him.

Corwin also oversaw the hangings of the convicted witches, which happened at a place named Proctor's Ledge. The ledge is a wooded hillside that now bears a memorial to those who lost their lives during the witch trials. It is easy to miss, and many visitors to Salem do miss it completely. Proctor's Ledge, the true hanging site, lies directly adjacent to a Walgreens pharmacy and a private residence.

Was the curse effective? Perhaps, or perhaps not. George Corwin was only 30 when he suffered a fatal heart attack in 1696. It is often stated that ill health, cardiac conditions, and premature death and disabilities have dogged sheriffs of Salem ever since, but there is little in the way of evidence to bear out that claim. Anything and everything that could be blamed on the curse over the years has been, ranging from individual mishaps and deaths to major fires. It's said that Giles Corey's ghost returned to haunt the cemetery that now stands in the spot where he died. The appearance of his apparition is said to presage disaster for the people of Salem.

Considering the pain, misery, and tragedy that befell those who were falsely accused, convicted, and executed during the witch trials, it comes as no surprise that the town has more than its fair share of ghost stories. Fellow author Sam Baltrusis has spent years collecting and researching Salem hauntings. You can read all about them in his book *Ghosts of Salem: Haunts of the Witch City*, which I recommend doing before paying Salem a visit.

Proctor's Ledge is a memorial to those who were unjustly accused of witchcraft and executed by hanging on the hill beyond.

I've been fortunate enough to spend several weekends wandering around Salem, delving into its history and its hauntings. Perhaps the most famous haunted property is known as the Witch House. Purchased in 1675 by Judge Jonathan Corwin (Sheriff George Corwin's uncle), the imposing residence is said to be the only home in Salem still standing that can trace its lineage all the way back to the 1692 witch trials. Standing outside, looking up at the gray wooden edifice, it was hard not to find the place intimidating. Corwin and his colleague Judge John Hathorne were directly responsible for trying the defendants. Neither man proved himself to be compassionate or merciful, offering little in the way of leniency or even open-minded fairness to those who stood accused before them. Although none of this took place in what was originally called the Corwin House, something about the proceedings seems to have left a psychic stain on the place. Those who work within its walls have heard disembodied voices and phantom footsteps, beyond even what one would expect from a creaky house that's more than 350 years old. Paranormal investigators have recorded EVPs inside the home, which has been the scene of deaths numbering in the double digits.

The gravestones in Salem's burial grounds are a veritable Who's Who of the town's troubled history.

Whenever I'm in Salem, I make a point of staying at the Hawthorne Hotel. Not only is it comfortable, friendly, and centrally located, it's also notoriously haunted. Wandering through the lobby is like stepping back in time. One soon encounters framed memorabilia from the popular TV show *Bewitched*, which filmed episodes at the Hawthorne in June 1970. The show has a complicated relationship with Salem; a nine-foot-tall statue of its star, Elizabeth Montgomery, draws crowds to pose with photographs but drew strong opposition from some locals, who believed that it tarnished the memory of those who died during the witch trials.

The hotel was built in the 1920s and is named after the writer Nathaniel Hawthorne, author of *The Scarlet Letter* and *The House of the Seven Gables*. (Hawthorne was a relative of Judge Jonathan Hathorne and added the extra letter to his surname in an effort to distance himself from the ignominy associated with that lineage.)

One of the ghosts said to haunt the Hawthorne is that of Bridget Bishop, who was the first to be hanged by Sheriff George Corwin during the trials—convicted on the basis of her allegedly having a third nipple. Others attribute the haunting to none other than the author Nathaniel Hawthorne. Both are good stories, but they probably aren't rooted in fact. When it comes to one specific room at the Hawthorne, we are on firmer ground.

The sound of crying children has been reported by more than one guest spending the night in Room 325. Others have the unnerving experience of waking up in the night and feeling phantom hands touching them beneath their bedclothes.

My own nights at the Hawthorne have been uninterrupted by ghostly visitors, but there's no shortage of guests who experience a brush with the otherworldly between its walls.

One question that has fascinated students of the Salem witch trials for centuries is: What happened to the bodies of those who were executed during the trials? It is believed that they were dumped in a temporary grave close to Proctor's Ledge and that some of them were subsequently recovered by their next of kin under cover of darkness and reburied elsewhere. They could not be buried in consecrated ground because of their status as witches. Even today, historians are not sure of their final resting places. Some believe that their bodies lie beneath the hill of Proctor's Ledge to this day, though no evidence has been found to confirm it.

In the fall of 2023, I visited Proctor's Ledge with some fellow paranormal investigators. We conducted an impromptu EVP session while there. For once, I was pleased to *not* get any EVPs during a session. Those poor souls already suffered more than enough at the hands of greedy and ruthless men of power. Hopefully they have found the peace in death that eluded them during their lifetimes.

Visitors often leave flowers and coins as tokens of remembrance for those lives cut tragically short by the Salem Witch Trials.

Human beings have an unerring capacity for failing to heed the lessons of history. As we look back on the witch hunts that tore apart communities on both sides of the Atlantic, it should be remembered that the true darkness did not usually lie within those who were charged with being witches but rather within the hearts of their judges and accusers.

SOMETHING MONSTROUS

THAT ABOMINABLE (SNOW)MAN

Although Westerners named it (rather rudely) "the Abominable Snow-man," the enigmatic humanoid creature that has been reported by generations of Nepalese people in the Himalayas is more appropriately known as the Yeti. Sightings of Yeti go back hundreds of years, at least to the late eighteenth and early nineteenth centuries—some authors believe the first accounts date back thousands of years—yet the popular term Abominable Snowman came into being in 1921. For this, we have a reporter to thank. Henry Newman, stationed in India, interviewed British mountaineers who had just returned from an expedition to climb Mount Everest. Although they hadn't seen the creature in person, the team had spotted an unusual footprint in the snow, which the sherpas believed had been made by a Yeti. Newman found the regional term for the creature difficult to translate, hence the bastardization that made its way into his report—and stuck.

The "wild man of the snows" story had been passed down from generation to generation of Tibetans, sometimes used as a means of frightening children into good behavior. ("Go to sleep or the Yeti will come and get you!") The expedition's leader, Charles Howard-Bury, took the Yeti story with a grain of salt, believing instead that the print had been made by a wolf. Others suggested that a bear was responsible. Despite Howard-Bury's mundane explanation, the story went viral, reprinted in various newspapers and proving the adage that people love a good monster story—the more mysterious and frightening, the better.

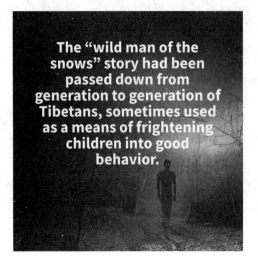

The "wild man of the snows" story had been passed down from generation to generation of Tibetans, sometimes used as a means of frightening children into good behavior.

Yet the claims were not easily dismissed. Others soon came forward to offer support, such as notable explorer William Hugh Knight, who took his own story to the newspapers in December 1921. While traveling in the eastern Himalayas with a large group of men, Knight had paused to give his horse a rest when he glimpsed movement off to the side of the track. He recalled that the figure was "a little under six feet high, almost stark naked in that bitter cold—it was the month of November. He was a kind of pale yellow all over … a shock of matted hair on his head, little hair on his face, highly splayed feet, and large, formidable hands. His muscular development in the arms, thighs, legs, back and chest was terrific. He had in his hand what seemed to be some sort of primitive bow."

After observing the figure undetected for about five minutes, Knight saw it sprint away downhill.

While the press (and subsequent authors writing about the Abominable Snowman) lapped this story up and used it to support claims of the Yeti's existence, Knight's account may not be all it appears to be. Indeed, after doing some digging, researcher Garth Haslam of the website *Anomalies* (anomalyinfo.com) found no evidence whatsoever of William Hugh Knight ever existing. One would think that a reputable explorer would be referenced in historical texts, but there's no trace of the man to be found. Haslam asserts that both Knight and his story were invented by a journalist to spice up a story on the Abominable Snowman, which leads one to wonder how many other sources need to be reevaluated with a critical eye.

Does this mean the Yeti does not exist? Absolutely not. Although Howard-Bury's footprint that captured the public imagination had a perfectly ordinary explanation, numerous other Yeti accounts also came to light.

The Yeti fires were stoked again in 1951 when mountaineer Eric Shipton climbed Everest accompanied by Michael Ward and Sherpa Tenzing, the latter of whom became one of the first two men to reach the summit of Mount Everest in 1953, alongside Edmund Hillary. Shipton was not attempting to summit the mountain. The intent was to reconnoiter it, in preparation for a future expedition. During the attempt, the climbers found tracks that were grossly similar to those of a human being but significantly broader, with splayed and separated toes. The size and anatomic differences strongly suggested that the tracks were made by no person. Shipton laid his ice pick alongside one of the footprints to provide a sense of scale and snapped a photograph that quickly became famous around the world. The Shipton picture is compelling evidence that *something* big and humanoid was walking around in the Menlung Basin—some 15,000

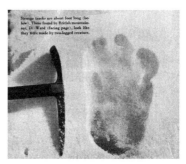

English mountaineer Eric Shipman discovered several footprints like this one in 1951. He placed a pickax next to the print to give an idea as to its size.

feet high. It should also be noted that any human who exposed their foot in such freezing temperatures would very quickly develop frostbite. Yet Michael Ward favored the theory that the source of the footprints was a local with deformed feet, rather than the Yeti. The controversy continues to this day.

During the 1950s, it was all the rage to mount a private expedition to the Himalayas in search of the Yeti. In 1959, the U.S. embassy in Kathmandu felt compelled to issue regulations pertaining to it.

On November 30, counselor Ernest H. Fisk declared that any prospective Yeti seekers would have to pay the Nepalese government 5,000 rupees for a permit. Hunters were given permission to photograph or capture alive any Yetis they encountered but were expressly forbidden from shooting at them—unless in self-defense. (One is forced to wonder how many hunters would actually have obeyed this rule.) Lastly, any

Although concrete evidence of the elusive creature was thin on the ground, there was no shortage of anecdotal reports.

evidence for the Yeti's existence was to be submitted to the government of Nepal and approved before ever being shared with the media.

Obviously, the U.S. government was taking the matter seriously. Although concrete evidence of the elusive creature was thin on the ground, there was no shortage of anecdotal reports. Some involved the Yeti attacking yak and other livestock, ripping them apart and feeding on their remains. Those who see Yeti report that the creatures sometimes walk upright like a human but other times can be seen loping on all fours in the manner of an ape.

Yeti sightings continue to be reported today. In January 2014, author Amanda Woomer visited a monastery in Khumjung, Nepal, and discovered that belief in the elusive creature is more prevalent today than ever before. Her Tibetan guide said that there are, broadly speaking, three types of Yeti: one that is kind and friendly, one that is aggressive if approached, and a third that seems more neutral, preferring simply to be left alone.

Fascinated by the stories, Amanda was shown a locked wooden case that was kept inside a locked metal cabinet. Inside was a cone-shaped scalp covered in tufts of coarse gray and rust-colored hair. This, she was told, was the scalp of a Yeti. Some 300 years ago, a lama was walking along a mountain trail one day when he happened upon one of the more aggressive types of Yeti. According to the story, the creature attacked, and in the scuffle, the lama cut off the top of the creature's head.

The scalp was found by mountaineer and conqueror of Mt. Everest Edmund Hillary in 1960, in the care of Tibetan villagers. Analysis of the "scalp" revealed that it wasn't a scalp at all and had a rather more mundane origin: it was made from goat hide. Nevertheless, the scalp is still displayed to visitors for a modest donation and is known as the Khumjung Yeti scalp.

The scalp that is supposedly from a Yeti is kept in the monastery at Khumjung.

This tends to be par for the course when it comes to physical evidence of the Yeti. Bones, nests, and tracks occasionally turn up and generate a buzz of excitement, only to turn out to be hoaxes or simple misinterpretation. Most notably, the actor Jimmy Stewart smuggled what was said to have been a Yeti finger out of India and into the United Kingdom in 1957. It was secreted amongst his wife's underwear, of all places, perhaps in hopes that officials of Her Majesty's Customs and Excise service would not check there.

Stewart was wrong about the customs officers *and* wrong about the legitimacy of the bone, which was deemed to be human in nature.

As the saying goes, *caveat emptor*—let the buyer beware.

The stories of Yeti encounters persist, however. The fact that nobody has recovered a carcass or remains does not prove that the creature does not exist. Absence of evidence is not evidence of absence. Many of the eyewitness reports are consistent with one another.

Those sightings are not restricted to the Himalayas. China, Russia, and Siberia have their own Yeti stories, and the creatures have been blamed for one of Russia's strangest mysteries: the Dyatlov Pass incident. The pass is a remote and lonely location in the northern Urals. In February of 1959, a group of nine cross-country skiers died while camping in the now-infamous mountain pass.

When the bodies were discovered, in two separate groups, it became evident that some had suffered significant blunt trauma to the head and torso. Others had died of hypothermia after running away from the camp site—barefoot and dressed only in their underwear. Some had lost their eyes or tongues. Some had sustained third-degree burns. Something had desperately panicked the campers—but what?

Hypotheses put forward in the 65 years since the incident took place vary, running the gamut from an avalanche to UFOs to attack by human beings, bears, or Yetis, which were reputed to live in the region. The avalanche theory is the most widely accepted, but that acceptance is by no means universal.

In other words, the Abominable Snowman isn't off the hook yet. Perhaps it never will be.

THE MONSTROUS LAMBTON WORM

The word "worm" conjures up images of little creatures used to bait fishing hooks. Yet in pagan mythology, the worm (or wyrm) was a giant serpent, essentially a dragon but without the wings, the legs, or the capacity to breathe fire. They were nonetheless terrifying for all that. It was believed that huge worms would slither their way out of their lairs, usually at night, to prey upon animals and, under certain circumstances, humans. The origins of this belief may lie with the ancient Irish deity Crom Cruach, which originally represented fertility and a bountiful harvest—so long as it was appeased with a regular supply of human sacrifices.

When Christianity arrived on Ireland's shores and began to take root, Crom Cruach made a useful villain. Thus, we get the story of St. Patrick confronting the god, which assumed a demonic worm-like form to square off against the saint. St. Patrick was said to have been the victor, consigning Crom Cruach to the infernal depths of hell and driving all of the snakes out of Ireland (a somewhat unlikely tale, considering that there were no snakes *in* Ireland during the fifth century, when St. Patrick first arrived).

Worms and snakes also featured prominently in Norse mythology, which is replete with stories of monstrous serpents lurking beneath the earth. Little wonder that such stories were popular among the British during the Dark Ages and beyond.

> Worms and snakes also featured prominently in Norse mythology, which is replete with stories of monstrous serpents lurking beneath the earth.

One of the most popular monsters of the time was the Lambton Worm, and its story is still told in and around the English county of Durham. The tale takes place in the early 1400s, when a young man named John Lambton decided to play hooky from church one Sunday morning, choosing instead to spend the day fishing. Perhaps not the best idea, as rather than hooking a tasty fish for dinner, Lambton instead landed an ugly-looking worm. Somewhat dispirited by his failure, John went home. On the way, he tossed the worm down into a well and gave the creature no further thought.

Big mistake. John Lambton grew older, became a knight, and sailed off to war. In his absence, the worm grew and grew, until finally it rose up out of the well in search of something to eat. The creature split its time between hanging out on a rock in the middle of the river and coiling its now-massive length around a hill nearby. (Unsurprisingly, this hill became known as Worm Hill, and remains so today.) In an effort to placate the monster, locals left nine barrels of milk as a daily offering. When they didn't, it had a tendency to snatch their livestock, their children, and sometimes even grown adults to eat. The entire region was being held hostage by a giant worm.

Cue the return of John Lambton, heir to the Lambton estates and now a combat veteran. Acknowledging his responsibility for the distressing state of affairs, the knight resolved to kill the creature. Donning his suit of armor and taking up his sword, Lambton set out to confront the worm. Although he did not lack courage, the knight's direct approach wasn't initially successful. No matter how many times he hacked at the worm's coils, they came back together and re-knitted themselves.

An illustration of the Lambton worm from the 1894 book *More English Fairy Tales.*

Frustrated, Lambton sought the advice of a local wise woman, who told him to upgrade his armor with a bevy of razor-sharp blades embedded in the metal. This he duly did and went down to the river for a final confrontation. The worm coiled itself around him. The tighter it constricted around the knight's armor, the more lacerated it became. Wading deeper into the water, John Lambton slashed and cut with his sword. Each individual segment of the worm was swept downstream, prevented from reuniting with the others by the fast-flowing water.

Finally, he was victorious. With the worm now dead and capable of terrorizing the populace no more, the weary knight splashed ashore. There was a special debt to be paid, for the wise woman had made him swear an oath to kill the first living thing he encountered after finishing off the worm. If he did not, the soothsayer cautioned him, no Lambton lord would die peacefully in his bed for the next nine generations.

Thinking himself a clever man, Lambton let out a shrill whistle, summoning his dog. His idea was simple: he would kill the dog cleanly and discharge his oath.

Unfortunately for John Lambton, his father beat his dog to the punch. Ebulliently running down to congratulate his son, he put John in an impossible position. How could he be expected to kill his own father in cold blood? (If you're anything like me, you're thinking exactly the same thing about the dog!)

John understandably stayed his hand, refusing to take his father's life. While the region had been freed from the worm's predations, victory had come at a cost: the Lambton male line was now cursed. Several sub-sequent Lambton heirs did indeed die violent deaths. Some were accidental. One, Colonel Sir William Lambton, died in the English Civil War. On July 2, 1644, he was killed fighting for Royalist forces in defense of the crown at the Battle of Marston Moor.

It seems that the Lambton Worm may have gotten the last laugh.

ROCKY MOUNTAIN BEASTIES: THE AUGERINO AND THE SLIDE-ROCK BOLTER

Stories of paranormal worms are not restricted to medieval Britain. When I relocated from my native England to the western United States in 1999, I became fascinated with its monster lore. From my adoptive Colorado and its neighboring Rocky Mountain states come tales of the Augerino, a large worm that burrows through rock in a twisting, auger-like manner—a sort of burrowing organic corkscrew. Descriptions of the Augerino call to mind images of the giant Sandworms from Frank Herbert's *Dune* or the carnivorous monsters from the *Tremors* movie series. According to legends told around campfires by woodsmen and farmers, Augerinos were reputed to bore through dams to drain them of water. The giant worms got the blame for disrupting pieces of infrastructure that related to water, including drainage and irrigation ditches. Why? Supposedly, the worms need an environment that is as dry as possible in order to thrive.

As if the burrowing Augerino wasn't enough for Coloradans to worry about, there's also the Slide-Rock Bolter—a huge beast that's said to live high up in the Rockies (at least, mountain communities are where most Slide-Rock Bolter sightings came from). Picture something akin to an enormous land-bound eel or worm. The creature is said to have a gaping maw filled with sharp teeth, and a hooked tail. After climbing to the top of a mountain and latching onto the summit (quite how the Slide-Rock Bolter gets up there in the first place has never been made clear), the creature casts around for its prey, which usually comes in the form of people. Orienting itself in their general direction, the Slide-Rock Bolter then propels itself downhill with all the speed and aggression of an artillery round being fired. Before the stunned victims can react, the beastie has snatched them up in its jaws, then uses its momentum to power itself up an adjoining slope to the top, where it fastens onto another peak and restarts the entire cycle, all the while chewing and eating its luckless human dinner alive. Slide-Rock Bolters are said to be incredibly patient, lurking on top of steep slopes for as long as it takes until an unwary traveler or two happens along. Then the monster dives into action.

Does the Slide-Rock Bolter actually exist? It seems unlikely. For one thing, no skeletal remains have ever been found. The earliest stories featuring it date back to Colorado's pioneer days, when miners and lumberjacks lived a rough and hardy existence on the mountainsides. Landslides and avalanches were an ever-present danger. It's likely that the Slide-Rock Bolter was a personification of these all-too-natural hazards. One can only imagine the terror that would have been evoked when stories of the ravenous beast were told around campfires late

Rather like the worms in Frank Herbert's *Dune* series, the Augerino is said to be a giant limbless monster with a gaping, fang-filled mouth.

at night, with alcohol flowing and the men keeping a wary eye on the dark mountains looming above them. It would have taken very little effort for the mind's eye to conjure up images of the Slide-Rock Bolter lying motionless up there in the shadows, biding its time, just waiting for its moment to strike.

Perhaps it hangs there still, lurking at the top of one of Colorado's mountains, patiently waiting for its next meal to stroll on by.

BRITISH BEASTS OF EXMOOR AND BODMIN

In 1983, the British press was abuzz with stories of a creature they dubbed "the Beast of Exmoor." Witnesses began to come forward with reports of encountering a large black cat, usually out in the wilds on the moors. Exmoor, a national park, is a lonely and desolate place that has its own windswept beauty. Sightings of the mysterious cat with glowing yellow eyes went back to the 1970s. Large feline paw prints were discovered in the mud, proving that the eyewitnesses were not delusional or simply making up stories.

Following the principle of "if it bleeds, it leads," the tabloid newspapers reported that farm livestock were found dead in the tens and then the hundreds, savagely killed and eaten by the so-called Beast. Although there was some skepticism about the existence of a big black cat roaming the moors, the British government didn't want to be seen to do nothing.

The Ministry of Defense deployed a team of elite Royal Marines Commando snipers onto Exmoor, with orders to track down, stalk, and then shoot the Beast dead. The snipers were equipped with night vision technology, which was somewhat rudimentary by twenty-first-century standards but still gave them an advantage in the darkness. The marines set up hunter's hides and settled in to wait. Catching sight of what they thought was their quarry, one of the marines fired off a shot. When they went to investigate, the commandos found no dead animal or any indication that they'd scored a hit. However, from that day on, the frequency of black cat sightings plummeted, although they didn't completely stop, with reports continuing into the 2010s and beyond.

Searching for an explanation, some put forward the hypothesis that the Beast of Exmoor was in fact a dog. However, the sheer savagery with which lambs were ripped apart makes this unlikely. Nor were the poor animals' bones chewed up, something a dog would have done instinctively. Panthers, pumas, and other great cats are not native to the United Kingdom. Another possible answer would be one of the creatures having been reared in captivity and then released into the wild, either escaping or being put there intentionally—and though it's difficult to fathom a motive for

Exmoor is a moorland located in southwest England and covering about 267 square miles, which is plenty of space for a large black monstrous cat to roam.

doing so, an article from Britain's *Daily Mirror* newspaper claims that a zoo owner named Mary Chipperfield released a group of pumas onto the moors when her own zoo was forced into closure in 1978.

Some paranormal believers have put forward the idea that the Beast of Exmoor travels interdimensionally, phasing into our reality, running down its prey, and then phasing out again. Others have hypothesized that it is a phantom or a ghost, although the sheer carnage it visited upon hundreds of sheep would argue against that. Every once in a while, a new photograph emerges on the internet purporting to be the beast. Often the resolution is poor enough that it's impossible to determine for certain whether the black shape in question truly could be a great cat. There is also the question of Photoshop and digital manipulation to contend with. We live in an age where if something looks too good to be true, it usually is.

Great cat sightings are not restricted to Exmoor. Nearby Bodmin Moor has its own, the Beast of Bodmin, which is also black and panther-like. Those reports also date back to the 1970s. At the time of writing, encounters with large black cats are on the rise across the U.K. Clearly, *something* strange is going on. The question is, what?

FROM THE DEPTHS: THE LOCH NESS MONSTER

Moving away from the moorland of Britain, we now turn our attention to its lakes … and lochs. Although stories of lake monsters come from around the world, unquestionably the granddaddy (or possibly grandmommy) of them all is Scotland's Loch Ness Monster—otherwise known as Nessie.

Although it's said that stories of there being a large, dinosaur-like creature in Loch Ness abounded for generations—a contention that is not backed up by documented evidence—it is a fact that the long-necked beastie didn't become widely known until the 1930s, when there was a surge in reported Nessie sightings and the appearance of several photographs that claimed to show the beast. One of the earliest, taken in 1933 by a dog walker named Hugh Gray, was said to show the creature's long, thrashing tail. Skeptics have pointed out that the image could just as easily depict the head of a dog swimming toward the camera, holding a stick between its jaws.

As the decade went on, the Nessie sightings began to stack up. In terms of consistency, the creature's size varied from six to eight feet

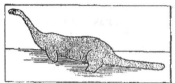

The Loch Ness Monster, As Sketched by Mr. A. Grant From Lieut.-Commander Gould's Interesting Monograph Upon the Subject.

A 1941 sketch of Nessie based on the 1934 alleged siting of the lake creature.

long all the way up to the rather nebulous "huge" and "massive." The creature was usually seen in the loch, swimming, surfacing, or diving, but at least one eyewitness reported stopping his vehicle because the monster was waddling across the road in front of him, on its way back to the water. Commonly reported characteristics were the long neck, angular head, and flippers. Often, all that was seen above the surface were humps, believed to be the creature's back.

One notable picture appeared to show the head and neck of the creature rising up out of the waters of the loch. Snapped in 1934, it became known as "the surgeon's photo" because it was taken by a physician, R. Kenneth Wilson. Then, as now, doctors were held in high regard, and Wilson's status as a medical man gave his picture a special credibility. For decades, the surgeon's photo was hotly debated, considered a prime piece of evidence for Nessie's existence by some and either a misconstrued object or outright fraud by others.

Unfortunately, it was most likely a hoax. At least, there was a confession, elicited by Nessie researcher Alastair Boyd, from the only surviving member of the alleged group of hoaxers. A young boy at the time of the sighting, but an old man at the time of his admission, Christian Spurling claimed to have manufactured the head and neck of the "monster" himself using some simple home materials and a toy submarine, which he then deployed into the loch to be photographed. It's a credible explanation, though not one that is accepted by everybody.

Is it really possible that there could be a creature of some sort in Loch Ness? Almost 800 feet deep in places, there are certainly plenty of places for a creature (or presumably a family of creatures) to hide. According to *The Official Loch Ness Monster Sightings Register* (lochnesssightings.com), a website dedicated to tracking Nessie's movements, in 2023 there were ten reported sightings. (The site has entries for over 1,150 sightings in total at the time of writing.) Some are eyewitness accounts, and others are photographs. Yet in an age of 4K resolution, with cameras more accessible and widespread than at any other point in history—not to mention round-the-clock webcam coverage of the loch's surface—we have yet to find the smoking gun of Nessie photographs. The images that are submitted tend to be relatively low-resolution blurs and blips, usually taken from a great distance, their subject indeterminable.

As large bodies of water go, Loch Ness is surprisingly busy. A multitude of tourists frequent the loch, each of them hoping to catch a glimpse of its elusive celebrity cryptid. Boats of all descriptions frequently sail across it, and a wide range of animals exist on, above, and under the water. This means that many mysterious wakes that are attributed to Nessie could actually be caused by eels, otters, or other marine animals. Otters are often seen to have multiple humps when partially submerged, which could explain a number of reported Nessie sightings.

The loch has been investigated numerous times over the years since 1933, with everybody from enthusiastic amateurs to professional scientists trying their best to find a trace of the elusive monster. Long lines of boats equipped with sonar arrays have trawled Loch Ness from one side to the other. Sensitive microphones are dipped beneath the surface, listening to the sounds of the loch, in attempts to isolate noises possibly made by the creature. Twenty-first-century Nessie hunters have employed drones with thermal imaging cameras to peer into its cold depths. DNA samples have been collected, turning up traces of various different types of marine life living in and around Loch Ness, none of which have proven to be inexplicable. There's no definitive biological proof of the monster's existence.

Skeptics point out that there have been no anomalous bones or carcasses found that might belong to such a creature. If Nessie really does

A statue of the Loch Ness monster by the lake affords photo opportunities for tourists.

exist, it would be virtually impossible for there to be just one such animal. There would have to be families, containing not just breeding partners but also their offspring. The presence of multiple generations means that there should statistically speaking have been *some* organic matter found, such as fossils, either in the loch or somewhere upon its shores.

In August 2023, the biggest organized search for the Loch Ness Monster in over 50 years took place. Volunteers traveled from across the United Kingdom and all around the world. Sadly, the search found no evidence to support the existence of Nessie.

Yet there are hypotheses of a paranormal nature that purport to explain the creature. Some have suggested that the Loch Ness Monster is none other than the ghost of an aquatic dinosaur. The descriptions given by eyewitnesses do bear striking similarities to the plesiosaur, which, contrary to long held belief, did indeed live in freshwater environs in addition to bodies of saltwater. Loch Ness is landlocked and contains freshwater, which skeptics have long insisted ruled out the possibility of Nessie having been a plesiosaur. Despite its size, the loch is also considered by experts to be too small for plesiosaurs to live in for any length of time.

If a plesiosaur or something similar to it had made it to Loch Ness before the species' extinction 66 million years ago, is it really possible that people would see its ghost today? It's an intriguing idea, but there are a few problems with it. For starters, if we entertain the notion of dinosaur ghosts, then where are all the phantom Tyrannosaurus rexes and velociraptors, diplodocuses, and triceratops?

Many paranormal enthusiasts accept the concept of a link between large bodies of water and ghostly activity, but the oldest ghost sightings on record date back to the era of ancient Rome.

Outside of the occasional scraps of folklore, why were there no reliable reports of the beastie until 1933—and then a veritable explosion of sightings? Many paranormal enthusiasts accept the concept of a link between large bodies of water and ghostly activity, but the oldest ghost sightings on record date back to the era of ancient Rome. This took place in the cellar of the Treasurer's House in York, England, where in 1953, the ghosts of Roman auxiliaries were seen marching through the basement along the path of what was once a major Roman road.

The Romans left Britain around 410 C.E., making the ghostly soldiers a maximum of 1,500 years old. That's a long time for an apparition to stick around—if apparition it was, as opposed to a time slip or an interdimensional event. To this author's knowledge, there are no reports of ghost sightings older than 2,000 years, and certainly none that measure their age in millions, let alone *tens of millions* of years.

Be that as it may, as time goes on, the Nessie sightings continue. Whether they are caused by wishful thinking, misidentified marine animals, or even the ghost of a long-dead plesiosaur remains a matter of discussion. As technology progresses and our ability to probe the depths of the loch improves, we may someday learn the definitive answer. For now, at least, what lies beneath the surface of Loch Ness remains an enduring and alluring mystery.

LURKERS IN THE DARKNESS: WENDIGO AND PUKWUDGIES

In the spring of 2022, I accepted an invitation to move into one of the most infamous haunted houses in the United States for a few days. Located in New York, the Hinsdale House was rotting away and on the verge of demolition when it was purchased by Daniel Klaes. Restoration of the house is an ongoing project, and in the meantime, Klaes has opened the property up to paranormal investigators, many of whom experience strange phenomena inside the house.

Yet the house itself isn't the only thing worth investigating. The land on which it stands is every bit as intriguing, if not more so.

During the early 1970s, the Dandy family (Phil, Clara, and their children) lived in the house. Their time was a turbulent and disturbing one.

Much about the house's history and reputation is uncertain and open to multiple interpretations. Dating back to the mid-1800s, there are stories of murders having taken place there when it was used as a way station for coaches. It's also said that a tree that once stood on the property was used as a hanging tree.

Several bodies are believed to lie in potential burial shafts, which are sited in close proximity to the pond that stands close by the house. If local legends concerning a Native massacre are true, even more may lie in the ground just a little further afield in the land that surrounds the house. This has yet to be confirmed, but efforts are underway to gather evidence.

Clara Miller (formerly Clara Dandy), matriarch of the family, chronicled the strange and disturbing experiences over a period of years in her memoir *Echoes of a Haunting*. Over a four-year period, these weird occurrences ran the entire paranormal gamut. Unidentified flying objects hovered over the property—on at least one occasion, flooding the entire house with light. Windows and doors opened and closed by themselves. Items disappeared, only to reappear later, sometimes in different parts of the house, where none of the family members had moved them. Disembodied voices and phantom footsteps were heard. Rooms suddenly became ice cold for no apparent reason, no matter what the temperature was outside.

Apparitions were seen walking on the grounds. A young man vanished into thin air while in plain sight of multiple observers. This took place at the edge of the pond—where Dan Klaes and friends would later discover evidence suggestive of human burials.

The Hinsdale House is built upon troubled ground, as its restless spirits will attest.

Mechanical equipment, particularly vehicles, either became unreliable or flatly refused to work. The breakdowns weren't restricted to the family. No friend or visitor who dropped by the house could be assured that their car would start again when it was time to leave. More alarming still, the Dandys were plagued by multiple car crashes, some of which were very serious. It started to seem as if the family was accident prone and receiving far more than the average amount of bad luck.

These are just a few elements of the haunting. The entirety would take several books to catalog, and efforts have already been made to do exactly that. The Dandys finally brought in a priest to exorcise their home, which reportedly caused the entire house to shake upon its foundations. Despite best efforts, even decades later, the Hinsdale House remains a prime case for a dark haunting.

During my own stay at the house, my fellow paranormal investigators and I distinctly heard the sound of a cat meowing while sitting in the living room. No cat was present at the time, and after checking with Dan, he informed me that phantom cats and dogs have been encountered in the house by more than one visitor. I might be tempted to put it down to the power of suggestion, were it not for the fact that the *meow* was picked up clearly on the voice recorder I had left running on the coffee table.

Of particular note, the Dandy family heard the sound of singing coming from the woods on more than one occasion. The vocal harmonies were reminiscent of a choir. They ventured up the hillside and into the trees to investigate but found no source for the invisible chorale. I was interested not just in the ghostly singing but also claims that two entirely different entities could be found lurking in the shadows of the trees at Hinsdale: wendigo and pukwudgies.

Legend has it that wendigo (or windigo) are supernatural beings that prowl the North American forests. Extremely tall and gaunt, humanoid in body, they are said to sport a rack of antlers that would give even the most impressive elk, moose, or buck a run for their money. Those same legends say that wendigo not only eat human beings but are sometimes capable of possessing people and making them attack others. In many stories, wendigo start out human, only to twist and transform into a cannibalistic perversion of their former selves. Historically, savage wilderness murders or disappearances have been laid at the door of this particular beast, particularly in isolated locations.

The lonelier and more socially distanced an individual or a setting is, the more vulnerable they are thought to be to the wendigo.

It was with no small degree of trepidation that we climbed the muddy slope behind the Hinsdale House one dark night until only the glow from its windows was visible through the trees. A small group of us sat quietly, letting our eyes adjust to the dark. *Something* seemed to be moving out there among the trees. We could see the shadows moving. Whenever we went to check, nothing was seen. Fortunately for us, we weren't pounced on by a huge carnivorous monster with antlers. (It's a lot easier to believe in the possibility of wendigo in the middle of pitch-black woods than sitting in a comfortable chair in a well-lit living room.)

According to two different psychic mediums with whom we consulted, those woods may have been home to an entirely different variety of paranormal dweller: pukwudgies. I first encountered stories of these mischievous goblin-like humanoids while investigating the Hartford City Jail in Indiana, which was allegedly beset by small, scampering creatures running from room to room and visible only for brief instants. Ranging anywhere between two and four feet tall, pukwudgies have porcupine-like quills running down the length of their back.

The author and his fellow paranormal investigators heard (and recorded) the sound of a cat in the living room of the Hinsdale House.

Indiana has many pukwudgie reports, though few of them are urban. Pukwudgies are said to live in forests and rural areas, avoiding contact with humanity where possible.

Pukwudgie sightings also arise from parts of New England, particularly Massachusetts. New York has its own accounts—particularly at the Hinsdale House. The creatures are sometimes said to be outright hostile, attacking humans and causing them injuries. In general, it's a wise idea to stay on their good side. Could they account for the movement we glimpsed and heard on the hillside that night, or was it simply the normal movement of nocturnal woodland critters?

A strange coda to this story took place when I involved a psychic medium from the U.K. to remote-read my location without revealing its identity to her. Detailing her impressions during a transatlantic phone call, she described seeing a gaggle of small, human-shaped beings standing on the grounds, peering intently at the house.

Being completely unaware of my whereabouts, it's highly unlikely that the remote viewer would have randomly guessed the pukwudgie connection with the Hinsdale House. When I went to sleep that night, it was only after peering out of the window and checking the lawn for an ocean of twinkling eyes looking back at me. There was none to be seen, but I locked every door and window just to be on the safe side.

A VISITOR COMES CALLING: THE VAN METER CREATURE

In 1903, the sleepy town of Van Meter, Iowa (so named because of the Dutch family who founded it), played unwitting host to a creature that still bears its namesake: the Van Meter Creature. I first learned about the case from documentary filmmaker Josh Heard, who based a movie named *1903* on the incident. The sightings happened over the space of several nights, spanning the months of September and October.

Foreshadowing future sightings of the much more widely known Mothman, the mysterious creature had a horned head fronted by a beak, a body estimated at eight feet tall, and a pair of huge bat wings that allowed it to soar through the air above the town or leap from one high vantage point to another. There was a distinctly avian, pterodactyl-like quality to the creature. One of its more peculiar characteristics was that the horn emitted a bright glow, perhaps a means of lighting the creature's path through the darkness. Equally piercing was the loud shriek that accompanied it as it moved.

It's a safe assumption that strange beings turning up in small-town America during the earlier part of the twentieth century were never going to receive a friendly greeting. Sure enough, each time it appeared, the creature was met with gunfire from whichever of the townspeople saw it. The brightly glowing horn must have made for a highly attractive target. The creature was agile enough to dodge some of the lead that was sent its way. When those gunshots did hit home, the strange visitor seemed impervious.

Witnesses also said that the creature stank, emitting an odor that was similar to sulfur. It is worth noting that some individuals believe the smell of sulfur heralds the arrival of a demonic entity. Finally, in early October the people of Van Meter tracked the entity to a disused coal and clay mine and waited for it to reappear. When it did, the creature had company: a smaller creature that looked very similar shot out of the mine alongside what may have been its parent or older sibling.

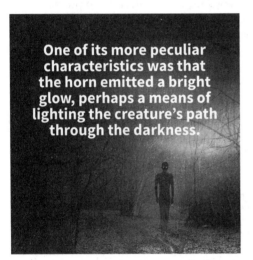

One of its more peculiar characteristics was that the horn emitted a bright glow, perhaps a means of lighting the creature's path through the darkness.

The locals waited for the two to return, and when they did, all hell broke loose. The creatures returned to their lair, which the armed group of townsfolk set about sealing up. They presumably remain inside today. I say "presumably" because the region still has its share of bizarre bird-like creature sightings right up to the present day.

Were it not for veteran researcher Chad Lewis, who investigated the case extensively and co-wrote a book about it (*The Van Meter Visitor: A True and Mysterious Encounter with the Unknown*), we might not ever have heard of the Van Meter Creature (or Visitor, as he termed it). It would have remained one of the many local pieces of cryptid lore that don't garner wider attention. Josh Heard's film also served to bring the baffling case before a larger audience, all of whom would like to know just what the Van Meter entity really was—alien, cryptid, hallucination, figment of the imagination, or something else?

"An incident 100 percent absolutely *happened*," Heard opined during our interview. "On the very last night, the entire town went out and took pot shots at this thing. They ran right alongside it, shooting and reloading. There are just too many eyewitnesses for this thing not to have taken place."

Could it simply have been a case of hyperactive imagination, spreading from person to person within Van Meter until the town was in the grip of mass hysteria? Heard doesn't think so.

"The initial reports were made by professional people. Doctors, lawyers, bankers … people with solid public reputations. Each of them had something tangible to lose if they were thought to be making up unsubstantiated stories about weird flying creatures. Considering everything they had to risk—their reputations, their livelihoods—then why lie?"

After the initial sightings, the townsfolk gathered. All of them saw the Visitor. It's a stretch to try to write them all off as having been drunk, hallucinating, or simply making it all up.

Once I read various accounts of what happened in Van Meter, I found myself wondering why they didn't simply bring in the army. Josh Heard offers up a plausible answer: "They had enough ammo in town to wipe out a whole regiment! Certainly more than enough to take out a single flying creature … or so they thought."

Yet apparently the pistols, shotguns, and rifles weren't enough. There was no indication that the creature or its smaller companion were harmed in any way by the guns fired at them by the townspeople.

A 2021 episode of the Josh Gates–fronted TV show *Expedition X* described the Van Meter incident as being the "most corroborated cryptid sightings of all time." More intriguing still, the show highlighted the fact that sightings of the creature didn't end in 1903. Shockingly, it—or something very much like it—is still being seen today.

Eyewitnesses describe the creature in an almost identical way: tall, black, and bird-like, with leathery bat wings. Back in 1903, nobody was carrying a cell phone equipped with a high-resolution still and video camera around with them. Today, almost everybody does. Unfortunately, none of the modern-day witnesses took photographs or video footage of whatever bat-winged creature they thought they saw.

One of the advantages of a TV show budget is that Gates's co-stars were granted access to the land on which the old coal mine—said

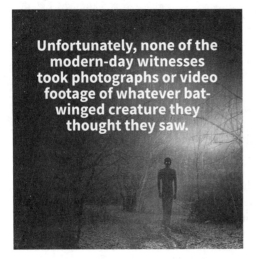

Unfortunately, none of the modern-day witnesses took photographs or video footage of whatever bat-winged creature they thought they saw.

by some to still contain the creature—is buried. The mine shaft has long been disused and was challenging for the production team to locate. When they excavated using heavy digging equipment, there was neither hide nor hair of a monster.

Expedition X ends without having gathered any evidence to support the existence of the Van Meter Creature, and Gates proposes that the closest natural explanation may come in the form of a turkey vulture. Like the creature, turkey vultures are black, large, winged, and avian. Crucially, however, they are not bulletproof, something to which hunters can testify. To accept this explanation, we'd also have to accept the possibility that a large group of rural Iowans failed to recognize a turkey vulture back in 1903—a possibility that may be harder to believe than the existence of a monster.

"I think that whatever this thing was, is still down in that mine today," Heard stated. "It's more than likely just a pile of bones at this point. I don't buy that this was some kind of interdimensional being. Whatever that thing was, it was flesh and blood."

A ROYAL SCANDAL: THE MONSTER OF GLAMIS

Every castle has its ghost story. Indeed, most castles have more than one—but few of those fortresses are said to have their very own monster. One exception is Scotland's Glamis Castle, which is reputed to have been the home of a mysterious creature that was equally to be pitied and feared.

The castle dates to the 1400s and has seen numerous British monarchs pass through its stone walls. The likes of King James V and Mary Queen of Scots resided there, as did Lady Elizabeth Bowes Lyon, future Queen Mother (the mother of Queen Elizabeth II). It is a sprawling stronghold with an array of turreted towers that gives the place a distinctly Hogwartian air. Much like Hogwarts, Glamis Castle supposedly has its very own chamber of secrets.

Glamis is alluded to in *Macbeth*—sorry, "the Scottish play"—but by far the darkest association it has involves a hidden room and a guilty secret going back to the early 1800s. Inside the room—which can only be accessed by the master of the castle, the current Lord Glamis—was said to live a horrifically deformed being that was the true heir to the castle and the title that went with it. So terrible was the occupant reputed to be that simply being in its presence could frighten an unwary visitor to the edge of insanity.

The boy's given name was Thomas. According to family accounts, he was born at Glamis on October 21, 1821. The accounts hold that he did not survive his first day in the world, but rumors to the contrary soon spread like wildfire. If the stories are true, the unfortunate boy spent his life confined to a single stone chamber, only let out after dark when most of the castle inhabitants were asleep, to exercise under close supervision. One worker who supposedly caught sight of Thomas "the monster" ended up leaving the country and emigrating overseas.

Unlike many legends, this particular story may be more truth than fiction. Given the British upper-class propensity for inbreeding to maintain a certain "purity of the bloodline," it was not remotely unusual for first cousins to marry and procreate. Assuming that Thomas Bowes

Glamis Castle in Angus, Scotland, has a long and storied history, including being the childhood home of Queen Elizabeth (the Queen Mother) and the birthplace of Princess Margaret and home to the Earl of Strathmore and Kinghome.

Lyon was born with severe deformities and labeled a monster, it is likely that he did not live to old age—yet no gravestone bears his name, and the whereabouts of his final resting place are unknown. Could it be that he was interred within the secret chamber at Glamis and that his body is still there? This would explain why, more than a century after even the most optimistic lifespan estimate, no trace of the hidden room has ever been made public.

In addition to its frightening secret, Glamis Castle is home to a range of ghosts, including a phantom boy who froze to death and, of course, the archetypal Grey Lady seen in so many British haunted locations. Something unique to Glamis is the story of a card game that took place there one dark night between the notorious "Earl Beardie" (as Alexander Lindsay, 4th Earl of Crawford, was known) and a mysterious stranger who came knocking at the castle door requesting entry. It should have served as a clue to the Earl that the man had presented himself exactly at the stroke of midnight. Saturday night had just given way to Sunday morning, and it was forbidden to play cards on the holy sabbath. Not that Earl Beardie cared about such matters. He did care very much about gambling, a trait that would turn out to be his undoing.

By the time the sun came up, the Earl had entered such a losing streak that he had gambled away every penny in his accounts, every item of value that he owned, even Glamis Castle and its estates, all to the enigmatic stranger who simply smiled and outplayed him at every hand.

Finally, with nothing left to wager but determined to win back his losses, Earl Beardie frittered away the very last thing in his possession: his soul.

The stranger, of course, was none other than the devil himself, and the story says that their game continues to this day, somewhere deep within the bowels of Glamis Castle. Earl Beardie continues to play cards, and continues to lose, locked in an eternal contest with Lucifer for the ultimate in high-stakes gambling.

The odds of his winning back his soul are not good.

STRANGER THAN FICTION

BLACK-EYED KIDS

Although they can often be mischievous, children are generally considered innocent. Deep down in our core, adults are hardwired to protect them from the cruelties of the world. Why else would there be so many instances of grown men and women giving up their own lives to save children from a burning house or an icy pond?

Yet there are exceptions. In recent years, one of the most notable has come in the form of Black-Eyed Children—also known as Black-Eyed Kids or BEKs. Although accounts date back to the 1990s, this appears to be primarily a late twentieth- or early twenty-first-century phenomenon, and members of the paranormal community remained divided on whether the BEKs are an entirely fictitious urban legend or terrifying entities who mean us the gravest of harm.

Many BEK experiences start out in a similar way. There's a knock at the door or a tap on the car window. Standing there are children aged somewhere between 5 and 15, usually two or more. The BEKs behave in a predatory manner, approaching their intended targets when they are most vulnerable—usually when they are alone.

Any pretense at sweetness and innocence is dispelled when the eyewitness looks at their eyes, which are said to be as black as coal and utterly devoid of either emotion or the spark of life. Some of those who encounter BEKs have described them as seemingly soulless; others recall them emanating a feeling of either dread or even outright evil.

The BEKs tend to have a hook: they want something. That specific something varies but usually involves either giving them something, such as food or transportation, or letting them in—inside a house, inside a car, access to someplace that would isolate their target from the outside world and keep them in close proximity to the BEKs. Which leads to the next logical question: What happens then? What exactly do the Black-Eyed Kids want, once they are sequestered alone with their target and away from prying eyes?

Although it may not be the earliest case, the classic BEK encounter comes to us via journalist Brian Bethel and dates to 1996. Bethel recounted his chilling experience to researcher Dan LaFave. He was approached by a pair of eerie children while sitting in his car, minding his own business. Both were preteen boys. They wore hoodies and had strikingly pale skin.

One of the children asked Bethel to give them a ride home. Bethel recalled later that the BEK's manner of speaking was so smooth, so "quasi-hypnotic," that it almost seemed practiced, in the manner of an actor who had rehearsed their lines prior to putting on a performance. As the first child talked, Bethel grew increasingly afraid—a fear that was compounded when the veteran reporter caught sight of the child's completely black eyes. The eyes of the second boy, who had thus far been a silent partner, were the same: black.

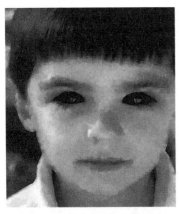

The creepy Black-Eyed Kids might arrive at your home or by hitchhiking, asking for food or shelter or transportation before becoming more sinister in nature.

Wisely, Bethel drove away before the BEKs could open the car door, leaving the two BEKs standing there in the street. His story later went viral and entered the mainstream paranormal lexicon. Numerous other stories surfaced, all of an equally sinister bent. Writing in 2018, author Nick Redfern challenged the idea that the arrival of BEKs on the paranormal scene was only around 20 years old. In his book *Paranormal Parasites: The Voracious Appetites of Soul-Sucking Entities*, Redfern relates his interview with a Louisiana woman who declared that her great-grandmother had encountered a BEK in 1923. Like all such encounters, all we have to go on is anecdote.

I am unaware of any compelling video or photographic evidence of the existence of Black-Eyed Kids, and even if it did exist, the likelihood is that skeptics would dismiss it anyway. They point out that black eye lenses are relatively cheap and easy to obtain. Could the BEK accounts conceivably be explained by flesh-and-blood children playing pranks? It is certainly possible, although Bethel, a trained observer and reporter, stands by his own account and remains deeply shaken by the experience even decades afterward.

Theories as diverse as vampires, demons, angry ghosts, alien entities, and shapeshifters have all been advanced as potential explanations for the BEK phenomenon. Many dismiss BEKs as nothing more than a modern-day myth or urban legend. For this author, the jury is still out—but if a child with black eyes should knock on my door late one night, there's no way on earth I would ever let them in.

THE PHILADELPHIA EXPERIMENT

Although his educational background was in linguistics, author Charles Berlitz gained widespread popularity and became renowned for his writing. Speaking multiple languages fluently, he wrote about the nuances and function of those languages and became greatly respected in his professional field. Yet now, decades after his death in 2003, his linguistic achievements are not what he is best known for.

Berlitz was a man of many interests, a true polymath. He found widespread publishing success when he wrote about the weird and bizarre, choosing subjects on the fringes of science and culture. A reading public who had made the works of Erich von Däniken into massive bestsellers lapped up books such as *The Bermuda Triangle*, in which Berlitz waxed lyrical on the subject of disappearing ships and airplanes in the Pacific Ocean. The notion of UFOs, whirlpools, or giant waterspouts swallowing the missing vessels whole has been thoroughly debunked, but at the time of its publication in 1974, such hypotheses were believed by many.

It was during his research for *The Bermuda Triangle*, Berlitz claimed, that he first hit encountered claims about a supposedly top-secret experiment said to have been conducted by the U.S. Navy during World War II. Unofficially dubbed the "Philadelphia Experiment" because it took place in the Philadelphia Naval Yard, the aim was to take a destroyer and, by using an exotic combination of energy fields, somehow render it invisible.

The destroyer was the USS *Eldridge*, and to be clear, the claims surrounding the ship have nothing to do with radar invisibility. Modern warships are designed and built to have low profiles on radar, absorbing rather than reflecting radar waves back to the sender. The same principles hold true with stealth aircraft. Such technology dates to the 1980s and 1990s. What is said to have happened with the *Eldridge* was something different: an attempt to quite literally turn the warship invisible to the naked eye.

Sometime in October of 1943 (the precise date is suspiciously unclear), the experiment went ahead. The efforts of the scientists were, it was said, successful—a little *too* successful, if accounts are to be believed. According to some, the *Eldridge* was almost immediately engulfed in an eerie glowing mist. The ship was then teleported from its mooring point at the Philadelphia Naval Yard, presumably passed through some other dimension, and emerged hundreds of miles away in Norfolk, Virginia—and then bounced right back to Philadelphia again.

The story doesn't end there. Members of the crew allegedly suffered bizarre and disturbing side effects after the termination of the experiment. In what sounds like a transporter malfunction from an episode of *Star Trek*, some found themselves stuck inside the ship's hull and superstructure when the *Eldridge* re-materialized, their body parts supposedly bound and fused with the metal at the molecular level. Some, it is said, were driven insane or were haunted by the experience for the rest of their lives.

The implications of these events, if they truly happened, would be extraordinary. For one thing, our understanding of physics and the laws of the universe would be proven grossly inadequate.

The U.S. Navy destroyer USS *Eldridge* is seen here in 1944 a year after it disappeared while moored at the Philadelphia Naval Yard only to reappear near Norfolk, Virginia.

If they truly happened.

Fast-forward more than a decade. Enter Morris Jessup, also known as M. K. Jessup or Dr. Morris K. Jessup (author Joe Nickell observes that, although he was often referred to by that appellation, Jessup did not in fact finish his doctorate; his highest level of education was a master's degree). Jessup was an avowed UFO enthusiast who took a deep dive down the rabbit hole of 1950s UFOlogy, which was in its infancy and enjoying massive popularity. In 1955, he published *The Case for the UFO*, which outlined a number of esoteric hypotheses on the potential origins of flying saucers and other strange phenomena.

Popular belief holds that one year after its publication, a copy of the book was mailed anonymously to the Office of Naval Research. Three different writers had annotated the book with what can best be described as fantastical references to secret government experiments that were on the cutting edge of physics, if not beyond. These same men then sent letters to Jessup that contained details about the Philadelphia Experiment. He duly turned the correspondence over to the U.S. Navy authorities.

Thus was the entire Philadelphia Experiment phenomenon—we use the word "phenomenon" in the cultural rather than physical sense—born.

One of Jessup's three letter writers was a man by the name of Carlos Miguel Allende. He claimed to have been an eyewitness to the experiment when it took place and had been responsible for writing two of the letters sent to Jessup. Veteran UFO researcher Kevin Randle, who dug into the matter extensively, notes that, after swearing that the stories concerning the disappearance of the *Eldridge* were absolutely true, Allende later did an about-face and admitted that the entire thing was a hoax. No sooner had the dust settled from that particular revelation than he reversed course a second time, claiming that he had been forced into concocting the hoax story at the behest of the CIA.

What can be deduced from this tangled web? One thing, for certain: Carlos Allende was not a reliable, trustworthy source of information. In October of 1980, researcher Robert A. Goerman published an article to that effect in *Fate* magazine. He spoke with the father of Allende, who also went by the name of Carl Allen, and reviewed personal documents such as Allen's military records. A clearer picture emerges of Allende as not just a reclusive figure but also as a fabulist, somebody who loved to bamboozle the credulous with fantastic stories.

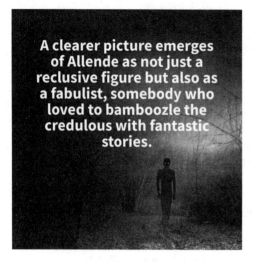

A clearer picture emerges of Allende as not just a reclusive figure but also as a fabulist, somebody who loved to bamboozle the credulous with fantastic stories.

He had been the author of all three sets of annotations on Jessup's book and had written the letters himself, posing as all three of the different correspondents.

Great kudos are due to Goerman for putting in the legwork to track down Allen's family. He corresponded with Allen and tried his best to arrange a face-to-face interview to settle the matter forever, but Allen was his typical, evasive self when it came to the specifics. It is safe to say that his claims of having witnessed the disappearance and reappearance of the *Eldridge* from the deck of a liberty ship, moored at very close proximity to the destroyer (which is, in itself, an unlikely detail, considering the volatile nature of the experiment), can be comfortably dismissed.

Carl Allen died on Saturday, March 5, 1994, at the age of 68, in Greeley, Colorado. He took the truth of the matter to his grave. The lack of supporting evidence overwhelmingly suggests that the Philadelphia Experiment never took place. We do know that, contrary to Allen's claims, the USS *Eldridge* wasn't even in port when the event is said to have happened. The ship served convoy duty during the final quarter of 1943, and while it did berth in New York, it never entered the Philadelphia Naval Yard during that time. Of course, conspiracy theorists may simply state that ship's logs and other official naval records could have been falsified, an answer that provides a comfortable security blanket for those who insist on believing.

Morris K. Jessup died on April 20, 1959. His body was found inside his car, which he had driven to a Florida park. Unsurprisingly, his connection with the Philadelphia Experiment and the supposed conspiracy of silence that surrounded it only served to fuel rumors that he had been murdered, presumably at the hands of a government and defense establishment that thought he had gotten a little too close to the truth.

Alternatively, perhaps Jessup had reached his emotional breaking point and tragically chose to end his own life—a far likelier explanation than some vast, overarching conspiracy theory involving assassins and secret military projects.

It is telling that, of the hundreds of participants and eyewitnesses involved with the Philadelphia Experiment, Carlos Allende, aka Carl Allen, was the only person to come forward and make such claims. These claims formed the foundation for the books of the 1970s by Berlitz (*The Bermuda Triangle*) and William L. Moore (*The Philadelphia Experiment: Project Invisibility*) through which the Philadelphia Experiment entered the public consciousness and gained widespread awareness. Indeed, as recently as 2021, the ship made an appearance in the Marvel TV series *Loki*, where it was sent into the void between worlds. It's an entertaining twist on a very persistent tale, which is unlikely to go away anytime soon.

It is safe to say that the U.S. Navy has had its fill of answering questions about the Philadelphia Experiment, and it's not difficult to see why. Despite there being absolutely nothing in the way of credible evidence to support the so-called experiment ever having taken place, rumors and stories have swirled around it ever since Berlitz wrote on the subject. The more vigorously the Navy might deny it, believers say, the more likely it is that it is simply covering something up. For the Navy, it's a case of damned if it does, damned

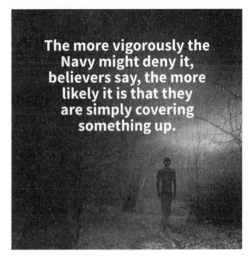

The more vigorously the Navy might deny it, believers say, the more likely it is that they are simply covering something up.

if it doesn't. No matter what it says, those who believe in the reality of the Philadelphia Experiment will continue to believe.

Still, in an attempt to set the record straight, the Navy's Office of Naval Research maintains a web page and fact sheet devoted to telling its side of the story. It states definitively that "ONR has never conducted any investigations on invisibility, either in 1943 or at any other time." This has been the Navy's official stance on the matter since the statement was issued in 1996.

So, what *really* happened to the USS *Eldridge*, if anything? The likeliest explanation is that the "experiment" was in fact nothing more than a degaussing of the ship's hull. In addition to U-boats, the mine was one of the things that World War II–era sailors dreaded. Mines were drawn toward target ships via magnetism. The process of degaussing, or demagnetizing, the hull made the vessel less likely to attract a mine toward it by making it more difficult for the mine to "sense" the presence of the ship. Degaussing weakened the hull's magnetic field and was achieved by running electrical cables along the entire length of the ship, then powering them up. To the uninitiated, this might have appeared both fascinating and futuristic—perhaps even like some kind of high-tech secret experiment.

Then again, maybe the truth is far stranger than anything a science fiction writer could dream up.

FROM THE SHADOW: THE ARRIVAL OF THE SHADOW PEOPLE

Paranormal tourism and field investigation experienced an explosion in popularity that began during the 2000s and shows no sign of slowing down at the time of writing. Although the classic tropes have always been with us—the lady in white, the haunted mansion, the banshee—the shadow person seems to be a relatively new phenomenon. But is it really? They may perhaps have been with us for a very long time.

The term "shadow people" (or "shadow figures") refers to humanoid shapes that appear to be extremely dark, if not entirely black in appearance. They are usually found in the proximity of people, places, or objects that have a reputation for being haunted. When I embarked upon my career as a paranormal investigator in the mid-1990s, few people seemed to have heard of shadow people, let alone seen one. After I relocated to the United States in 1999, a number of the locations I was called in to investigate had claims of these mysterious shadowy figures haunting their rooms and hallways.

It struck me that shadow people seemed to be particularly prevalent in abandoned hospitals, prisons, and asylums—the type of places in which emotions ran strong, particularly negative emotions, and especially those facilities that ran a pressure-cooker environment, with negativity constantly simmering and ready to boil over.

The paranormal community came to perceive shadow people as being inherently malevolent in nature. Partly this had to do with the way they were portrayed on reality TV shows, not to mention the fact that some of them could behave violently. A case in point: I investigated the Farrar Elementary School in rural Iowa over an extended period of time. The dominant entity that is said to haunt the former schoolhouse is a very tall—possibly seven feet tall—shadow person known as "the Principal."

Class has long since ended, but ghosts still walk the halls of Iowa's Farrar School.

Whether or not this truly *was* the principal of the school during the entity's physical lifetime remains unclear, though I suspect this was not the case. This entity has been given the nickname because it seems to be an enforcer, stalking the halls long after the last child has left for pastures new. It has been seen by numerous visitors, who describe its height and shadowy appearance, and most of whom note that the Principal has the build and mannerisms of an adult male.

Crossing the Principal can be a very bad move indeed, as one investigator found when he was slammed forcefully into a wall after being knocked off his feet by an invisible force, almost sustaining a serious head injury.

The Principal's motives are unknown but seem to focus upon respect: respect for the school and for the memory of those who once walked its hallways, whether they taught or learned in its classrooms. Those visitors to Farrar who show the proper decorum rarely have anything to fear from this particular shadow person.

Despite having spent days investigating the school and interviewing several eyewitnesses who had seen the Principal with their own eyes,

I did not encounter him in person—though I did stick to my standard policy of being respectful when researching a haunted location. Rather than see this entity as being evil or somehow "bad," I tend to think of Farrar's Principal as being a protector, keeping a watchful eye over the school and making sure that the people inside it don't get out of line. Whether the Principal was ever human, let alone was a "he" or a "she," is still open to question.

I've been fortunate enough to catch glimpses of what I *think* are shadow people at several different haunted places through the years and heard countless stories from paranormal investigators and eyewitnesses that I respect, but it wasn't until I set foot in the old South Pittsburg Hospital in Tennessee that I became truly, unequivocally convinced of their reality.

The hospital closed its doors after giving decades of dedicated service to the people of South Pittsburg. When I was invited to spend a working week investigating the building along with a small team of fellow researchers, I jumped at the chance. After we set foot inside the place for the first time, it quickly became apparent that there was so much square footage that we would never be able to cover it all. Because of that, I asked staff members where some of the most paranormally active hot spots were. We were directed to the nurses' station on the second floor.

Having found some comfortable chairs, my colleagues and I settled in for what felt like it could be a long wait. Twilight was just giving way to night when I saw what I at first thought was another investigator standing behind the desk the nurses had once used for filling out patient charts. Although it was dark in the hospital at that point, there is no doubt that I was looking at a very solid black silhouette of an adult human being. So fully realized was it that I called out to the person I thought it was, only to realize that they were more than a hundred feet away at the end of a long hallway.

> There was nowhere that a flesh-and-blood person could have run to, and while it is possible that my eyes were playing tricks on me, if that was truly the case, then this was the single most vivid optical illusion or hallucination I have experienced in my entire life.

Just like that, it was gone. I was up and out of my chair in a flash, heading straight for it.

There was nowhere that a flesh-and-blood person could have run to, and while it is possible that my eyes were playing tricks on me, if that was truly the case, then this was the single most vivid optical illusion or hallucination I have experienced in my entire life.

Nor am I the only person to have seen shadow people in that same spot.

There was no sense of threat or fear either before, during, or after my encounter with the shadow person. Not everybody is lucky enough to say the same, however. There is no shortage of people who report being menaced by them and, in some cases, even physically attacked.

I have personally interviewed a number of healthcare workers and family members who report seeing increased shadow person activity in the nursing homes and healthcare facilities in which they work. Of particular note is that many of these nurses, nurse aides, and administrators claim that the intensity and frequency of shadow person sightings increases up to and during the time at which an individual is about to pass.

It has become traditional for visiting paranormal investigators to sign the chalkboards at the Farrar School. Thousands have come to attempt communication with the spirits here.

A number of those reports come from hospice and palliative care facilities and from several different countries.

Shadow people come in different shapes and sizes, ranging from adults to smaller humanoid figures two to three feet high. I hesitate to label them as children, because there is doubt whether they are human at all. Some researchers believe that shadow people may be aliens or extra-dimensional in nature. Others have speculated that they may be time travelers from our future, returning to observe events of the present day, for reasons known only to themselves.

Those who live in the Western world have projected evil and frightening purpose onto shadow people, and while that might be true in some cases, there are alternatives to be considered. During a conversation I once had with occult researcher John E. L. Tenney, he raised the belief held by other cultures that shadow people are the spirits of departed loved ones, appearing in shadow form as they manifest in our own reality for brief periods of time. As a potential explanation, it is no less likely than their being vengeful spirits that stalk and prey upon the living. It also lends credence to the accounts of palliative care workers who experience shadow person activity while tending to patients on their deathbeds. Many believe their purpose to be one of easing the transition of the dying person into the next realm.

As with so many aspects of the paranormal, shadow people can behave in both good and evil ways; they can help or they can harm. Some are ambivalent, lurking in the darkness, watching the living, observing their behavior, but not interfering. If you should happen to encounter one yourself, it's best to remain calm. Some researchers believe that shadow people are drawn to, if not fueled by, the energy of fear.

Consider the situation carefully. It may be that the shadow people in question are simply curious or seek only to help. In locations with a darker history, however, the intentions of these mysterious entities may be equally dark, if not outright threatening. In such cases, discretion may prove to be the better part of valor.

FACE TO FACE WITH DEATH:
THE DOPPELGÄNGER

To meet one's doppelgänger, the German term ("doublegoer") for an exact double of oneself, is believed to be a very bad sign; in fact, for centuries people have believed that a doppelgänger encounter signifies death for the living person who sights themselves. Some cultures held the belief that it was simply a sign of bad things to come.

But not so fast—a number of cases can be explained by medical science, as some people have an almost identical double who is not a brother or a sister. The key word here is "almost." Such unrelated look-alikes can still be distinguished from one another upon close inspection; they can easily be mistaken for one another but don't stand up to close scrutiny.

In paranormal terms, a true doppelgänger is something akin to an evil twin. It looks, sounds, and dresses like you—any differences will be extremely subtle, if they are present at all. Yet even though somebody who knows you might think that the doppelgänger actually *is* you, there's often a catch. Perhaps the doppelgänger acts in a way that's just subtly different enough from your own manner of behavior that it raises the hairs on the back of the acquaintance's neck. Some people believe that these are evil spirit entities that have the capacity for mimicking the living

Formerly the Teller County Jail, the Outlaws and Lawmen Jail Museum has a claim to being the most haunted building in Cripple Creek, Colorado.

almost perfectly. Doppelgängers have been reported at several locations I've investigated. At Asylum 49, owner Kimm Andersen's double was such a good copy of him that it fooled his own first cousin. These phantom "twins" have also been seen at the Waverly Hills Sanatorium in Kentucky, impersonating volunteer staff.

My own doppelgänger put in an appearance one night at the old Cripple Creek jail in the mountains of Colorado. It was during a charity paranormal investigation, and I was joining an ensemble of ghost hunters all doing our bit to help raise money. Now operating as the Outlaws and Lawmen Jail Museum, the jail is built on two levels. After climbing up to the second floor, one of my colleagues encountered me standing on the upper walkway, apparently just minding my own business. I didn't speak or acknowledge his presence in any way. He thought nothing of it at the time and simply continued on his way along the exterior landing until he came to the first cell that was occupied.

Stepping into the cell, he passed another paranormal investigator who had been standing in the doorway for the past 15 minutes. Then

A mannequin illustrates the manner in which the jailers may have been dressed during the late nineteenth century.

he saw me, sitting in the middle of the floor, conducting an EVP session. My colleague stopped dead in his tracks, turning pale white and giving life to that old phrase "He looked as though he'd just seen a ghost." Which he may very well have done.

Of course, my companion was able to testify that I'd been inside the cell the entire time. Whoever it was that the other colleague saw—assuming it wasn't a hallucination—couldn't possibly have been me. A check of the entire jail confirmed that there was nobody else in the building who could have fit the same description. He was certain that the impostor's facial features, physical build, haircut, and most of his clothing were an exact match for my own. The one key difference: his shirt was a different color.

Whether this was indeed a doppelgänger—as opposed to some kind of time slip or extra-dimensional version of me, or some other as-yet unexplained phenomenon—remains unclear to this day. The good news is that my presumed doppelgänger and I never came face to face. I can only wonder how severe the consequences might have been if we actually had.

THE SCREAMING SKULL OF BURTON AGNES HALL

Elsewhere in this book, we delved into the curious case of the Hexham Heads in the north of England. Equally bizarre is a paranormal phenomenon that seems to be almost exclusively British in nature: that of the screaming skull. Thanks to its being highlighted by the work of ghost-hunting authors such as the late, great Peter Underwood, arguably the best-known case is that of "Owd Nance."

Located in the East Riding of Yorkshire, the grand manor of Burton Agnes Hall has a history dating to the year 1170, although the majority of the current building was constructed around 1610. Britain has numerous such historic stately homes, many of which come with their resident ghost (or ghosts). The phantom of Burton Agnes dates to the year 1620, when a daughter of the household, Anne Griffith, was set upon and badly injured by a gang of robbers. As she lay on the brink of death (or so the story goes), Anne made a truly macabre request. She loved her new home so much that she wanted to become a permanent part of it—to which end, once she was dead, her head was to be cut off and kept within Burton Agnes Hall forevermore. Her family, uncer-

Burton Agnes Hall in East Yorkshire, England, has a history dating back over eight centuries. Naturally, such an old building must have a ghost, and in this case it is that of Anne Griffith, who insisted her head always remain inside her beloved home.

tain whether this was truly her wish or the ramblings of a dying brain, promised faithfully that they would adhere to her request, only to renege and have her buried in the consecrated ground of the local cemetery.

As most keen students of ghost lore are aware, this broken promise constitutes a classic reason for a restless spirit to return from the grave to haunt the living. No sooner had Anne Griffith been buried than her beloved Burton Agnes Hall was plagued with unearthly screams, shrieks, and moans fit to curdle the blood. Legend has it that Anne's sisters went to her grave and had her casket opened, only to find she had somehow been decapitated since her burial! Reluctantly, after enduring night after sleepless night of hideous screaming, they brought Anne's head back to Burton Agnes Hall.

The disturbances immediately stopped.

The hall remained at peace until such times as the skull of "Owd Nance," as the family took to calling her, was removed, which happened on several occasions. Whenever it was taken from the premises for any reason, all hell broke loose. The spirit of Anne Griffith had no compunction about expressing her displeasure, and nobody slept peacefully until the skull was restored to its rightful place, which is where it remains today—although nobody is sure exactly *where* it can be found. According to the current owners of the property, Anne Griffith's skull was incorporated into one of the walls of Burton Agnes's great hall. It has never screamed since.

Anne's story does not end there, however. It is said that her ghost returns to her beloved home once each year, to commemorate the day of her death—a classic anniversary haunting.

NOT OF THIS EARTH

THE COMING OF THE SAUCERS

Although there's a tendency to think that strange lights in the sky and reports of encounters with otherworldly beings began in the twentieth century, the fact is that sightings of UAP (unidentified aerial phenomena) go back centuries. Some stories date as far back as ancient Egypt and the Roman Empire, according to writings and images. Admittedly, those documents are open to interpretation, and there are many who don't find these so-called "ancient aliens" theories believable. It's also worth noting that the specifics of UAP sightings have changed with the times. Whereas ancient sightings involved chariot-like objects, the Victorian era brought with it reports of bizarre-looking airships, strange craft that had a definite Steampunk vibe to them, if the descriptions given by eyewitnesses are to be believed.

During World War II, Allied airmen encountered mysterious multicolored lights that trailed their aircraft while flying over the European mainland. Sometimes there would be only a single light; on other occasions, there were enough of them to constitute a squadron. They were far too agile to be airplanes, and flight crews gave them the nickname "Foo Fighters." Although by late 1944 and early 1945 the Nazi regime was desperately pinning its hopes on a series of so-called wonder weapons, none of the experimental aircraft on the drawing board, including jet fighters, were capable of moving as nimbly as the Foo Fighters could. Despite the best efforts of skeptics to write them off, no credible explanation was ever found.

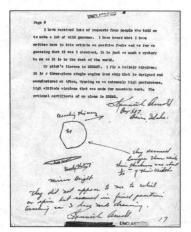

A page from Kenneth Arnold's unclassified report on his sighting of unidentified objects near Mount Rainier, Washington, in 1947.

Word of these military encounters with UAPs didn't go mainstream until years after the war had ended. The first real entry of strange phenomena in the sky to garner widespread public attention was on June 24, 1947, when a civilian pilot named Kenneth Arnold was flying in the vicinity of Mount Rainier, Washington, searching for a crashed U.S. military transport plane. There was a hefty cash reward on offer for whoever located the down aircraft, so Arnold kept his eyes peeled that afternoon. There was plenty of daylight left, and the rays of the sun glinting on a flying object soon caught the pilot's attention. It was not the missing transport, however, but a group of nine round, metallic objects flying in a diagonal line formation known as the echelon.

Arnold was a highly experienced pilot with over 4,000 logged flying hours. He was skilled at estimating the air speed of other planes. By his best estimate, the formation of strange craft was flying well in excess of one thousand miles per hour. There's some debate over whether he actually described the UAPs as being saucers or even saucer-like, but once the story hit the media, the term "flying saucer" was coined. Alongside its sibling, UFO (unidentified flying object), it was a description that would reign supreme until well into the twenty-first century.

Much like the 1880s airships and the 1940s Foo Fighters, no satisfactory explanation ever came to light for whatever it was that Arnold saw. Stories of unidentified objects and lights in the sky grew as the Cold War between East and West intensified. That same month, one of the most incredible incidents took place just outside the New Mexico town of Roswell.

SKYFALL: THE ROSWELL INCIDENT

Today, more than 75 years after what came to be called the Roswell incident, there is still no consensus on the nature of the object that crashed on rancher William "Mac" Brazel's land in June 1947. That it was wreckage of some sort was clear. Later, stories would emerge about some of the lightweight materials having remarkable properties, acting in a way unlike anything manufactured by human beings. Some pieces were inscribed with writing that matched no earthly language.

Brazel voluntarily turned in some of the wreckage to the authorities. The military took an interest in the crash, not least because stationed at Roswell was the world's only atomic bomb–capable bomber squadron, the 509th Bombardment Group. Security at the airbase was tight, and any aircraft crashing in the vicinity was something its commanders wanted to know about. Jumping the gun, a press release was put out for distribution stating that the wreckage came from none other than a flying saucer.

Despite a retraction and claims that the object was really nothing more than a weather balloon, countless conspiracy theories would arise from the flying saucer claim. Although the military said that bodies recovered from the crash site were those of "anthropomorphic test dummies" used as part of the weather balloon's experimentation setup, others claimed that they were extraterrestrials, members of the ship's crew that were killed on impact or died shortly afterward. Accounts of alien autopsies followed, along with claims that the bodies and their crashed ship were transported to Wright Patterson Air Force Base in Dayton, Ohio.

Even before the events of summer 1947, the number of flying saucer sightings reported in the United States had skyrocketed. After the Kenneth Arnold sighting and the Roswell incident, they continued to rise, and reports in other countries followed suit. With strange lights appearing more often in American skies and sightings of unusual objects, it soon became clear to all but the most hardened skeptic that *something* strange was intruding upon North American airspace. The question was ... what?

Pilots are trained observers. They know the difference between a lenticular cloud and an unidentified light or craft hurtling through the skies alongside their aircraft. As both civilian and military pilots began to encounter these oddities more frequently, the military paid lip service to the idea of investigating UFOs with programs such as Project Grudge and Project Sign. Many of the encounters between aviators and these aerial phenomena were perplexing

Major Jesse A. Marcel sorts through debris from Roswell, which the military concluded was merely parts of a weather balloon.

but not hazardous. Not all were so benign. At least one case was much darker, resulting in the loss of two American lives with no satisfactory explanation.

TRAGEDY AT KINROSS

Built by Northrop, the F-89 Scorpion jet fighter was tasked with a single purpose: to intercept and, if necessary, destroy hostile aircraft invading United States airspace. It was well equipped for its role. Powered by two jet engines, the Scorpion was capable of speeds in excess of 400 miles per hour. A single pilot flew the plane, and a back-seat radar operator served to guide him to the target, which could then be blown out of the sky with AIM-4 Falcon air-to-air missiles—when the notoriously unreliable weapon worked properly, that was.

In 1953, F-89 squadrons were part of the United States' integrated air defense network. Had the Cold War suddenly turned hot, these fighters were to have intercepted incoming Soviet bomber formations intent on devastating the American heartland. Yet on the night of November 23, something completely different was encroaching on the skies above Lake Superior. The radar contact was unidentified, and its pres-

An F-89 Scorpion on display at the Hill Aerospace Museum in Roy, Utah.

ence triggered the launch of a single F-89C from Kinross Air Force Base, Michigan. It's unlikely that the two-man crew or the controllers who dispatched them were overly worried; there's a big difference between a single radar trace and a mass influx of enemy warplanes, and the bogey in question was thought to be a Canadian transport flight.

Soon after the USAF fighter closed in with the unidentified contact, things took a turn for the strange—and deadly.

First Lieutenant Felix Moncla Jr. was piloting the Scorpion. In the back seat was Second Lieutenant Robert Wilson. Both were highly trained and experienced military aviators. Vectored in by ground-based radar, the track of the F-89C converged with that of the mysterious return it was sent to intercept ... before it suddenly disappeared from the scopes. Just a few minutes prior, radio traffic from the fighter plane had ceased. Its IFF (identification, friend or foe) transponder had also stopped transmitting responses.

Fearing a mid-air collision, the Air Force launched a search and rescue mission. No trace of the missing Scorpion was ever found, not even the smallest fragment of debris. The official U.S. military story claimed that Lieutenants Moncla and Wilson had collided with a Royal Canadian Air Force transport plane, a C-47 Dakota. This claim is problematic for several reasons, not least that the Canadian authorities denied it had happened. What reason would they have to lie about a missing aircraft? Presumably the Canadian flight crew would have had families who would speak up about the accident, if it had truly taken place.

The top speed of a C-47—a propellor-driven airplane, not a jet—is around 220 miles per hour. The radar contact that was pursued by Moncla and Wilson was moving more than twice as fast. While it's true that a C-47 *was* flying through the area that night, its pilot confirmed to researcher Gord Heath that they hadn't seen hide nor hair of the USAF interceptor, let alone collided with it. In their report on the case, researchers from *The Open Skies Project* point out that it was not unheard of for F-89Cs

No trace of the missing Scorpion was ever found, not even the smallest fragment of debris.

to crash, sometimes breaking apart in mid-air. While this is a more feasible explanation for the Kinross incident than a fictitious collision with a transport aircraft, it fails to explain how *both* contacts disappeared from radar screens, and why no debris from either was ever found.

In the years after the disappearance of Lieutenants Moncla and Wilson, stories emerged that claimed they had been abducted by a UFO. The United States was still experiencing a high volume of UFO sightings in 1953, with books and articles regularly covering the subject in print. Whether they were abducted by the occupants of whatever craft they were chasing or lost their lives in a tragic crash during their final intercept mission may never be known. Both men are still missing, presumed dead. What can be said for certain is that they gave their lives fulfilling their duty to protect the citizens of their nation, and regardless of the cause, they should be remembered as heroes.

UNDER SIEGE: THE CURIOUS CASE OF THE HOPKINSVILLE GOBLINS

In 1951, a flying saucer landed in Washington, D.C. Its occupants were met, predictably, with gunfire from the U.S. Army, which fortunately did not kick off an interplanetary war.

This was not an alien invasion but scenes from the classic science fiction movie *The Day the Earth Stood Still*, a classic cautionary tale about humankind's capacity for destruction rapidly outpacing its wisdom and, well, humanity. Extraterrestrial visitors, some of them friendly and some decidedly not, were much on the mind of the American public during the 1950s, thanks to a string of alien invasion-themed movies such as *The War of the Worlds*, *Invasion of the Body Snatchers*, *Invaders from Mars*, and *Earth vs. the Flying Saucers*. There were countless more. UFO cinema in the 1950s was much like the superhero genre of today.

What about a *real* alien invasion? One of the strangest incidents on record took place on the night of August 21, 1955, in rural Kentucky. The scene was the Sutton family farmhouse in the town of Kelly. The sun was descending toward the western horizon at 7 P.M. when a house guest standing in the backyard watched in astonishment as a metallic flying object flew above the farm, on a descent trajectory toward the ground. When it broke the story the next day, a local newspaper report would describe it as "a flying saucer."

Skeptics such as Joe Nickell and Blake Smith would later suggest that this was actually a fireball or meteor, any number of which blaze their way through our skies on a nightly basis.

It wasn't long before the presumed spacecraft's occupants made an appearance, in the form of small, silver-skinned humanoids that were somewhere between three and four feet tall. Their bulbous heads had large, swept-back ears and large eyes located at the side of the head. There was no nose, meaning that the creatures were mouth breathers, had some sort of hidden respiratory system (possibly gills), or maybe did not need to breathe at all. The creatures' physiques were a study in contrasts, with a muscular upper body but thin legs and no apparent feet, as we would recognize the appendages. Their claw-like hands were large by comparison to those of a human being, and their long, webbed fingers tapered to sharp points.

Just like actor Michael Rennie's alien character Klaatu in *The Day the Earth Stood Still*, these visitors to Earth were greeted not with open arms but by gunfire. For the next three hours, the occupants of the farmhouse—some 11 people in all—fought off their uninvited drop-ins, using shotguns and rifles. Either they were not very good shots or the creatures were bullet proof, because no bodies were later found at the site, and no liquids that might pass for bloodstains. None of the creatures had shot back, though it would later be claimed that one of them had made a grab for the head of one of the family members.

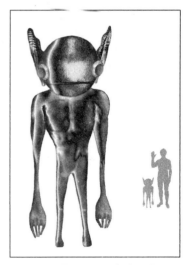

The adult eyewitnesses estimated the number of intruders at 12 to 15, though it must have been difficult to tell in the dark. The creatures popped up, were shot at, and disappeared again. At around 11 P.M., the family decided to make a run for it. There were enough cars on the property to get them all to the closest police station in Hopkinsville, where officers working the night shift listened to their story in disbelief. Still, the family, adults and children alike, were absolutely terrified by the ordeal they had just endured. No matter what the cause actually was, the fact was that multiple shots had been fired over at the Sutton farm, and officers had a duty to investigate. A cadre of law enforcement officers was quickly assembled and drove out to the farm. Who knows what they were expecting to find, but all was still and quiet when they ar-

An artist's depiction of what the Hopkinsville Goblin might have looked like, based on descriptions from witnesses.

rived. Spent cartridges lay everywhere, proving that the besieged family had definitely been shooting at *something* … but of that something, there was no sign. Nor was there any evidence of any kind of craft having landed on the property.

Few law enforcement agencies have a protocol for investigating flying saucer landings, not even at the height of the flying saucer flap of the 1950s. After searching the scene and making sure that nobody had been hurt, the responding police officers withdrew. However, the terrorized family's ordeal was not over. Shortly after they retired to bed in the early hours of the morning, the creatures returned. They were seen standing outside the windows of the farmhouse, peering inside. Apparently, the one-sided firefight and the ensuing visit from the authorities had failed to scare them off.

> The officers who investigated the scene found no evidence of alcohol having been consumed at the farmhouse, nor did the terrified residents seem intoxicated when they ran into the police station to breathlessly beg for help.

This leaves the question: what happened on the Sutton farm that hot summer night in 1955? It is tempting—and lazy—to simply dismiss it out of hand as having been drunken shenanigans. The officers who investigated the scene found no evidence of alcohol having been consumed at the farmhouse, nor did the terrified residents seem intoxicated when they ran into the police station to breathlessly beg for help. Claims to the contrary are out there, but they have been roundly debunked by researcher Blake Smith, co-host of the *Monster Talk* podcast. Irked by the number of myths that have sprung up surrounding the Hopkinsville case, Smith has gone out of his way to dispel them. There is no evidence to suggest that any member of the family was intoxicated. Neither, contrary to popular belief, was this incident the source of the phrase "little green men" entering common usage.

Of course, the family could just have been making it all up—but why? Admittedly, the family made a little money in the aftermath, letting the curious visit and poke around the farm. Yet they didn't appear to have been seeking fame or notoriety (though that would come shortly afterward when the story hit the national news). It could perhaps have been a shared delusion, but that explanation seems like something of a stretch. Not many shared delusions seem so real to those who experience them that multiple people feel compelled to try to shoot them dead.

The creatures are now immortalized in the history books as "the Hopkinsville goblins" or "aliens," but there may be a more down-to-earth explanation: owls. Several researchers, particularly skeptic Joe Nickell, have pointed out the resemblance between the reported creatures and great horned owls, not least the grayish color and swept-back appearance of their heads. While the two sets of appearances do indeed match up, it seems strange that not a single owl, living or dead, was found at the farm later that night during the police search.

Almost 70 years have passed since the bizarre events of that night. The people of Kelly commemorate the siege each year with an extraterrestrial-themed festival. Whether the creatures that sparked the kerfuffle were owls, aliens, or something entirely different remains one of the most enduring mysteries of American folklore.

> Whether the creatures that sparked the kerfuffle were owls, aliens, or something entirely different remains one of the most enduring mysteries of American folklore.

As if aerial and terrestrial encounters with potentially alien intelligences weren't scary enough, the 1960s ushered in the era of a new and even more alarming phenomenon: abduction. It remains one of the most controversial aspects of the UAP/UFO quagmire. For skeptics, there's not a shred of evidence to support the mountain of claimants who say they have been taken aboard extraterrestrial spacecraft, either voluntarily or against their will. For believers, their conviction that aliens are present in our skies and oceans, and that the creatures like nothing better than to swoop in and snatch up human beings and animals for their own purposes, is unshakable. The debate has raged for decades and dates back to the 1950s and 1960s. It's fair to say that some abduction experiences are far more disturbing than others.

TAKEN: THE ABDUCTION OF BETTY AND BARNEY HILL

On the night of September 19, 1961, a married couple named Betty and Barney Hill were driving on a lonely New Hampshire road. The Hills were far away from city lights and urban population centers when they realized that they were being followed—not by another car but by a strange light that jinked and dipped through the skies above them. Based on its pattern of movement, this was clearly no aircraft or shooting star. Barney pulled to the side of the road, and the strange light came straight at them.

Once it had come close enough, the Hills realized that the mysterious light was in fact some sort of flying craft controlled by a team of small humanoid figures. The couple seemed powerless to return to their car and drive away. What happened next would become a matter of intense debate and remains so to this day. Betty and Barney experienced a period of missing time that was about three hours long. It was as if a chunk of their respective memories had been surgically cut out of their minds.

The Hills regained consciousness miles away from the site of their encounter, some 90 minutes before sunrise. Both knew that they should have reached home hours before. Betty's dress had somehow gotten ripped. Neither had any idea what had taken place during that window of missing time and had forgotten all about the flying craft's inhabitants … until the Hills allowed themselves to be placed in a state of hypnosis, when an astonishing—and horrific—scenario emerged.

The author poses with a historic plaque at the site of one of history's most famous UFO abduction cases.

The couple relived the experience of being abducted by the short humanoid entities that were the flying vessel's crew. Once on board, Betty and Barney recalled being subjected to medical assessments that were both physically and emotionally traumatizing. These evaluations took place in a chamber that was reminiscent of an operating suite and included the Hills being poked with sharp needles and having tissue samples harvested from various locations on their bodies.

Betty and Barney became famous on the strength of their seeming encounter with extraterrestrial life forms, yet not everybody believed their story. While it was almost universally admitted that the Hills seemed like honest and upstanding citizens, things get tricky when the human mind is hypnotized. Unless questions are asked in a very specific and unbiased way, it is easy for an interviewer to plant or nourish false ideas and memories while their subject is in such a vulnerable state. It is impossible to state with any certainty whether the Hills' recollections of being taken aboard an alien ship were genuine memories—events that objectively happened, were obscured, and then were recovered under hypnosis—or fake memories, constructed partly in response to the questions put to them while they were in an impressionable state.

Experts who questioned Betty and Barney afterward were impressed with their honesty. The couple went on to become prominent speakers in the field of UFOlogy. Barney died in 1969 at the age of 49. Betty claimed further extraterrestrial contacts in the years after her husband's death, some of which she depicted in a book titled *A Common Sense Approach to UFOs*. Unfortunately, the later UFO sightings she described were less than convincing and cost her much credibility.

Betty Hill lived to the age of 85, passing away in 2004.

TERROR IN THE WOODS:
THE TRAVIS WALTON ABDUCTION

The Hills were far from the first people to claim a close encounter with some form of extraterrestrial life. There was no shortage of individuals who said they were in contact with beings from Venus, Mars, and other worlds. One such example was California resident George Adamski, who claimed in the 1950s to have conversed with beings from Venus and produced a photographic trove of what he purported to have been their spaceships. The Venusians allowed Adamski to come aboard their craft and experience spaceflight, which provided him with plenty of material to write books about the subject. While many mocked his photos and wild stories, Adamski did not lack for supporters.

The passage of time was not kind to George Adamski and his claims. Probes sent to Venus not only failed to uncover any signs of life, let alone the thriving civilization Adamski insisted was there, but found the conditions to be completely incompatible with the sort of humanoid life that he reportedly encountered. This lack of extraterrestrial life held true for the rest of the solar system as well, in direct opposition to his claims. Until the day he died, George Adamski nevertheless insisted that he had told the absolute truth about Earth's cosmic neighborhood teeming with alien life and the fleets of spacecraft that carried it.

Author and ufologist George Adamski gained fame in the 1950s for his books claiming to have traveled on several occasions with Nordic-looking aliens.

One key difference between Adamski's story and that of Betty and Barney Hill was the matter of consent. He had *agreed* to be a contactee. If the Hills' story was accurate, they had been given no choice in the matter. They were captured, not invited, and stripped of their most basic rights to bodily autonomy. No matter how benevolent some of the abduction stories that emerged in the wake of the Hills' experience seemed to be, many had an element of kidnap and non-consensual medical procedures that is impossible to ignore.

Take the case of Travis Walton. Many have heard of Mr. Walton through the Hollywood adaptation of his abduction incident, the 1993 movie *Fire in the Sky*.

On November 5, 1975, a logging crew working in the Apache-Sitgreaves National Park near the town of Snowflake, Arizona, became the center of a furor after they encountered something otherworldly. The seven-strong crew was driving through the woods when they saw a bright light in the night sky. Reminiscent of the Betty and Barney Hill case, the loggers encountered a glowing flying disk.

One of their number, 22-year-old Travis Walton, got out of the pickup truck, seemingly drawn toward the hovering craft. A beam of energy lanced out, hitting him in the chest and blasting him backward. Panicking, the remaining six men sped away in the truck. After driving a short distance, they were overcome with remorse at having left Travis behind. Gathering up their courage, the crew drove back to the site of the encounter. The craft was gone. There was no sign whatsoever of Walton.

What followed were some very difficult conversations with law enforcement. Understandably, the sheriff's deputies and detectives who interviewed them weren't buying the crew's outlandish story. The more likely explanation seemed to be that Travis had been killed and disposed of by his own crew. Yet things didn't add up. The loggers were tough men and were clearly terrified by whatever it was had happened out in the forest. After a huge manhunt, there was still no body. Equally interesting was the fact that there had previously been UFO sightings in the region.

Then, five days after his disappearance, Walton phoned home … from a telephone booth in Heber, Arizona. Medical testing yielded no answers. As with the Hills, there was a period of missing time, but in this case, the duration was not hours but *days*. Walton also agreed to be placed under hypnosis and regressed in an attempt to learn what had happened to him. If the results of the regression session were to be believed, Walton had been subjected to medical assessment by short, non-human creatures aboard a flying craft, and after interacting with beings aboard the ship, he was then returned, dazed and confused, to Earth.

Travis Walton is shown here at an International UFO Congress conference in 2019.

As soon as Travis Walton returned, a controversy blew up that remains unresolved almost 50 years later. He was roundly accused of faking the entire incident himself or engaging in a conspiracy to do so in conjunction with some or all members of his logging crew. The motive ascribed for this was financial gain, with Walton selling his story and penning a book, *The Walton Experience*, in 1978. Yet he also has staunch defenders, some of whom claim that what has come to be known as the Travis Walton Incident represents one of the most compelling cases of alien abduction to go on record.

THE INTIMIDATION GAME: MEN IN BLACK

The year 1997 saw the release of *Men in Black*, a Hollywood blockbuster starring Will Smith and Tommy Lee Jones as a pair of agents working for a mysterious organization with the remit of "protecting the Earth from the scum of the universe." Although the movie version of the Men in Black, or MIBs, are figures of fun, their real-world counterparts are more like figures of fear. They first appeared on the scene in the late 1940s, with an increasing number of encounters being reported from the 1950s onward.

MIBs represented themselves as delegates of U.S. law enforcement or intelligence agencies—or of organizations so secretive that the public was never made aware of their existence. Driving shiny black cars, MIBs tended to turn up shortly after an encounter with a UFO. Their apparent objective was to cajole, threaten, or intimidate eyewitnesses into keeping

> More bizarre still were those instances in which the MIBs didn't speak at all, instead communicating with a form of telepathy, "beaming" their thoughts directly into the mind of the witness.

quiet about what they had seen. The message was always clear: shut your mouth, or you and your loved ones might end up hurt—or worse.

The term "Men in Black" was coined because of the formal black suits, shoes, and sometimes hats that they wore. Often, the MIBs wore sunglasses. As time went on, reports of Women in Black also emerged. Whether male or female, the MIBs always seemed slightly "off" to those who encountered them. Their speech patterns seemed scripted and artificial, almost as if they were actors playing a role or speaking a language that wasn't natural for them. In certain cases, the MIBs sounded more like automatons than human beings, speaking in a drab, monotone manner that was completely devoid of inflection and emphasis. More bizarre still were those instances in which the MIBs didn't speak at all, instead communicating with a form of telepathy, "beaming" their thoughts directly into the mind of the witness.

Although governmental interest in investigating the UFO phenomenon soon waned—or so the government claimed—there was no shortage of people researching on their own time. If they poked their noses too deeply into UFO cases, the MIBs would come calling. Whenever those who had a run-in with the Men in Black would check on their credentials, contacting the agencies the MIBs claimed to represent, their inquiries were met with stonewalling or outright denial.

Far from being relegated to the golden age of UFO encounters, the MIBs continue to surface in the twenty-first century. They have been seen by none other than *Ghostbusters* star and *Saturday Night Live* alumnus Dan Aykroyd, who claims he was under observation by a Man in Black—complete with the classic all-black car—in 2002 when Aykroyd was involved with a documentary series on UFOs. Both the MIB and his vehicle disappeared in a split second. Shortly afterward, the plug was pulled on Aykroyd's documentary, without any explanation.

One can only wonder what might have become of the comedy legend if he had continued to push the issue, potentially falling afoul of the MIBs and their mysterious agenda.

SHIFTING SHAPES

HUNGRY LIKE THE WOLF

Throughout human history, there have been stories of men and women who possessed the ability to change into the form of an animal. By far the most common beast with which these special humans were said to have mingled was the wolf.

Peering down on humanity from the skies above for the entirety of our existence, the moon has long held a position of power for those of a mystical persuasion. Since time immemorial, humankind has believed that the appearance of the full moon heralded the arrival of the lycanthrope, also known as the werewolf.

Werewolves were a convenient explanation for those exhibiting what we would today recognize simply as homicidal behavior. Take the case of Gilles Garnier, who lived in sixteenth-century France. The antisocial and hermetical Garnier was blamed for the disappearances and savage killings of children from the nearby community of Dole. Upon questioning by the authorities, Garnier confessed to being a werewolf and to tearing apart the missing children to feast upon their bodies. He became a lycanthrope after making a deal with the devil, who furnished him with a magical ointment to slather on his skin to cause his transformation from man to wolf.

Believing that the surest way to kill a werewolf was by incineration, the authorities had Garnier burned at the stake. History remembers him today as the Werewolf of Dole. Assuming that Garnier truly was guilty of the child murders—something that was never definitively proven—why did he confess? Some scholars believe that he was beaten and tortured into confessing. Others have posited the possibility that he was mentally ill. Whatever was the truth, it was far more palatable for the public and the authorities to believe that a ravening werewolf was to blame for abducting and murdering their children than to consider the possibility that the evil deeds were carried out by a human being who looked just like they did.

Psychologically speaking, they took comfort when their monsters actually *looked* monstrous.

Making bargains with the devil was a common way of gaining werewolf powers in sixteenth-century Europe. A German farmer named Peter Stump (or Stubbe, Stumpp, Stumpf, or other variations, depending on the source) held a reign of terror that included the murder and cannibalization of 13 children, three adults, and an unknown number of animals. Upon closing the deal, the devil had furnished him with a magic wolfskin belt that turned him into a werewolf with superhuman strength whenever he put the garment on.

In the past, centuries ago, deranged homicidal behavior was at times explained away by saying the killer was a cursed werewolf. This helped people cope better with the idea that a human being could be so insanely violent.

Stump's 1589 torture and trial was a public scandal, not least because in addition to carrying out the savage killings, the accused man also claimed to have engaged in sexual congress with a demoness and with his own children. Of particular horror was the ripping of two fetuses from the wombs of their mothers. One of Stump's murder victims was his own son. Because of the deeply grotesque and therefore, to some, titillating nature of the case, accounts of it were printed up and distributed widely for money in the same way that newspapers are today. This was the sixteenth-century equivalent of exploitative, trash "journalism," and it sold like hotcakes. It's unclear how much of the little primary source material that survives was exaggerated to attract a bloodthirsty readership.

After butchering and eating his way through this mass of humanity and livestock,

Stump was finally captured and brought to trial. As was the case with Gilles Garnier, the man who was now given the nickname "Werewolf of "Bedburg" promptly confessed to the slew of killings. Stump was then tied to a wheel, his arms and legs were fractured, and his flesh was repeatedly burned and pinched with scorching hot pincers, before the executioner finally put an end to matters by cutting off his head. His broken body was then burned to ashes to prevent the werewolf from returning to life and exacting bloody revenge. For good measure, Stump's daughter and his mistress were also executed, just in case they were tainted by the pact he had supposedly made with dark powers.

The French and German people certainly believed that Garnier and Stump were, quite literally, werewolves. Their respective confessions, which were most likely extracted by intimidation and torture, fit within the people's frame of reference at the time. Such beliefs were particularly strong in rural areas, where it could be disturbingly easy to find oneself put on trial for the crime of being a werewolf and, if convicted, executed.

ON THE PROWL: THE BEAST OF BRAY ROAD

Nearly 500 years after the European werewolf mania, we have learned that there are no such things as lycanthropes. Haven't we?

Perhaps not, when certain bizarre events that have taken place in the vicinity of Elkhorn, Wisconsin, are taken into account. Elkhorn is a rural city that around 10,000 people call home. For almost 50 years, stories have circulated regarding a huge wolf-like creature that has become known as the Beast of Bray Road. They have continued into the 2020s.

The late journalist and author Linda Godfrey spent years researching the case. She was an acknowledged expert in the lore of not just the Beast of Bray Road but also similar encounters from further afield. (Wisconsin and the rest of the American Midwest seems to have more than its fair share of wolfish cryptids.) She spent decades tracking sighting after sighting of the predatory creature, which has confronted human eyewitnesses and allegedly slaughtered livestock, tearing them apart with its jaws and claws. Many of those who see it describe the beast as large and wolf-like, moving quickly and nimbly from cover to cover. The creature seems to walk on two legs and run on four.

Particularly notable are the orange-reddish eyes, which can appear six or seven feet above the ground. This implies that whatever it is that the Wisconsinites are seeing, it must be large—either human-sized or

Elkhorn is a modest town of about 10,000 human residents in southern Wisconsin.

an animal standing on its hind legs. This characteristic of the creature often being seen on two legs rather than four has been reported by multiple individuals and sets it apart from typical wolf behavior—though it can happen in the animal kingdom. Moving on hind legs is a behavior commonly associated, for example, with bears.

Paw prints that have been spotted at the scene of some sightings are of the canid variety—the sort of tracks that would be made by dogs, jackals, foxes, or wolves. The prints are large enough and spaced a sufficient distance apart that the creature that made them must have an abnormally long stride.

Why do so many sightings occur in the vicinity of Bray Road? Perhaps it is because much of the land bordering the road is covered with crops and woodland, ideal terrain in which a predator could stalk its prey.

Skeptics have either dismissed the existence of the Beast of Bray Road entirely or suggest that many of the sightings could simply be of an actual wolf. Yet the sheer volume of testimony from locals and visitors alike suggests that *something* bizarre prowls the fields and woods in the vicinity of Elkhorn. Whatever that something is, I'm not sure I'd like to come face to face with it on a pitch-black night … or under the light of a full moon.

AN EVIL MAGIC: THE SKINWALKER

The Navajo people have a tradition of spirituality stretching back countless generations. While primarily positive and light, that tradition has its dark side … and there can be few things darker than the Skinwalker. According to legend, Skinwalkers are human beings with the capacity to shapeshift into ferocious otherworldly creatures. They are commonly believed to have been witches or shamans who took a dark path in pursuit of power and forbidden knowledge that would give them an advantage over their rivals. Like all dark power, this came at a price: the would-be Skinwalker was required to murder a loved one or family member as a form of "paying their dues."

The form into which Skinwalkers can transform themselves varies but is usually predatory in nature. Commonly resembling a human hybrid with a wolf, coyote, or jackal, the shifted Skinwalker is said to be a creature with gleaming fangs and razor-sharp claws. Sometimes, other beastly forms are taken, such as a stag with huge antlers but still possessing claws. They can outrun any human being and have strength far beyond that of even the most highly trained adult. Some are even said to have powers of mind-control over potential victims. No wonder they are considered to be so fearsome.

In some of the Navajo oral traditions, Skinwalkers are all but immune to ordinary blades and even bullets. That isn't to say a Skinwalker cannot be killed, although doing so takes significantly more effort (and luck) than killing a human being would. Lore holds that Skinwalkers are more vulnerable in their human form than in their animal form. Weapons coated in ash or silver are said to be most effective.

A Skinwalker is an evil magical creature who can take a beastial form such as a wolf, deer, or coyote. They gain their transformational powers through the murder of a loved one.

Once they are back in human form, the Skinwalker is incapable of hiding their true nature from others. In addition to sensing something obviously "off" about them, radiating an aura of danger and evil, those who have encountered Skinwalkers say that there is a feral, animalistic quality to the eyes of a Skinwalker—eyes that sometimes glow with an ethereal light.

Skinwalkers are said to be most prominent in states such as Arizona, Utah, and New Mexico, though they have been reported in other places as well. You might run into one while out hiking or camping in the wilderness or traveling in the vicinity of a reservation.

While researching my series of books on the paranormal aspects of medicine and healthcare, I interviewed Richelle (not her real name), a wildland firefighter who reported her own encounter with what may have been a Skinwalker. As a Comanche herself, Richelle fit in comfortably with the wildland crew, who all shared a similar heritage. One of the firefighters was a young man nicknamed Wolf Man, for reasons that soon became apparent.

The crew were dropped off by vehicle and then hiked in toward their assigned place on what turned out to be a huge, sprawling fire incident. Passing through some woods, they began to hear the distinctive beat of tribal drums coming from all around them in the trees. It would be disconcerting at the best of times, but it became even more so when Richelle checked and found that there was nobody out there to account for the source of the drumming. Stranger still was the ritualistic chanting that followed.

A little freaked out by the experience, Richelle did her best to shrug it off. She and the crew worked hard on the fire all day, then retired to their camp at night to rest. Lying in her tent and trying to drift off to sleep, she heard movement. Peeking outside, Richelle saw a huge wolf prowling through the camp. As she watched in stunned silence, it slunk away into the shadows.

> **Peeking outside, Richelle saw a huge wolf prowling through the camp. As she watched in stunned silence, it slunk away into the shadows.**

Wolf Man took a lot of good-natured ribbing from the crew the next morning—jokes about what a long and exhausting night it had been. It was only when Richelle heard the same sounds outside her tent that second night that she understood what they meant—because this time, it was Wolf Man she saw lurking in the darkness before finally vanishing into the woods at the edge of the camp. The path he took was identical to the one followed by his namesake the night before.

As I listened to her story, I could see that both fear and deep respect were present in the veteran firefighter. This was somebody who had gone into burning buildings time and again. She didn't scare easily, but she was definitely scared telling me this story.

"I don't want to give you any more details," Richelle apologized as we wrapped up our interview. "Wolf Man is real, and he is out there. If I say too much, you or I might wake up one night to find that wolf standing in our own backyard—and who knows what would happen then?"

SKINWALKER RANCH

Now we move on from Skinwalkers to a place named after them—the infamous Skinwalker Ranch. Although the plethora of strange goings-on at this remote former homestead in Utah's Uinta Basin have been public knowledge for years, the ranch itself only generated mass interest with the debut of the History Channel's hit TV show *The Secret of Skinwalker Ranch*.

Claims of a wide range of strange activities taking place at Skinwalker Ranch go back decades. As any paranormal investigator worth their salt will attest, when delving into claims of mysterious occurrences at a given location, one of the first orders of business is to study the history of the land itself. Like most of Utah, the land Skinwalker Ranch sits upon once rightly belonged to the indigenous people of North America, specifically the Ute tribe.

Skinwalkers have long been said to prowl the more desolate parts of the Uinta Basin, and while the residents of Salt Lake City and other major population centers might laugh at stories of Skinwalkers roaming the mesa at night, for those who lead a more solitary existence in the wilderness, the existence of shapeshifters is taken as a matter of the utmost seriousness.

The Sherman family lived at Skinwalker Ranch during the 1990s, and it was during their residency that many of the weird events took place. In 1996, *Deseret News* reporter Zack van Eyck broached the subject of UFOs at Skinwalker Ranch in an article titled "Frequent Fliers?" Tellingly, the nickname of the ranch was not mentioned.

The Uinta Basin had been a UFO hot spot ever since the 1950s, when flying saucers hit the mainstream. Skinwalker Ranch appeared to be exceptionally active, however. Van Eyck interviewed Terry and Gwen Sherman, who had seen UFOs in the skies above the ranch for the past year. One was described as "a huge ship the size of several football fields." The entire Sherman family reported witnessing incredible sights, such as energy portals opening in midair and lights zipping past them several feet above the ground—including one that pursued Gwen as she was driving. (Shades of the Betty and Barney Hill abduction case, which is covered elsewhere in this book.)

The high strangeness taking place at Skinwalker Ranch wasn't restricted to aerial phenomena. Poltergeist activity, disembodied voices, and phantom sounds were also thrown into the increasingly spooky mix—as were cattle mutilations, which accompanied so many UFO sightings throughout the twentieth century and still continue today (albeit less frequently). The portals lead one to consider whether the UFOs were of an interdimensional, rather than interplanetary, nature.

The entrance to Skinwalker Ranch near Ballard, Utah, is unassuming enough, but the 500-acre ranch is a mecca for UFO and paranormal activity.

Whichever was the case, when the ranch was put up for sale, it was snapped up by entrepreneur Robert Bigelow, who had a passion for both civil aviation and UFOs. It was an opportunity too good to pass up, and the businessman wasted no time in converting the ranch into a nonstop, year-round scientific research center, with the intent of getting to the bottom of the outlandish phenomena said to be taking place there. Over the course of their years-long investigation, Bigelow and his team found whatever it was that manifested at Skinwalker Ranch to be maddeningly elusive when it came to capturing solid evidence on film.

After Bigelow decided it was time to move on, another highly successful businessman took ownership of the ranch in 2016: Utah native and real estate empire builder Brandon Fugal, a man who has taken the investigative baton from Bigelow and run with it. The research team put in place under Fugal's auspices runs a network of high-tech monitoring equipment working to gather as much data as possible concerning the anomalies reported at Skinwalker Ranch. Researchers have also devised and constructed a panoply of scientific experiments, some of which have formed the basis of episodes of *The Secret of Skinwalker Ranch*.

Virtually all of Fugal's staff members have their own accounts of odd occurrences during their tenure at Skinwalker, ranging from puzzling electronic glitches to full-blown medical emergencies (one member of the team was sent to the emergency department after falling victim to a seemingly inexplicable illness). Strange objects are still being seen in the sky some 30 years after the Shermans left.

Virtually all of Fugal's staff members have their own accounts of odd occurrences during their tenure at Skinwalker, ranging from puzzling electronic glitches to full-blown medical emergencies....

By partnering with a TV production, Brandon Fugal has brought a welcome tide of transparency to the table; yet five seasons into their televised exploration into the mysterious property, it seems that more questions are being raised than answered. Potential explanations have ranged from the land supposedly being cursed (for which there's no firm evidence), to the ranch being an interdimensional nexus of some kind, to hauntings, witchcraft, and the ever-popular catch-all of "aliens."

In October of 2023, Fugal told *Deseret News* reporter Meg Walter that "whatever mechanism is at work appears to amplify consciousness and even intent." If that truly is the case, then potential visitors to the difficult-to-access location should beware. One never quite knows how Skinwalker Ranch will react to newcomers.

THE GOATMAN COMETH

On first hearing the name of Goatman, it seems like an elevator pitch for the lamest superhero ever: a creature that's part man, part goat, and lurks in the woods and scares the living daylights out of those who encounter it. For those residents of Denton, Texas, who *don't* scoff at the stories, it's considered wise to avoid the Old Alton Bridge after nightfall. Indeed, the historic iron truss bridge, which dates back to 1884, is known to all and sundry as Goatman's Bridge. It was built to span Hickory Creek, which separated the town of Denton and the former village of Alton. Alton was a ghost town by 1860, but Denton continued to grow and thrive. Even though there were no living souls left in what had once been Alton, there was still a need for locals to go back and forth across the creek on a regular basis.

The bridge was restricted to foot traffic in 2001; vehicles could now drive across a newer and safer span nearby. Yet Goatman's Bridge remained a popular destination for hikers, outdoor enthusiasts, and those with a passion for the paranormal. The area is steeped in legend and folklore, none of which is particularly pleasant. There are claims of occult rituals involving animal sacrifices taking place in the woods around the bridge. A myriad of ghost stories is also attached to the area, but none is as disturbing as that of the Goatman.

Built in 1884, the Old Alton Bridge near Denton, Texas, is on the National Register of Historic Places and continued to serve traffic until 2001.

According to local lore, during the 1930s, Ku Klux Klan members lynched an African American goat farmer named Oscar Washburn at the Old Alton Bridge. Yet somehow, after the lynching, the noose was empty. There was no sign of Washburn's body. Presumably spooked by the sudden disappearance of their victim, the mob of Klansmen stormed the dead man's farm, set fire to the place, and murdered his family. Washburn had been nicknamed "the Goatman" because of the superior dairy products he sold. Could this be why a monstrous human/goat hybrid has been sighted in the vicinity of the bridge?

It's a tale suitable for spawning a horror movie, which seems appropriate because there's no Oscar Washburn to be found in the local records, nor any evidence of his murder, that of his family, or a farm having been burned to the ground. Many towns have stories like these, usually passed down by children and teenagers from one generation to the next. Drive out to Goatman's Bridge at midnight, the stories say, flash your lights or rap three times on the iron structure, and you'll see the glowing red eyes of the Goatman glaring back at you out of the darkness.

Some believe that occult rituals have conjured up a demonic entity, suggesting a reason for the creature having a goat-like appearance. It may also be a case of the Goatman legend having been repeated so many times that it has simply taken on a life of its own, reinforced by scary stories and the power of fear multiplying from one year to the next. In January 2017, Goatman's Bridge was featured on an episode of the TV show *Ghost Adventures*. It quickly became a fan favorite. According to cast member Jay Wasley, the paranormal activity they experienced at the bridge was so intense that it contributed to the breakup of his marriage. Wasley's wife, *Ghost Adventures'* still photographer Ashley Richardson, was deeply affected in the woods near the bridge. The couple would ultimately divorce.

Denton, Texas, isn't the only place said to be stalked by a Goatman. Prince George's County, Maryland, has its own version of the tale—actually, several different variants. The Old Line State's Goatman has been blamed for killing animals and frightening the unsuspecting few who caught glimpses of it in the darkness ... which only encouraged youths to drive out looking for the creature at night. Tales of the Goatman go back decades, yet none of the origin stories appears to hold any water. In some, he's an axe-carrying hermit. In others, he's the archetypal mad scientist. Yet another story has the Goatman being a genetic lab experiment that escaped and ran amok in the woods.

Animal cries and howls coming from the woods at night are attributed to the Goatman of Prince George's County. Researcher and author Mark Opsasnick talked to eyewitnesses who claimed to have seen Goatman and concluded in an October 2008 interview with *Washington Post* reporter Lori Aratani that "the people I interviewed actually believed they saw Bigfoot in Maryland, or the Goatman in Prince George's County. Now, what they actually saw, I don't know."

Other states have their own Goatman stories. Some have been ex- plained away, such as the Goatman spotted on the side of a peak in Ogden, Utah, that sparked a brief media circus until the real explanation came to light: a hunter was approaching a herd of goats on the moun- tainside, testing out a homemade goat suit. Yet not all sightings can be debunked so easily, and any reader who would care to find out for them- selves may consider traveling out to the Old Alton Bridge after dark or to Fletchertown Road in Prince George's County, to spend some time peering into the darkness. Who knows what might be looking back?

LOST SOULS AND ANGRY SPIRITS

The arrival of the automobile at the turn of the twentieth century ushered in a new era of freedom and mobility for the masses. As with any world-changing innovation, however, the motor car brought with it a darker side—a new way for people to die or be seriously injured. In 1913, 4,200 Americans died in automobile crashes. Fast-forward to 2021, and that number jumped to 46,980. Around the world, thousands of drivers, passengers, and pedestrians have been killed in collisions. Predictably, the roads and highways have more than their fair share of ghost stories. In this section we'll delve into some of the more noteworthy cases.

THE WANDERING WOMAN AND OTHER PHANTOMS OF BLUE BELL HILL

One of the most tragic highway hauntings comes from Britain. The A229 is one of the busier roads in Kent and has a number of steep hills with which drivers must contend. On the night of November 19, 1965, a car containing four members of a bridal party was involved in a high-speed collision on one of them—the now-infamous Blue Bell Hill. Australian bride-to-be Suzanne Browne was celebrating her upcoming marriage to her sweetheart, a photographer who served in the Royal Air Force. She would not survive to be wed on the following day; she died later after surgery. Neither would two of her friends, one of whom was killed at the scene, while the other also died of injuries sustained in the collision. The fourth woman survived, albeit with injuries.

The story should have ended there. Instead, the fatality crash was just the beginning. In the years that followed, witnesses began coming forward to report terrifying nocturnal encounters with ghosts on Blue Bell Hill.

In the summer of 1974, a man named Maurice Goodenough made a police report stating that he had struck a girl of about ten years of age while driving on Blue Bell Hill. Notably, Mr. Goodenough distinctly recalled the jarring force of impact, suggesting that he had hit something all too real and solid. He got out of the car and wrapped the wounded child in a blanket.

Goodenough drove off to fetch the police. When he returned, the blanket was still where he had left it. The girl was gone. Officers searched the surrounding area and found nothing. A public appeal made by the police turned up no reports of a missing child. The incident remained a mystery, though it soon became a part of Blue Bell Hill's extensive ghost lore. The hill developed a reputation for being haunted, and despite the fact that the strange encounter did not seem to relate to the 1965 car crash, it became commonly accepted that the little girl had been a ghost.

Goodenough drove off to fetch the police. When he returned, the blanket was still where he had left it. The girl was gone.

One of the more disturbing encounters happened in the 1990s to a driver named Ian Sharpe. It involved a woman who jumped out in front of the unsuspecting driver's vehicle and disappeared underneath it, as though she had been run over. The driver then stopped, understandably horrified at the prospect of having killed somebody, only to find no trace of a body on the road or anywhere nearby. Nor was there any damage to the bodywork of the car, which would not have been the case if he had collided with a living human being.

Although the phantom of Blue Bell Hill is widely known as "the Ghost Bride," we must bear in mind that Suzanne Browne did not die on the hill—one of her companions did. Reflecting this, some accounts name the deceased bridesmaid as the Blue Bell Hill ghost—or one of them. Stories of phantom hitchhikers have also sprung up, muddying the waters even further.

Not every ghost haunts the scene of its death. It is entirely possible that the physically and emotionally traumatic events of November 19, 1965, were so severe that echoes of them could potentially be felt for decades afterward.

They still resonate today. On February 1, 2019, heavy snow caused pandemonium on the road at Blue Bell Hill. Traffic was gridlocked due to the appalling weather conditions. Stuck in long traffic jams, motorists soon grew frustrated. Some reached the point where they pulled to the side of the road, which had become a sheet of solid ice, abandoned their vehicles, and walked home. Others, stuck in their vehicles with nothing else to do, pulled out their phones and took to social media.

One driver posted a photograph that contained a strange anomaly—what appeared to be a dark figure standing on the median separating the two stretches of road. The image was grainy and pixelated. Predictably, opinions on social media were polarized, with some believing it to be the ghost of Blue Bell Hill, and others suggesting it was more likely the back of a signpost, eerily lit between the swirling snow and headlights of passing vehicles.

Blue Bell Hill is an unremarkable rise in Aylesford, Kent, England, yet for such an unimpressive place it seems to be a favorite hangout for ghosts!

DARK SPIRITS: MONSTERS, DEMONS, AND DEVILS

In his own extensive study of the case (inarguably the most balanced and thorough currently written), *The Ghosts of Blue Bell Hill & Other Road Ghosts*, researcher and author Sean Tudor notes that there have been many car crashes on Blue Bell Hill, a number of them resulting in deaths. Assuming that the eyewitness reports are genuine, rather than mistakes or hoaxes, we should not jump to the conclusion that ghostly encounters bear any relation to the events of November 19, 1965.

Yet due largely to countless media articles and news segments, 60 years after the tragic crash that claimed the lives of Suzanne Browne and her friends, the tale of their Blue Bell Hill haunting continues to circulate. If you should find yourself driving on the A229 bound for Maidstone or Chatham, take it slowly as you approach Blue Bell Hill. Offer up a prayer for those who lost their lives, if it suits your belief system to do so—and keep a watchful eye out for ghosts.

RESURRECTION MARY: THE QUEEN OF GHOSTLY HITCHHIKERS

The hitchhiking phantom seems to occur in so many cases that it has long since become a trope. The ultimate account of a ghostly woman haunting the scene of her fatal road accident comes to us from the opposite side of the Atlantic from Blue Bell Hill, in a case that straddles the border between fact and folklore: it's the story of Resurrection Mary. It's a tale shrouded in mystery and contradiction. An excellent attempt at cutting to the core truth of it all has been made by researcher and author Troy Taylor in his book *Resurrection Mary: The History & Hauntings of Chicago's Archer Avenue*. Within its pages, Taylor makes a strong case for the haunting being a genuine one.

Mary died in a hit-and-run accident right there on Archer Avenue, her killer never identified—or so the stories claim.

Resurrection Mary's story dates to the 1930s and a falling out between the young lady and her date during a night out at a Chicago ballroom. This building, named the Oh Henry at the time but later renamed the Willowbrook Ballroom, was located on Archer Avenue; it sadly burned to the ground in 2016. An irreplaceable slice of Chicago history was lost with it.

Mary died in a hit-and-run accident right there on Archer Avenue, her killer never identified—or so the stories claim. It's a shade under four miles from the Willowbrook to Resurrection Cemetery, where Mary's body was said to be buried.

Beginning in 1934 and continuing for many years after her death, motorists traveling along Archer Avenue on the stretch of road between the ballroom and the cemetery encountered a beautiful blond woman dressed in a flowing ball gown, trying to hitch a ride. (Taylor points out that some sightings involved a woman with darker hair.) No matter how inclement the weather, her mode of clothing never varied. A flesh-and-blood woman would have contracted hypothermia on some of those winter nights. In a handful of terrifying cases, she was seen either walking or running out into the road, almost as though she was deliberately trying to get hit by one of the passing cars.

Not all of the encounters with Mary took place at the side of the road. Some drivers met her in social establishments such as dance halls and nightclubs and offered her a ride home after hours. At times, she requested that they pull over to the side of the road, only to exit the car and run toward the gates of Resurrection Cemetery and vanish into the night—sometimes, before their very eyes. On other occasions, the phantom was sitting in the passenger seat of the vehicle one minute and gone the next, disappeared into thin air, usually as the car was passing by that same cemetery.

The entrance to Resurrection Cemetery in Justice, Illinois, where Mary's body was laid to rest; however, her spirit apparently remains restless and wandering.

One way or another, Resurrection Cemetery was the end of the line for poor Mary.

There is a fascinating physicality to some of the encounters with Resurrection Mary. Some drivers claim to have literally run her over, hitting the phantom with their car and feeling a sickeningly solid impact. After slamming on the brakes and bringing the car to a screeching halt, the shaken driver hops out of the vehicle, walks all the way around it, checks underneath, and finds ... absolutely nothing.

In certain cases, Mary opens the car door, something that requires physical contact and energy. In others, she appears inside the vehicle without touching the door at all. The reverse is also true. The ghost has by turns thrown the door open wide to get out and, conversely, just vanished into thin air right in front of the astonished (and deeply shaken) driver.

On one occasion, Mary's hands left scorch marks on the iron gates at the entrance to the burial ground, partially crushing the metal rods. It was as if the poor woman was trying to force her way out of the cemetery. (The *Chicago Tribune* offered an alternative explanation: a truck driver backing into the gates accidentally, warping the bars so much that a blowtorch was used to try to bend them back into their original shape. Instead, the high heat only mangled them even more.)

After considering the evidence, Taylor believes that Resurrection Mary is not one single woman but rather multiple women. An October 25, 1992, article in the *Chicago Tribune* identified her as 21-year-old Mary Bregovy, who was indeed killed in a car crash in 1934 and buried in an unmarked grave in Resurrection Cemetery. One key point to bear in mind is that Mary Bregovy's death did not take place on or even near Archer Avenue but in the Windy City itself, some 20 miles away.

Taylor identifies the second possible candidate as Mary Miskowski, a young woman who also loved dancing and was killed by a speeding vehicle in 1930.

Taylor's hypothesis concerning there being at least two dead women behind the Resurrection Mary apparition sightings makes a great deal of sense. There's no other way to explain the differences in physical description that are reported (unless you happen to believe in a ghost that regularly dyes her hair).

Over the span of several decades, Chicago-based author Ursula Bielski has documented a trove of spirit encounters that span the length of Archer Avenue and beyond. She is extremely well versed in the story of Resurrection Mary. Writing about the case in her 2024 book *You Cannot Follow: Resurrection Mary and Other True Ghost Stories of Chicago's Haunted Archer Avenue*, Bielski doesn't find Mary Bregovy to be a credible candidate for being the ghost. More credible in her view is a 13-year-old Lithuanian girl identified by local resident and enthusiastic Resurrection Mary researcher Frank Andrejasich: Anna Norkus.

Over the span of several decades, Chicago-based author Ursula Bielski has documented a trove of spirit encounters that span the length of Archer Avenue and beyond.

Anna was killed in a car crash on the night of her thirteenth birthday in 1927. Her father was driving her home after a celebratory night out at a dance hall. She was buried in Resurrection Cemetery.

Bielski makes a solid case for Anna Norkus being the spirit who came to be known as Resurrection Mary. The main drawback, however, is that the vast majority of sightings report Mary as being a young woman rather than a young teenager. Are those unwary drivers who pick up the ghostly hitchhiker unable to tell the difference between a 13-year-old girl and someone several years older ... or could Troy Taylor and Ursula Bielski have identified not just two but *three* separate and distinct ghosts that are all collectively reported as being the same spirit?

Whatever the truth may be—and it is likely that we will never know for certain—in all likelihood, it will turn out to be stranger than fiction. If you, dear reader, should find yourself driving along Archer Avenue some night, you are advised to keep a sharp eye out. Perhaps the figure in the flowing dress who emerges from the darkness at the side of the road is an entirely real, flesh-and-blood young woman—or perhaps you'll be heading for your own close encounter with the legendary Resurrection Mary.

MOST HAUNTED (OR HYPED): 50 BERKELEY SQUARE

"When the legend becomes fact, print the legend." So goes a famous line from the 1962 motion picture *The Man Who Shot Liberty Va-*

lance. This principle often applies to claims of paranormal activity—especially hauntings. When ghost stories seem too good to be true, they often are.

Such is the case with what came to be known as the most haunted house in London: the infamous No. 50 Berkeley Square, located in the historic heart of the British capital. Although it was the home of several notable people, including Prime Minister George Canning for more than 50 years, once the property was abandoned and began to deteriorate, tales of horrifying paranormal activity began to circulate about the place in the late 1800s. The stories included one visitor who was found dead while alone in the house, literally scared to death, and another who was driven insane by whatever dark forces they encountered within its crumbling walls. It was even said in some quarters that nobody who spent the night in the most haunted room at No. 50 ever survived with their sanity intact, and some paid with their lives.

Writing in issue 335 of *Fortean Times* (December 2015), author Jan Bondeson places much of the responsibility for these tales at the door of an issue of *Mayfair* magazine and the early twentieth-century author and self-styled ghost hunter Elliott O'Donnell, a man who rarely let the truth get in the way of a good story—and boy, No. 50 Berkeley Square had some good stories! Tellingly, there was little consistency between them, and no concrete evidence to back any of it up.

THE "HAUNTED HOUSE," BERKELEY SQUARE.

A 1907 illustration of the Berkeley Square building from the book *Haunted Houses: Tales of the Supernatural* by Charles George Hall.

There were deaths within the house, but this is almost inevitable for any property that is more than a hundred years old. None of them were suspicious or gruesome in nature. Yet the legend of No. 50 continued to spread and does so to this day. In 1980, when I was seven years old, I received a copy of Daniel Farson's *The Hamlyn Book of Ghosts* as a Christmas gift. Farson recounted stories of a sailor who had broken into the abandoned home being so frightened that he jumped to his death from an upper-floor window, having been attacked by an evil entity in the haunted room. Although Farson was writing more than half a century after O'Donnell had begun telling tales of the dark haunting in Berkeley Square, he did little to question the lurid stories. To his credit, Farson at least attempted to offer an alternative explanation:

that the abandoned house was taken over by a gang of criminals who created and encouraged ghost stories to keep people away from their base of operations. Although there is no more evidence to support this hypothesis than there is for the ghost stories, the principle of Occam's razor would make it easier for many people to accept.

For almost a hundred years, the house has been home to the antiquarian bookseller Maggs Bros. According to the owners and staff, the ghost stories are simply that: stories.

Based upon good, old-fashioned research, checking the records and identifying owners of No. 50 down through the years, Bondeson was able to show up many of the ghost stories for the fictions they truly are. As a young boy, I eagerly devoured the terrifying tale in Farson's book. As an adult, I have since learned better. Yet please indulge me, dear reader, and try a simple experiment: type the words *50 Berkeley Square* into your favorite internet search engine, and then spend a while scanning the results. Then do the same

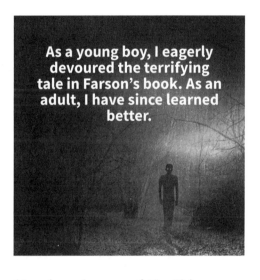

As a young boy, I eagerly devoured the terrifying tale in Farson's book. As an adult, I have since learned better.

thing on YouTube. The truly scary thing about the story of No. 50 has nothing to do with the ghosts, which likely never existed in the first place: of far greater concern is how unwilling many people are to question long-standing legends and folklore.

OFF WITH THEIR HEADS: THE BLOODY TOWER OF LONDON

On a cold New Year's Eve in the mid-1990s, I stood shivering in the darkness with a small group of equally weird friends. While the rest of the country was celebrating, we were standing watch in Bradgate Park, Leicestershire, waiting for the arrival of an anniversary ghost. Our chosen stakeout position was the crumbling ruins of Bradgate House, an early sixteenth-century manor that was once home to Lady Jane Grey—famous for having been the Queen of England for just nine days.

Jane's meteoric rise and stratospheric fall took place between 1553 and 1554. She was just 15 years old when political machinations contrived to place her on the throne. Jane was married to Guildford Dudley, whose father, John Dudley, was the Duke of Northumberland, a highly influential advisor and confidante of King Edward VI. As the king's health deteriorated in the summer of 1553, John Dudley convinced him to declare Jane to be his successor. She was intended to serve as little more than a pawn for Dudley's ambitions; he would be the puppet master, pulling her strings from behind the scenes.

There was a fly in the ointment, however, in the form of the dead king's sister, Mary Tudor. Four days after his death on July 6, 1553, Jane ascended to the throne. Mary came out swinging—with the full backing of Parliament. By July 19, Jane was replaced on the throne by the newly crowned monarch Mary I, who wasted no time in declaring her rival a traitor and tossing Jane in the Tower of London. She would never leave alive and, in February of the following year, was beheaded by the royal executioner. Her feckless husband, Guildford, was executed as well. Jane never returned to her beloved Bradgate.

The Tower of London was the prison of a number of famous figures in history, including Sir Walter Raleigh, Guy Fawkes, Rudolf Hess, and two of Henry VIII's wives: Jane Grey and Anne Boleyn.

Or perhaps she did. According to a long-held local legend, every New Year's Eve, a black coach pulled by four headless horses speeds through the park and the nearby town of Newtown Linford. The sole occupant of the coach is none other than Lady Jane Grey, sitting with her decapitated head resting upon her knees. The horses gallop up to the shell of her once-proud childhood home, where they, the coach, and their phantom passenger all disappear into thin air.

The phantom coach and horses are said to appear at midnight. If so, they took the night off when I was waiting for them, patiently sipping hot tea from a flask and listening to the sounds of Bradgate's many peacocks strutting about the ruins. Perhaps this really is just a legend. On the other hand, there is a variation that holds that the night of Jane's return is Christmas Eve, rather than New Year's. By all accounts, she is a busy ghost, for Jane is also said to appear in London, walking along the battlements of the White Tower, on February 12, the anniversary of her grisly demise.

For centuries, the Tower of London served as both Death Row and execution chamber for those who were declared traitors to the British monarchy. Torture chambers were used to extract confessions, some of which were genuine, others of which were screamed out in a desperate attempt to make the agony stop. Public executions took place on Tower Hill, outside the walls of the fortress. These were extremely popular events, the Super Bowls of their day. Crowds of thousands assembled, either to bay for the blood of the condemned or, in some rare cases, to express respect and support. Vendors sold food, ale, and souvenirs to the crowds, who cheered and cat-called each beheading or hanging.

For a select few of the elite, including queens such as Jane Grey, executions were carried out on Tower Green, a stretch of land within the walls of the Tower itself. This afforded the prisoner a small shred of privacy, as the mob were unable to see the execution take place. All the condemned man or woman could do was pray that the headman knew his craft. In some cases, a sword was used for the beheading. In others, a heavy axe. A skilled executioner could lop off the head in a single stroke. Occasionally, things would be badly botched. In 1541, 67-year-old Margaret Pole was sentenced to death for the crime of treason. She did not go quietly. Contemporary accounts say that it took 11 blows of the axe to kill her and that the executioner was forced to chase the shrieking Margaret across Tower Green when she fled. Little was left of her head and upper body by the time she finally died. Margaret Pole's terrified screams were heard for many years after her death, reverberating from the high stone walls surrounding the Green.

A painting of the doomed Anne Boleyn awaiting execution in the Tower of London by artist Édouard Cibot.

Considering such brutal stories as this, it should come as no surprise that the Tower is known as the most haunted building in London, if not the entire country. King Henry VIII kept his executioners busy with a steady stream of visitors to the chopping block. One such unfortunate was his wife, Anne Boleyn. Rather than divorce her, Henry had Anne declared an adulteress and thrown in the Tower. Her execution went off without a hitch; Anne's head was lopped off with a single stroke of the sword. She was buried in the chapel of St. Peter ad Vincula, close to the site of her execution on Tower Green. Yet Anne Boleyn refused to remain quiet after her death. Her body was seen inside the chapel late one night by an astonished guardsman. She was leading a procession of apparitions slowly down the aisle, which must have been challenging, considering that she lacked her head.

The Tower has many ghosts, yet few tug at the heartstrings more than the two young princes Edward and Richard. Edward became King of England at just 12 years of age, following the death of his father, Edward IV. King Edward V's reign was to be short-lived—just two and a half months. His uncle Richard, the Duke of Gloucester, was supposed to care for the fledgling king and guide him. Instead, he took the throne for himself (Edward had never actually been crowned) while Edward and his nine-year-old brother were already living in the Tower, awaiting Edward's coronation.

The two princes disappeared in 1483, and Richard of Gloucester was crowned King Richard III. There are theories that the boys may have been spirited away to live quiet lives of anonymity in Europe, but the most commonly accepted explanation is that Richard had them murdered, thereby removing the biggest obstacle standing between himself and the throne of England. He had declared Edward's claim to be invalid but feared that even with the crown sitting upon his own head, he would never be able to rest so long as the two brothers drew breath.

Richard III met a violent end himself, dying in battle at Bosworth Field two years later, in 1485. Of his nephews, there was no sign … until two centuries later. In 1584, structural alterations were being made to the White Tower. A section of staircase was knocked down, and beneath it were found the skeletons of two children, the ages of which approximated those of the missing brothers. Why had they been hidden away? It was deemed likely that these were the remains of Edward and Richard, and they were reburied in Westminster Abbey, the traditional final resting place of England's kings and queens. Two more children's skeletons were discovered at Windsor Castle in the 1700s, and some historians believe that these may have belonged to the missing princes.

While investigating there in 2002, I spoke with one of the Yeoman Warders who are tasked with guarding the Tower. A decorated, no-nonsense British military non-commissioned officer, he told me of the time when his young son accompanied him on his nightly rounds. The Yeoman Warder made his way through the White Tower, ensuring that all was secure for the evening. Impatient to move on, he turned to see his son dawdling several rooms back.

"Come along, it's time to go," the Yeoman Warder said.

"In a minute, Dad," his son replied. "I'm playing with these two boys."

There were no boys to be seen. Scooping up his son, he exited the White Tower as quickly as possible, without looking back.

Who could possibly blame him?

A MURDEROUS AFFAIR: MALVERN MANOR AND THE VILLISCA AXE MURDER HOUSE

Like so many towns across the American Midwest, Malvern is a railway town. Set on the western edge of Iowa, it's the sort of place where, although not everybody knows everybody else, most people do know one another—and often, one another's business. The people are friendly, and the neighborly spirit, now long lost from most big cities, lives on.

The building that is now known as Malvern Manor started life as a hotel. It was the sort of place where travelers could debark from the train and check in for the night, enjoying a hot bath, a cooked meal, and a cold drink—when Prohibition wasn't in effect, that is. Before the motor car became affordable and the advent of commercial air travel, the primary way to travel across the United States was by rail.

Once a hotel, then a nursing home, the echoes of Malvern Manor's former occupants still linger here.

The highways and airports didn't kill rail travel entirely, but they did come close to driving the proverbial stake through its heart. The flow of travelers slowed to a trickle, relative to what it had been before. Without railroad patrons to cater to, many of the smaller hotels eventually closed their doors, permanently. In the case of Malvern, the hotel in question became a residential facility, taking in those who could not care for themselves. The medically debilitated, the addicted, and those with mental illness all found a home there. It was a safety net, their last chance before being thrown out onto the streets to fend for themselves.

The men and women who worked there did their very best to care for the residents, sometimes under trying circumstances. Despite their best efforts, the facility began to decline in the twenty-first century, with a lack of funding sending it into a death spiral from which it never recovered. After the State of Iowa stepped in, the last patients and residents were shipped out to other facilities, and the doors were closed for the last time. The building was locked up and abandoned.

Apart, that is, from the ghosts.

Perhaps the most heart-wrenching aspect of the haunting involves a 12-year-old girl named Inez Gibson, who lived with her adoptive parents in Malvern at the end of the nineteenth century. Inez was distraught when she was told that her birth mother was coming back to reclaim her. She was found hanging by the neck from a jump rope in her closet. The tragic death was ruled accidental, but there were rumors that she had taken her own life. It's unlikely that the truth of the matter will ever be known. Inez is buried in the cemetery at Malvern, yet ever since the Manor (as it is now called) was opened to paranormal enthusiasts and investigators, there have been numerous reports of visitors encountering the ghost of a little girl that purports to be her.

Despite earlier claims to the contrary, Inez Gibson did not die at Malvern Manor…yet someone, or something, still claims to be her.

There's just one problem with that. Inez Gibson did not die at Malvern Manor. She died at her adoptive parents' home. Yet the Manor has a room named after her (complete with a closet), and until the staff learned better, it was believed that she did die there. The story was told repeatedly—in good faith—and it wasn't long before *something* picked up that ball and ran with it. Having spent many days sleeping at the Manor and investigating it, I'm convinced that what claims to be Inez is really nothing of the sort. What calls itself Inez is most likely to be either an opportunistic spirit masquerading as the young girl, for reasons best known only to itself, or an *egregore*, a thought form created by the continual retelling of Inez's story. Sometimes, directed thought and belief can literally take on a life of its own. In Tibet, these thought forms are known as *tulpas* and can be both created and destroyed at will by those who are practiced in the art and willing to put in sufficient effort.

Gracie was an older lady who was afflicted with dissociative identity disorder, or DID—the condition that used to be referred to as multiple personality disorder. A very sweet woman, by all accounts, she used to sit in her room and manifest a wide range of different personalities. Some were children. Some were adult men and women; some nice, some nasty. Of particular note was a gruff male who would repeatedly growl the phrase "the devil's coming to get me." So convincing was the voice that a new member of the nursing staff thought that Gracie had snuck a man into her room.

While it isn't known whether Gracie died at the Manor or not, some trace of her presence still lingers there in the room that bears her name. Personal items such as her spectacles are still there, sitting on a

Empty beds and long-abandoned rooms are the only reminder of the building's status as a former residential care facility … apart from some of the spirits who have remained behind.

small shelf above Gracie's bed. Paranormal investigators have recorded EVPs speaking in several different voices, which begs the fascinating question: in the case of DID, do some elements of each of those different personalities survive death? Or could they paranormally imprint on the environment somehow, even before the person has died, only to interact with others later on? Gracie's room remains a firm favorite for visitors to spend time in and, if they're brave enough, sleep in overnight.

There is nothing threatening about Gracie and her personalities, but the same cannot be said of the Manor's other entities. Walk 50 feet from Gracie's room and you come to the old medical wing. The doorways are wider here, indicative of the fact that hospital beds had to pass through them. Now, the wing has a more sinister name: the Shadow Man Hallway. The name derives from a former resident who used to live in Room 2, which is now permanently locked and inaccessible to visitors. According to former staff members who have returned to Malvern Manor to reminisce and share their stories, the long-term resident of Room 2 was a tall, thin male who had an extremely violent history. The staff were scared of him and used to treat him with kid gloves for fear that he might attack them. One of his favorite practical jokes was to wait for a nurse to come and check on him. When they left his room, he would slip out of bed and tiptoe after them, moving up so close that he was within inches of their back. Once the nurse turned around, sensing somebody right behind them, they would get the shock of their life.

On his more aggressive days, this patient would simply charge at the staff while they made their rounds, though he tended to stop short of physically attacking them. It would appear that his behavior hasn't changed much after his death. Several visitors to Malvern Manor have reported seeing a tall, skinny shadow figure walk out of Room 2—passing *through* the closed and padlocked door—and turn toward them. While the hapless visitor watches, usually

The infamous Shadow Man Hallway, in which a tall, dark figure has been known to aggressively rush at unsuspecting visitors.

rooted to the spot in fear, the Shadow Man charges toward them, typically vanishing into thin air just an inch or two in front of them. Paranormal author Josh Heard, acknowledged expert on the haunting of Malvern Manor, was one such person. He was rushed by the Shadow Man on no fewer than three separate occasions.

"I felt a sense of complete dread and fear," Heard recalled during our interview. "Just as soon as he hits you, the feeling's gone."

Only the bravest are willing to spend the night in the Shadow Man Hallway. Another sad spirit in this hall is that of a woman who was abandoned at Malvern Manor by her husband, who had rejected her. She would tear her hair out, screaming and crying. During my own investigation at Malvern Manor, I recorded the sound of a woman sobbing in that same stretch of hallway. It was just a couple of seconds long, but my colleagues and I heard the crying with our own ears, making it a direct voice phenomenon (DVP) rather than the more common electronic voice phenomenon (EVP). Female visitors tend to connect better with the poor anguished lady than do males.

At the top of the building lies the attic. When paranormal attacks take place at Malvern Manor, this is where they most often occur. The attic is a claustrophobic enclosed space, renowned for causing visitors to spontaneously vomit for no apparent reason. Offerings of cigarettes, beer, and liquor are often there to mollify the male spirit, who is said to still crave the vices of his earthly life. More than one visitor has been scratched shortly after climbing the steep, narrow staircase to the attic. Some have experienced blackouts and fainting episodes, although these cases are mercifully few and far between. More common are the growls that are sometimes heard when visitors encroach upon the attic space.

Although it's mostly conjecture, there may be a link between Malvern Manor and one of Iowa's most infamous haunted locations and dark tourism sites: the Villisca Axe Murder House. Situated some 40 miles to the east of Malvern, Villisca is a small town with a dark past. On the night of June 9–10, 1912, an intruder—or intruders, depending on which theory one happens to believe—made entry into the home of Josiah and Sarah Moore and their four children. All six members of the Moore family were murdered in their beds, bludgeoned to death with an axe. Also brutally killed were two visiting sisters, Lena and Ina Stillinger, who were asleep in the downstairs bedroom at the time.

The Villisca Axe Murder House may be linked with Malvern Manor. Some researchers believe that the killer may have stayed at the former hotel before or after committing the brutal murders in Villisca.

Suspicion for the crimes fell on several different individuals, including an itinerant priest and a local businessman, but the killer was never caught. In recent years, authors Bill James and Rachel McCarthy James have put forward the "man from the train" hypothesis, which proposes that the Moores and the Stillinger girls were the victims of a traveling serial killer who made his way across the Midwest by rail. If this was indeed the case, then it's entirely possible that the murderer could have spent the night at the hotel that was destined to become Malvern Manor.

The Villisca Axe Murder House has plenty of ghost stories of its own. As somebody who has investigated both locations, I can confirm that the place is haunted. By whom, or by *what*, is the key question. Although visitors to Villisca have experienced childlike phenomena, such as giggling and the pitter-patter of little feet across the floor in the empty children's bedroom upstairs, one hopes that the Moore and Stillinger children have long since moved on. Much like the case of poor Inez Gibson at Malvern Manor, it may simply be a case of the story having been retold and reinforced so many times inside the house that it has taken on a life of its own via paranormal means.

The children's room at Villisca, where the poor Moore children were murdered while they slept.

Both Malvern Manor and the Villisca Axe Murder House are open to respectful visitors. Neither is suggested for the faint of heart.

THE HANGING HOTEL: BODMIN JAIL

Built in the latter half of the eighteenth century, Bodmin Jail was the location of numerous deaths by hanging. Most of them took place just outside the walls as major public events that were attended by entire families, but the last two took place in a purpose-built execution shed that was constructed within the jail walls. The two men, both convicted murderers, received what is known as the "long drop," a technique in which the condemned man's weight is used to calculate the exact length of rope needed to break the man's neck. Use too much rope, and the prisoner would fall too far, too fast—sometimes ripping the head from the neck. Use too little, and the neck wouldn't break, leaving the helpless inmate to choke to death over long, agonizing minutes.

Men, women, and even young children were imprisoned at Bodmin for crimes as trivial as petty theft or—one shudders to think—bestiality. At the other end of the spectrum, condemned rapists and murderers were also incarcerated there. One part of the jail was turned over to the Royal Navy, becoming an official naval prison and housing British sailors and, during World War I, German prisoners of war.

Bodmin Jail's main gate. Not every prisoner who came in through the archway would leave alive.

Bodmin Jail stopped being a working prison in the 1920s. After the last inmate was transferred or discharged, it became a nightclub and a restaurant for a while, and it saw service as a military installation in World War II. At the time of writing, it is a museum and tourist attraction. Huge sections of the jail are in the process of being converted into a hotel. When the project is complete, guests will be sleeping in actual prison cells that once housed numerous prisoners. It promises to be a surreal and, I daresay, chilling experience.

The jail has long had a reputation for being haunted. Those who work there simply shrug the strange experiences off as being part of working there, but for some visitors, a brush with the spirits of Bodmin Jail can come as quite a shock. One local taxi driver I spoke to had taken his dog along on a tour of the jail. The poor animal became terrified as it reached one specific cell and flatly refused to go any deeper into the building, whimpering and shaking as though reacting to something that the human beings present couldn't see.

Shadow figures are commonly seen at Bodmin, and so are strange light anomalies. Disembodied footsteps and voices are also heard there, as is the jangling of keys and clinking of chains. Many visitors report feeling a sense of oppression come over them when they enter the jail. It is almost as if the atmosphere itself has somehow thickened, perhaps a consequence of more than a century's negative energy generated by those who served time within its walls. Several witnesses that I interviewed reported experiencing this unnerving sensation, which seemed to dissipate as soon as they left the foreboding main gate behind.

Those who were executed at the hands of the state were not allowed to be buried in a public churchyard or cemetery. Instead, they were interred within the grounds of the prison itself, their grave usually adorned with just a simple marker and a few flowers paid for by their family. Small wonder, then, that the ghosts of Bodmin Jail's condemned are reputed to still walk its hallways long after their deaths.

One such ghostly legend involves Selena Wadge, who was hanged there in 1878 for murdering her own child. As the story goes, Selina's phantom still haunts Bodmin Jail, sobbing and wailing in remorse for her awful crime. She is most often seen by children, who talk of "the upset lady in the long dress" after encountering this tragic figure on one of the upper floors.

Over the span of two years, I was fortunate enough to spend several nights investigating the jail alongside a team of researchers and aided by members of the Bodmin Jail staff. It was an extraordinarily active case, and one that would end up affecting me emotionally in a most surprising way.

We recorded multiple EVPs during our stay. The basement was particularly active, with several shadow figure sightings and an unseen voice joining in with one of our conversations. I was sitting in one of the cells, chatting with a fellow investigator about a mutual acquaintance. A digital voice recorder was running, and noth-

After extensive renovation and restoration, the jail (now a hotel) has been preserved for future generations to experience. What might the ghosts think of that?

ing out of the ordinary was noticed while we were speaking. On play-back, however, a male voice with a distinctly Liverpudlian accent broke in on our chat and declared: "You don't really know him."

On the ground floor, during a burst session, I asked whether there were any prisoners there with us. There was no answer. Then I asked about jailers, warders, or prison staff. A voice whispered, "Warders." This was clearly a direct response to my question, suggesting an intelligent rather than a residual haunt.

Two investigators were conducting a recording session at the top of a staircase. They recorded a voice saying: "He's coming up." A few seconds later, I came up that same staircase to join them—once again, another intelligent EVP.

The crumbling and ramshackle Naval Prison was closed off for construction, but my team and I were granted permission to spend a few hours in there, late one rainy night. Despite the inclement weather, we recorded voices speaking in German coming through our Spirit Box. Could this have been a residual auditory phenomenon linked to the German naval POWs who were imprisoned there during World War I?

In the main part of the jail, heavy emotional energies affected several of my investigators, even bringing one to the verge of tears. I don't usually experience strong emotional reactions at haunted locations, but Bodmin Jail was something else. On the last night of our investigation, I went down into the dank, water-logged hanging pit and spent 30 min-

The author standing above the execution pit at Bodmin Jail in Cornwall, England.

utes down there doing EVP bursts. When I emerged, my entire mood and affect were different. For no apparent reason I found myself overcome by a cold rage, stalking around snapping angrily at people for no good reason. This feeling of anger intensified throughout the night, spoiling what had until then been a very enjoyable investigation.

I felt as if I had somehow left the jail on bad terms. Don't ask me why, but I felt compelled to turn the car around when I was halfway to my hotel. I reached the jail before sunrise and was given permission by Kirsten, the resident paranormal guide, to walk through the building one last time. With her at my side, I went from room to room, apologizing to the spirits of the jail in case they felt my team and I had disrespected them or had given offense in some way. Up on the second floor, I was rewarded with a completely unexpected loud *boom* that I took as acceptance of my apology. Just like that, I instantly began to feel better.

As with so many other visitors, I was back to my old self again by the time I left the jail behind me. I have never experienced anything like it in my life, either before or since. Kirsten firmly believed that something attached itself to me in the hanging pit—something that was either appeased by my blanket apology or was unable to follow me once I had left the jail behind.

The hanging pit at Bodmin Jail. Capital punishment no longer takes place in the United Kingdom.

After my visit, Bodmin Jail underwent an extensive $70 million, five-year renovation and redevelopment process. Although the structure was preserved and upgraded, it was turned into a luxury hotel. Given that reconstruction can be a significant trigger or catalyst for paranormal activity, it should come as no surprise that the spirits seem to be as active as ever. Cells became hotel rooms, many containing photographs of and details about some of the former inmates.

I returned to the old jail in 2023 to carry out both public and private ghost hunts. My wife Laura accompanied me—a decision she regrets to this day. I was warned by a reputable psychic medium in attendance that one of the male spirits had taken a particular dislike to me. Late one night at the end of the public investigation, Laura felt her throat suddenly beginning to close up. Initially, I was concerned that it might be an allergic reaction, something I am trained to deal with in my capacity as a paramedic, but a quick examination found something far more disturbing. A series of red marks, not unlike those made by human fingers, ringed the front of Laura's throat. We wasted no time in getting Laura out of there and back to our hotel room.

The modern-day hotel is a far cry from the era in which each guest room was a prison cell.

After ensuring that she was okay, I went back to the scene of the ghostly strangling and read the entity the riot act. I'm happy to relate that the remainder of our stay was uneventful. I would encourage anybody with an interest in the paranormal to visit the Bodmin Jail Hotel, with its good food, comfortable rooms, friendly staff … and some not-always-friendly ghosts.

HOSPITAL OF HOPE AND HORROR: ASYLUM 49

The old Tooele Valley Hospital in Tooele, Utah, was a product of the 1950s, and it served the local community well. There is a U.S. Army depot in Tooele, which meant that a number of service personnel and their dependents also received care there.

As the years passed, a newer and larger facility was constructed nearby. Staff members began to leave, until finally the hospital could no longer keep its doors open. After the doors closed for the last time, most of the equipment and furniture was left behind. The structure was pur-

The author at one of his favorite haunted locations, the former Tooele Valley Hospital—now the full-contact haunt attraction known as *Asylum 49.*

DARK SPIRITS: MONSTERS, DEMONS, AND DEVILS

chased by a man named Kimm Andersen and his family, with the intent of turning it into a haunted house attraction for the Halloween season.

After taking ownership of half of the building, Kimm wandered the hallways and rooms, taking in the atmosphere and marveling at how much it still felt like a working hospital. All of the original patient beds were still there. The armature-mounted lights in the emergency room still worked. There was even an X-ray machine! The biohazard containers were brimming with used needles. It was as if everybody had just gotten up and left one day, leaving everything as is and locking the doors and never coming back—which was exactly what had happened.

Feeling invisible hands tug at his pant leg while he was walking around, Kimm learned the hard way that his new acquisition also came with an unadvertised feature: ghosts. It seemed that some of the hospital's former residents had not moved on when the last staff member left.

Not one to be frightened by the paranormal, Kimm set to work building his long-dreamed-off haunt with gusto. Yet it wasn't long before he and his fellow haunters began to notice strange things happening. Amidst all of the sawing, hammering, and painting, tools went missing. Somebody would set a hammer down beside them, for example, then turn back to reach for it a few seconds later, only to have their fingers close around empty air. The tool would be nowhere to be found and, despite a careful search, would not turn up until hours (sometimes days) later, usually in a completely different part of the hospital.

Then came the voices. People would hear their names called out loudly and clearly. When they went off to investigate, nobody was there. Shrugging, they would go back to their work, only to have the same thing happen over and over again. It would be tempting to dismiss this as being no more than practical jokes, but it happened so often that everybody's nerves were soon set on edge.

When it opened for the first time, the haunt was a huge success. Never one to do things tentatively, Kimm was running a full contact experience. The waiver that each customer had to sign before coming into the haunted

Countless patients walked or were wheeled along this hallway when the hospital was still functional. Not all of them left when the hospital was closed down.

house laid it out in very clear terms: the haunters had full permission to lay hands on you, grab you, and manipulate you however they pleased (within reason and the bounds of propriety). Many of the cast members were teenagers and older children, and it wasn't unusual to see grown men quaking in fear when a 12-year-old pulled them out of the waiting line and stuffed them inside a dark and stinky coffin.

Asylum 49, as it came to be known (because construction had begun on the hospital in 1949), was the place to go in Utah if you wanted to get scared. But nobody had bargained for the fact that in amongst the made-up actors, fake chainsaws, and latex monsters, some of the scares were very, very real. One customer complained that while the haunt itself was pretty cool, the actor playing a doctor in the emergency room was "kind of a dick." Wearing scrubs and a surgical facemask, the doctor simply glowered at her as the customer made her way hesitantly through the ER. It was as if her presence was an annoyance or an imposition, the customer explained, and it had put a damper on her experience.

Once she had gone, Kimm and his team looked at each other in bewilderment. There *was* no actor playing the role of a doctor in the emergency room that night.

Other spirits soon began to make their presence felt. The apparition of a little girl, somewhere between six and eight years old, was seen by some of the younger cast members, walking through the hallways and playing hide-and-seek with them. It may well be that the little girl was attracted to the other children, even though they were a little bit older than she was. Mediums visiting Asylum 49 claimed that there were at least three child spirits active there, two girls and a young boy.

Kimm and his partners were very open to the idea of psychics and paranormal investigators visiting Asylum 49 to learn more about the haunting. Interested members of the public were invited along to some events. Ghost hunts became a regular occurrence, and a large stack of evidence soon began to mount. There were EVPs galore, including the sing-song voice of a young child and that of an adult male stating his name very clearly and precisely on the recording—a name that was verified as having belonged to an imaging technician on the hospital staff.

Nor were the spirits camera-shy. Full-body apparitions showed up on video camera footage and in still photographs taken inside the building, almost always when nothing out of the ordinary seemed to be going on. One photo captured the image of a shadowy young child peeking

The cast and crew at Asylum 49 go all out to provide a scary experience for visitors during the Halloween season. Sometimes, the resident spirits like to lend a helping hand.

around the corner of a patient room. Another showed the figure of a tall, well-built man standing in the center of the main hallway, staring right back at the photographer –who couldn't see him at the time the picture was taken.

Many of the entities at Asylum 49 are friendly, or at the very least, mostly benign, but there are some notably vicious exceptions. The first is the spirit of a former patient named Wesley, who is said to haunt his old room at the hospital. Having been afflicted with Alzheimer's during his lifetime, Wesley can be either sweet and kind or angry and belligerent, depending on the day. His aggressive behavior stems from illness, not malice.

Far nastier is the entity known as the Guardian, so-called because during his lifetime, this individual liked to know and guard the secrets of his co-workers at the hospital. As the story goes, he was a member of staff with a particular nose for gossip and liked having as much dirt as he could on the people he worked with. Now that he's dead, the Guardian is even less pleasant to be around. Apparently, something of a misogynist, this spirit has an intense dislike for women and has been known to scratch, push, and shove them when they enter his part of the hospital.

At first, Kimm and his partners were only able to purchase half of the building. The other half was an operational nursing home, caring for retired senior citizens. In 2018, the staff and occupants of the nursing home moved to a newer facility, and now Asylum 49 comprises the entire hospital. Unsurprisingly, the nursing home side turned out to be as haunted as the other half. My team and I were the first to investigate there, just a month after the changeover took place. We witnessed doors slamming themselves shut in empty hallways and bizarre visual phenomena on what was once the psychiatric ward. A former staff member claims that one of the rooms was so haunted, nurses did their best not to put patients in there if they could avoid doing so.

Asylum 49 holds a special place in my heart as the most consistently active haunted location I have ever had the privilege of investigating. It also doesn't hurt that the cast and owners are some of the most big-hearted people you could wish to meet. They work in some very dark conditions. I spend each Halloween locked down there with my teammates, acting in the haunt until midnight and then venturing out into the hallways, trying to peel back one more layer of the enduring mystery that is the old Tooele Valley Hospital. Each year, our dossier of evidence grows. Visitors are made to sign waivers before entering, and with good reason. When the lights go out and the haunters emerge—some of them actors, some of them former staff and patients—the haunted hallways of Asylum 49 are no place for the faint of heart.

MAKING SENSE OF IT ALL

So here we are, at the end of our journey through the darker side of the paranormal world—and what a journey it has been. It's time to pause, take a breath, and consider some of the strange things we have learned along the way.

Places such as the suicide forest in Aokigahara, Japan, and the Hotel Cecil in Los Angeles, California, have taught us that while death, despair, and tragedy are very real things, the ghosts that are said to haunt them both can be a little harder to pin down.

Although the last living patients left long ago, the shadowy hallways of the Waverly Hills Sanatorium in Kentucky are still haunted by those who breathed their last in that space. Yet to focus only on the darkness at Waverly Hills is to ignore the bright, shining light of the healthcare workers who toiled selflessly to treat their fellow men and women. This was challenging, thankless, and often dangerous work— work for which some of the doctors, nurses, and orderlies paid with their lives. In the war against tuberculosis, they were true heroes.

The Bermuda Triangle, the London Underground, and Denver Botanic Gardens are visited by hundreds, sometimes thousands and tens of thousands of visitors each day. They each stand as a clear lesson that no matter what things look like above, there is often a darkness lurking beneath the surface—and sometimes it likes to reach upward, toward the living.

An acceptance of demons in one form or another is as old as humanity itself. Those who believe them to be all too real and fear the possibility of being possessed by one of these malevolent entities: take comfort in the possibility that ceremonies such as the ritual of exorcism exist. With dedication, effort, courage, and, above all, faith, it is believed that exorcists can cast out this particular form of evil and darkness and restore the innocent soul to its normal state.

Is possession what happened in the case of Ronald Hunkeler—or was he really nothing more than a disturbed young man, seeking to garner attention? Opinion remains divided to this day.

A devout Christian, Anneliese Michel paid the ultimate price for her faith. As happens in far too many cases, the process of exorcism turned out to be more hazardous to her health and well-being than whatever it was that caused her to act in such a bizarre manner. A case can be made that what truly killed her was, in fact, nothing more than ignorance, and that the very faith that representatives of the church rely on to cast out demons was what really cost Anneliese her life.

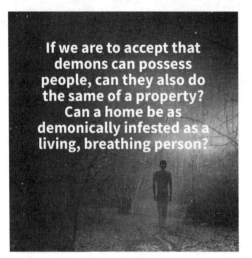

If we are to accept that demons can possess people, can they also do the same of a property? Can a home be as demonically infested as a living, breathing person?

If we are to accept that demons can possess people, can they also do the same of a property? Can a home be as demonically infested as a living, breathing person? If it can, then the so-called Demon House of Gary, Indiana, and the Monroe House of Hartford City, Indiana, would seem like possible locations for them to set down roots. Both of the respective properties have drawn the attention of those who consider themselves to be experts in the field of demonology, and although only one of the buildings remains standing, each case is equally fascinating—and disturbing.

Vampires can be by turns funny (the house-sharing comedic bloodsuckers from the hit TV series *What We Do in the Shadows*) and moody, such as the brooding, glowing-in-daylight vampires of Stephanie Meyer's *Twilight* saga. Hollywood has contrived to make vampires both cool and, in many cases, sex symbols.

From Transylvanian warlords with a penchant for impaling prisoners, to bloodthirsty Hungarian countesses, the label of vampire has been applied by the superstitious to demonize outsiders and vilify their enemies. In reality, their deeds were dark enough to begin with.

Throughout much of recorded history, human beings have lived in fear of the creatures of the night. Afraid of the restless dead rising from their graves and prowling for living victims, our forebears used decapitation, impalement, and a host of other brute-force methods to make sure that those buried stayed deep within the earth where they belonged. Only in relatively recent times has medical science overtaken superstition. Knowledge finally came to supplant ignorance. Yet a belief in vampires persists and shows no signs of disappearing anytime soon.

From fear of the undead, we move on to the fear of a lettered, numbered board. For as long as there have been talking boards, people have had disturbing experiences with them. Torture and even murder have been carried out at the behest of messages that came through what is still marketed as a toy. Perhaps that's all the talking board really is: a toy. Perhaps it's a conduit for the subconscious thoughts of those who participate. Or perhaps, depending upon what you believe, it might be a gateway to something much darker.

Belief is a powerful thing. Without it, curses have no power. For those who not only believe in them but are also convinced that they have been cursed, the effects can be devastating. Yet how are we to explain those cases of individuals or groups who apparently suffer the consequences despite being unaware of the existence of any curse or hex? Were some of those who entered the tomb of King Tutankhamun struck down by dark forces—influences that exacted retribution for the intrusion upon the pharaoh's final resting place—or were their misfortunes merely coincidence?

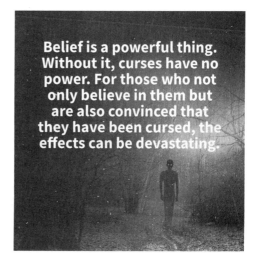

Belief is a powerful thing. Without it, curses have no power. For those who not only believe in them but are also convinced that they have been cursed, the effects can be devastating.

Curses don't apply just to places and people. Consider objects such as Robert the Doll and the numerous paintings of the Crying Boy. The first is a single item that may have been imbued with malevolent energies and, if the stories are to be believed, spread that psychic malignancy to those with whom it came into contact who lacked a sufficient degree of respect. In the case of the paintings, there is no clear-cut explanation for the origin of any curse, yet thanks to media coverage, tales of misfortune associated with ownership of the painting spread like wildfire. Even today, many people feel uneasy at the prospect of having a Crying Boy print hanging in their home—and who could blame them?

We live in an age where interest in both the paranormal and in true crime (particularly murder) is at an all-time high. It should therefore come as no surprise that many people are fascinated by places in which the two intersect. The hauntings of Fox Hollow Farm and the R Theater make total sense, given the atrocities committed by Herb Baumeister and John Wayne Gacy prior to their deaths. In both cases, however, it appears that the dark residue left behind is slowly being erased and replaced with positivity by the happy families who now live in those residences. In Wilder, Kentucky, the ghosts of Bobby Mackey's Music World may soon be moving into a new home; the building is scheduled for demolition after 45 years of entertaining patrons. But fear not: a replacement club is set to be built on the same spot. Considering that two of the most common and powerful triggers for a haunting to flare up are demolition and construction, one can only wonder what the work

Sometimes the worst monsters are the ones concealed behind a human mask.

DARK SPIRITS: MONSTERS, DEMONS, AND DEVILS

crews will encounter as they tear down the 100-year-old structure and build its replacement. Perhaps this will finally lay to rest rumors that at Bobby Mackey's lies the gateway to hell.

Witch hunts have cast a dark shadow over the history of Europe and North America. Although the practice thrives today, until very recently, being labeled a witch or warlock could result in one's incarceration, torture, or death. Even the most cursory glance at the events of the witch trials in either North America or Europe clearly shows that the outpouring of misery and death wasn't caused by the devil or his creatures. To explain how darkness came to hold sway over settlements such as Salem and St. Osyth, we need look no further than the fundamental inhumanity and willingness to abuse power by those authority figures who stood to gain from the persecution of their fellow human beings.

Say the word "monster," and what comes to mind? Serial killers such as the aforementioned Baumeister and Gacy certainly qualify. Often the monsters wear a human face, but there is no shortage of claims that monsters of the more traditional variety live in the lakes, forests, and wild places of our world—and sometimes, much closer to home. Many will flatly deny the existence of such mystical creatures. Others will have no problem believing that the wendigo stalks the woods, giant cats roam the moors, Nessie swims beneath the surface of the loch, and something savage and wolf-like hunts the edges of Bray Road.

For every friendly spirit haunting a comfortable old manor house, it seems as if there's a bitter, angry, and twisted entity that needs to be handled with care—or avoided entirely. At the edges of our sunlit world lie the dark places, the shadowy corners in which strange things sometimes happen. This is, to quote the Victorian author Catherine Crowe, "the night side of nature."

It is here that we encounter the dark paranormal, and if we are wise, we will tread carefully.

FURTHER READING

Anson, Jay. *The Amityville Horror*. New York: Gallery Books, 2019.

Baltrusis, Sam. *Ghosts of Salem: Haunts of the Witch City*. Charleston, SC: Arcadia Publishing, 2014.

Bell, Michael E. *Food for the Dead: On the Trail of New England's Vampires*. Middletown, CT: Wesleyan University Press, 2011.

Berlitz, Charles Frambach, and Joseph Manson Valentine. *The Bermuda Triangle*. St Albans, U.K.: Panther, 1977.

Blatty, William Peter. *The Exorcist*. Burbank, CA: Warner Bros., 1972.

Byers, Shannon Bradley. *Paranormal Fakelore, Nevermore: Real Histories of Haunted Locations*. Lilburn, GA: Paranormal Genealogist Publishing, 2017.

Estep, Richard. *American Hotel Story: History, Hauntings, and Heartbreak in L.A.'s Infamous Hotel Cecil*, privately printed, 2021.

Estep, Richard. *The Dead Below: The Haunting of Denver Botanic Gardens*, privately printed, 2019.

Estep, Richard. *The Devil's Coming to Get Me: The Haunting of Malvern Manor*. privately printed, 2018.

Estep, Richard. *In Search of Demons: Historic Cases & First-Hand Experiences from Experts & Skeptics Alike*. Woodbury, MN: Llewellyn Worldwide, 2024.

Estep, Richard, and Robert Graves. *The Horrors of Fox Hollow Farm: Unraveling the History & Hauntings of a Serial Killer's Home*. Woodbury, MN: Llewellyn Worldwide, 2019.

Estep, Richard, and Vanessa Mitchell. *Spirits of the Cage: True Accounts of Living in a Haunted Medieval Prison*. Woodbury, MN: Llewellyn Worldwide, 2017.

Farson, Daniel. *The Hamlyn Book of Ghosts in Fact and Fiction*. London, U.K.: Hamlyn, 1980.

Godfrey, Linda S. *The Beast of Bray Road: Tailing Wisconsin's Werewolf*, privately printed, 2015

James, Bill, and Rachel McCarthy James. *The Man from the Train: The Solving of a Century-Old Serial Killer Mystery*. New York: Scribner, 2017.

Kaplan, Stephen, and Roxanne Salch Kaplan. *The Amityville Horror Conspiracy*. Laceyville, PA: Belfry Books, 1995.

Kusche, Larry. *The Bermuda Triangle Mystery Solved*. Edison, NJ: Galahad Books, 2006.

Lewis, Chad, Noah Voss, and Kevin Lee Nelson. *The Van Meter Visitor: A True and Mysterious Encounter with the Unknown*. Eau Claire, WI: On the Road, 2013.

Manchester, Sean. *The Highgate Vampire: The Infernal World of the Undead Unearthed at London's Highgate Cemetery and Environs*. London, U.K.: Gothic, 1991.

Miller, Clara M. *Echoes of a Haunting: A House in the Country*. Philadelphia, PA: Xlibris, 1999.

Osuna, Ric. *The Night the DeFeos Died: Reinvestigating the Amityville Murders*. BookSurge Publishing, 2006.

Redfern, Nicholas. *Paranormal Parasites: The Voracious Appetites of Soul-Sucking Supernatural Entities*. Woodbury, MN: Llewellyn Worldwide, 2021.

Screeton, Paul. *Quest for the Hexham Heads*. Bideford, U.K.: Fortean Words, 2012.

Sloan, David L. *Robert the Doll*. Key West, FL: Phantom Press, 2014.

Smith, Dan. *Ghosts of Bobby Mackey's Music World*. Charleston, SC: Haunted America, 2013.

Taylor, Troy. *The Devil Came to St. Louis: Uncensored True Story of the 1949 Exorcism*. Jacksonville, IL: American Hauntings Ink, 2021.

Taylor, Troy. *Resurrection Mary: History & Hauntings of Chicago's Archer Avenue*. Decatur, IL: Whitechapel Productions Press, 2007.

Tudor, Sean. *The Ghosts of Blue Bell Hill & Other Road Ghosts: A Case-Centered Study of Phantom Hitch-Hikers & Phantom Jaywalkers in Folklore and Fact*. White Ladies Press, 2017.

Walton, Travis. *The Walton Experience*. New York: Berkley, 1978.

Weatherly, David, A. Dale Triplett, and Nicholas Redfern. *The Black Eyed Children*. Leprechaun Press, 2017.

INDEX

Note: (ill.) indicates photos and illustrations